Fuentes,
Terra Nostra,
and the
Reconfiguration of
Latin American
Culture

Fuentes, *Terra Nostra,* and the Reconfiguration of Latin American Culture

MICHAEL ABEYTA

University of Missouri Press
Columbia and London

Copyright © 2006 by
The Curators of the University of Missouri
University of Missouri Press, Columbia, Missouri 65201
Printed and bound in the United States of America
All rights reserved
5 4 3 2 1   10 09 08 07 06

Library of Congress Cataloging-in-Publication Data

Abeyta, Michael, 1964–
Fuentes, Terra nostra, and the reconfiguration of Latin American culture /
Michael Abeyta.
p.   cm.
Summary: "Grounding his study on the work of Derrida and Bataille, Abeyta
focuses on the theme of the gift in Carlos Fuentes's Terra Nostra. Analyzing
how gift giving, excess, expenditure, sacrifice, and exchange shape the
novel, he reveals its relevance to current discussions about the
relationship between art and the gift"—Provided by publisher.
Includes bibliographical references and index.
ISBN-13: 978-0-8262-1641-0 (hard cover : alk. paper)
ISBN-10: 0-8262-1641-2 (hard cover : alk. paper)
1. Fuentes, Carlos. Terra nostra. 2. Gifts in literature.   I. Title.
PQ7297.F793T432   2006
863'.64—dc22
2005036667

∞™ This paper meets the requirements of the
American National Standard for Permanence of Paper
for Printed Library Materials, Z39.48, 1984.

Designer: Kristie Lee
Typesetter: Crane Composition, Inc.
Printer and Binder: Thomson-Shore, Inc.
Typefaces: Adobe Caslon and Hiroshige

Contents

Preface

M Y FIRST READING of Carlos Fuentes's *Terra Nostra* (1975)
happily coincided with readings of Georges Bataille and Jacques
Derrida, specifically their works having to do with Marcel Mauss and the
question of gift giving (*The Accursed Share* and *Given Time: I. Counterfeit
Money*), or what Fuentes sometimes calls "gift economy." It became very clear
to me that Fuentes's rereading of Latin American history in *Terra Nostra*
confronted important changes during the initial encounter between Europe
and the Americas, the consequences of which have shaped the present. The
European discovery of the Americas occurred simultaneously with the spread
of the European market and the beginnings of a truly global culture. It also
coincided with a parallel transformation in Western culture: the shift from a
gift economy to an exchange economy, from a society or culture in which
economic relations were wrapped up in religious beliefs and practices that
bound communities together, usually based on sacrifices, tributes, or gift giving, to one in which market forces and the principle of exchange became predominant as the ethos of society (this is mostly true of the northern
European countries).

The question of the gift is one of the primary philosophical inquiries in
Terra Nostra, and it is the primary concern of this book. A number of related
issues and themes that appear in the novel will be treated here: money and
usury in the conflict between gift and exchange economies, gift giving's role
in art and narration, and the ostentation of the baroque in Latin American
culture. *Terra Nostra* also deconstructs the absolutist notions of identity and
the Hispanic tradition through the re-creation of very colorful, "conjectural"
literary characters, such as Celestina and Don Juan, a technique Fuentes still

uses in his most recent fiction. Last, underlying Fuentes's treatment of the gift and the role it has in the novel is a deep questioning of utopian thought and its impact throughout Latin America's history.

Since the end of World War II there has been an increasing awareness and intensification of the global economy, and along with that awareness the utopian impulse of modernity has come under scrutiny, especially from what was once considered the periphery of Western civilization—the Third World. *Terra Nostra* was written within the context of this questioning and of the resistance to capitalist modernization. In the postwar era, moreover, there was much discussion in anthropological circles and elsewhere about so-called primitive or premodern societies and the alternative models of socioeconomic life they seemed to offer. This nostalgic concern came out of a Europe exhausted from the two world wars and demoralized by the self-destruction of its own modern societies, and it had a great impact on intellectuals from the periphery of Western culture who were already engaged with their own searches for national identity (and inspired to struggle against fascism and colonialism during an era characterized by movements of national independence). Francisco Javier Ordiz notes that after the Second World War the loss of optimism, the loss of confidence in progress, and the breakdown of Eurocentrism led Latin American intellectuals to become conscious of "their belonging to a rich culture that no longer could be considered 'eccentric' and inferior, but rather integrated in the vast multiplicity of human cultures."[1] He cites Alfonso Reyes, who had an immense influence on the younger generation (including Octavio Paz and Fuentes), as one of the first in Mexico to pronounce and assert Latin America's place in the world.

In Mexico, the nationalist interest in indigenous and pre-Columbian motifs in Mexican art was colored in part by European nostalgia and exoticism, but also by this renewed appreciation of Latin America's cultural heritage. As Octavio Paz once put it:

> Nationalism in Mexican art is a consequence of European exoticism. Certain "very Mexican" painters are too similar to Gauguin or to Rousseau. All of this nationalist art simply flatters tedious Europeans and North Americans who have grown weary of civilization.
>
> (El nacionalismo mexicano en el arte es una consecuencia del exotismo europeo. Ciertos pintores "muy mexicanos" se parecen demasiado a

---

1. Ordiz, *El mito en la obra narrativa de Carlos Fuentes,* 16.

Gauguin o a Rousseau. Todo ese arte nacionalista adula el hastío de los europeos y norteamericanos, fatigados de la civilización.)²

Both Paz and Fuentes were very critical of this exoticism as a holdover from the earlier colonial and imperial appetites of the eighteenth and nineteenth centuries, but this does not mean that they themselves were not interested in recovering Mexico's and Latin America's rich cultural legacies, nor that they did not take seriously the inquiries of European anthropologists and other thinkers. Fuentes sought a critical reevaluation of the indigenous as well as the European and African roots of culture in the Americas, an integration that was to be neither reductionist, stereotypical, nor exclusive. In *Terra Nostra* and in *Cervantes, o la crítica de la lectura* (Cervantes; or, The Critique of Reading), Fuentes has a particular interest in recovering not only the indigenous legacy but also the Spanish legacy, which is why he depicts the Spanish baroque as a defining factor in Latin American culture.

Thus, Fuentes, as well as other writers and intellectuals from Europe's other former colonies, was both inspired by and critical of the writings of Marcel Mauss, Georges Bataille, and Claude Lévi-Strauss, who were themselves looking to the Third World for explanations for and parallels to the deep structures of the European psyche, of Europe's past and present cultures. The investigations of these authors led some to distinguish between, on the one hand, gift economies and the traditional communal institutions often identified with them (the traditions of gift giving served as the sacred-sacrificial base of ancient religions and socioeconomic organization) and, on the other hand, exchange economies, which characterize the modernization of capitalist society (hence Mauss's studies in sacrifice and "gift-exchange," Bataille's interest in "potlatch" and sacrifice, and Lévi-Strauss's interest in kinship relations, which he related to gift giving and exchange).

As the centers of political and economic power shifted from Europe to the United States, the search for national identity in countries such as Mexico came, in part, from their own social revolutions as well as their struggles for self-determination. Beginning, perhaps, with the writings of Jorge Luis Borges, which emphasized the heterogeneity of European culture, its debt to

---

2. This quote from Paz is cited in an unsigned article in *Revista Mexicana de Literatura* that Maarten van Delden attributes to Fuentes: "La burra al trigo," *Revista Mexicana de Literatura* 1 (September–October 1955): 93-94. See also van Delden's *Carlos Fuentes, Mexico, and Modernity*, 4-5. The quote shows that both Paz and Fuentes since the 1950s had been aware of the problem of the Anglo-American and European fetishization of Mexican culture and myth, and its reception in nationalist art. The English translation is mine.

the East, and the idea that the world does not in fact have a cultural and political center, many contemporary thinkers broke out of the straitjacket of
Eurocentrism. In this context, Fuentes and other Latin American writers felt
a particular need to articulate and understand two complementary problems:
on the one hand, the influence on the present of the syncretic legacy of the
Spanish and Portuguese colonies and the pre-Columbian cultures that distinguish Latin America from Anglo-American culture and, on the other
hand, the impulse toward industrial modernization and the pressures and en-
croachments of global mass culture, emanating primarily from the United
States. (This concern dates back at least to José Martí, if not earlier.)

The problem was how to adapt to modernizing forces without sacrificing
the rich, in its own ways modernizing, but also retrograde baroque heritage.
The difficulty lay in how to address this problem without falling into a roman-
ticized, utopian reaffirmation of a pre-Columbian past that also merited
scrutiny yet was crucial for the understanding of Mexico's and Latin America's
cultures. It is in this sense that Fuentes undertakes the profound rereading and
rewriting of Latin America's history and culture in *Terra Nostra*. Following
Bataille's profane study of the sacred and what he called "general economy,"
Fuentes also questions the work of art's value, function, and resilience for a
Latin American culture in the process of modernization. This led him to renovate and revise the Latin American baroque as an art of resistance. In this context, *Terra Nostra* is essential for understanding Fuentes's intellectual scrutiny
of Latin America's past, and it is the novel in his repertoire in which he most
directly reconfigures the role of Latin American fiction as a form of resistance.

Acknowledgments

M Y GREATEST DEBT of gratitude goes to Zunilda Gertel for
guiding me over several years in the preparation of this book; she has
been an invaluable mentor. Her questions, knowledge, and insights have been
essential for the development of the theory and the interdisciplinary approaches that inform the study. Georges Van Den Abbeele of the Critical
Theory Program at the University of California–Davis was also helpful to me
in my earlier struggles with the theory. I thank Raymond Williams and
Maarten van Delden for supporting this project, and for their suggestions for
improvement in style and scholarship. The College of Liberal Arts and the
Department of Foreign Language and Literatures at Colorado State University have also been supportive of me in my research and preparation for this
book. Last, I would like to thank all of my family, and especially my grand-
parents, for their patience and support.

I am grateful to the editors of *Hispanic Review*, *Revista Iberoamericana*,
and *Confluencia* for permission to reprint sections of the manuscript that ap-
peared in earlier versions in those journals.

Fuentes,
Terra Nostra,
and the
Reconfiguration of
Latin American
Culture

Introduction

CARLOS FUENTES is one of the most celebrated Mexican novelists of the twentieth century and is a major figure in Latin American literature. In 1975 Fuentes published *Terra Nostra,* his most ostentatious and far-reaching novel to date. *Terra Nostra* provides a critical reappraisal of Mexico's Spanish heritage in light of Spain's encounter with the indigenous reality of Mexico in the fifteenth and sixteenth centuries. In this novel, Fuentes seeks to recover the "authentic" Spanish legacy, that confluence of three cultures, Christian, Jewish, and Muslim, that flourished during the age of Alfonse the Wise. Spain's heterogeneous legacies were later repressed by the Inquisition, the expulsions, and the resurgence of "feudal" absolutism; this in turn set the stage for the destruction of the Americas' indigenous cultures during the conquest. Nevertheless, as Fuentes explains in *Valiente mundo nuevo* (Valiant New World), "We were born of the catastrophe of the conquest, we the Indo-Afro-Iberian Americans, and we created a culture of the counterconquest, as Lezama Lima called it" (De la catástrofe de la conquista nacimos nosotros, los indo-afro-iberoamericanos, y creamos la cultura que Lezama Lima llama de la contraconquista).[1] Following Fuentes's reading of the Cuban poet and novelist, the undercurrent of Indian, African, and Iberian values in Spanish American popular culture subverts those values that are "purely" European, and vindicates the specificity and difference of Latin American culture. Yet the tragic consciousness of this counterconquest

1. Fuentes, *Valiente mundo nuevo: Épica, utopía y mito en la novela hispanoamericana,* 214.

remains latent. It can emerge, however, through the revitalization of the baroque as a potential art of resistance. For Fuentes, the Spanish American baroque in the twentieth century contests the more ruinous legacy of Cortés and the colony, and reaffirms Latin America's Indian and mestizo heritage. Fuentes rejects, moreover, any Manichaean attempt to justify either the conquistador or the conquered, for in his writings he is equally critical of the absolutist tendencies of both the Spaniards and the Aztecs. This historical inquiry, moreover, is also a commentary on the authoritarianism of the twentieth century.

In this context, Fuentes seeks to renovate the literary language of the baroque from this critical standpoint. He explains in *La nueva novela hispanoamericana* (The New Spanish American Novel) that the contemporary Latin American novel seeks to reinvent a language that had maintained the hierarchical order inherited from the conquest and colonization of the continent. This critical renovation is by design the "profanation and contamination of a sacred rhetoric," a rhetoric, moreover, that was bound to the Counter Reformation and the culture it produced. Though expressive of a greater consciousness of social crisis in seventeenth-century Spain, according to José Antonio Maravall, baroque art, theater, and literature tended to reaffirm the centralized power of absolutist monarchy and to dissuade popular threats to the seigneurial order.[2] As a renovation of the baroque, *Terra Nostra* reexamines the crisis of the era and redeploys its language by turning it against its own conservative heritage. Through a process of self-contamination, the novel's figurative language plays a key role in the profanation of traditional seigneurial privilege and of the hierarchical, absolutist tendencies in the Hispanic tradition in general.

Although in *Terra Nostra* Fuentes's use of figurative language attempts to recover the critical humor of pun and parody that informed *Don Quixote* and *The Celestina*, it also integrates the rhetorical strategies of Nahuatl poetry as part of the "contamination" of baroque rhetoric. *Terra Nostra* reconstructs the chronicles and histories of the Indies coalesced with parallel Spanish literary texts: *Don Quixote, The Celestina, The Joker of Seville, The Solitudes, The Critick, The Life of Guzmán de Alfarache,* and *The Life of Lazarillo de Tormes.* Such intertextuality, as Juan Goytisolo points out, reflects an intense interrogation and rereading of the Hispanic tradition:

---

2. Fuentes, *La nueva novela hispanoamericana*, 30–31 (hereafter cited as *NNH*); Maravall, *Culture of the Baroque: Analysis of a Historical Structure,* 89–97.

Fuentes initiates a systematic "cultural looting" of the entire sphere of the Spanish language. . . . On the one hand, he appropriates entire phrases from Rojas, Cervantes or the chroniclers of the Indies and incorporates them into his own discourse (an operation typical of Cervantes); on the other hand, he converts the sphere of the novel into an imaginary museum in which unrelated literary characters cross paths and separate (which once again refers us back to the *Quixote*).[3]

The characters and events of these works, in turn, are integrated into the same textual spaces as the gods and events portrayed in Aztec and Mayan codices. Furthermore, the revival of baroque style in *Terra Nostra* integrates Nahuatl figurative strategies into the narrative discourse, particularly the use of parallelisms, and complements the representation of *general economies*.

As the novel traces the cultural values and sociopolitical hierarchies handed down from Hapsburg Spain, as well as from the Aztec Empire, it also investigates how these values and hierarchies are represented in cultural production. This representation implies an intimate relation between language and economy. Indeed, as *Terra Nostra* is the novel by Fuentes wherein he is most concerned with issues of literary theory, one of the main issues the novel explores is this relationship in literature. In particular, the tension between gift giving and an exchange economy is one of the fundamental conflicts that structure the novel. Much of this conflict is reflected in the novel's baroque style and its figural language. I use the term *figural* to refer to the rhetorical tropes and figures in literature that transgress conventional discursive communication by expanding or reducing the meaning of words, as well as through the employment of imagery. The study of these gains and losses at the level of figuration will complement the analysis of the specific "general economies" represented at the semantic level of the narration.

General economy, a term employed by Georges Bataille, approximates a science that studies the excesses of energy produced in the universe, excesses that by definition cannot be utilized. This useless waste or expenditure also implies an irreducible loss at the level of representation. In other words, the excess implies a loss in meaning. As a theoretical framework, moreover, general economy studies and posits a relation to this loss with regard to other economies that Bataille characterized as restricted economies. These would be the political economy of accumulation and epistemological systems that

3. Goytisolo, *"Terra Nostra,"* 250.

seek to establish absolute truth and fixed meaning. Political economy is restricted precisely because it is always concerned with wealth and value as common denominators. I bring this up because in *Cervantes; or, The Critique of Reading*, Fuentes points to Bataille for his own conception of economy's relationship to literature.[4] Indeed, Fuentes's relationship to Bataille, and to other poststructuralist thinkers, is a primary concern of this book.

Perhaps the first critic to take a serious interest in Fuentes's relationship to Bataille's thought is Wendy Faris. Of Fuentes's knowledge of Bataille's work, Faris states the following: "Given Fuentes's familiarity with French culture and criticism, and his presence in Paris at a time when Bataille's ideas were popular, I think it likely that Fuentes was familiar with the entire range of Bataille's thought, so that in the case of *Terra Nostra* we might posit a case of influence."[5] My position regarding Bataille's "influence," though I prefer to see it as an intertextual relationship or Fuentes's reading of Bataille, is that *Terra Nostra* shares many of the same concerns that Bataille raises and, indeed, is the book by Fuentes that addresses them directly. At issue for Fuentes, and for us, is the relationship among art, culture, and what Fuentes calls "the gift economy" *(la economía del don)*.

In *Terra Nostra*, the restricted economies of exchange, accumulation, and conservation are complemented and undermined by nonrestrictive economies functioning at different levels of the narration: these are the novel's baroque style, the excess of its figural language, the thematic representation of sacrifices, potlatches, gift giving, and other socioeconomic relations. In this vein, moreover, the concept of *herencia* (legacy, heritage, inheritance) has a dynamic function in the novel that fulfills both the temporal and the economic nuances of the term. Thus, the title, *Terra Nostra* (Our Land), refers not only to the past's repercussions in the present but also to the sense of a legacy bestowed and shared, as well as the corresponding debt to that legacy.

In Fuentes's novels up to the publication of *Terra Nostra* in 1975, the persistence of Mexico's past in its present was a central theme. *Where the Air Is Clear* (1958), *The Death of Artemio Cruz* (1962), and *A Change of Skin* (1967), for instance, illustrated the troubled relations of the postrevolutionary generations of Mexican society with their revolutionary and pre-Columbian indigenous past.

---

4. Bataille, *The Accursed Share: An Essay on General Economy*, 1:19–41; Fuentes, *Cervantes, o la crítca de la lectura*, 108–10 (hereafter cited as *CCL*). Published shortly after *Terra Nostra*, *Cervantes, o la crítca de la lectura* was designed to elucidate the novel's project. I do not cite the English translation, *Don Quixote; or, The Critique of Reading*, because it is abridged, and several key passages that I refer to were not included in that version.

5. Faris, "'Without Sin, and with Pleasure': The Erotic Dimensions of Fuentes' Fiction," 63.

These novels have also questioned the impact that the twentieth-century revolutions and world wars in Europe and Asia have had on Mexico. Likewise, the resulting hegemony of the United States appears as a constant antagonism in these works. Beyond this, Fuentes's shorter works from and after the early sixties demonstrate a more direct concern with the legacy of the conquest of Mexico.

Aura (1962), in particular, initiates in the author's writing a historical consciousness of this legacy that culminates in *Terra Nostra*. According to Zunilda Gertel, the story "Tlactocatzine, del Jardín de Flandes" from *Los días enmascarados* (The Masked Days) prefigures the writing of *Aura*. In turn, this brief novel marks the genesis of *Terra Nostra*. The narrator and protagonist of *Aura* suggests this himself when he states:

> If you can manage to save at least twelve thousand pesos, you can spend a year on nothing but your own work, which you've postponed and almost forgotten. Your great, inclusive work on the Spanish discoveries and conquests in the New World. A work that sums up all the scattered chronicles, makes them intelligible, and discovers the resemblances among all the undertakings and adventures of Spain's Golden Age, and all the human prototypes and major accomplishments of the Renaissance.[6]

The novels *Holy Place* (1967) and *Cumpleaños* (Birthday) (1969) and his essays collected in *The New Spanish American Novel* (1969) and *Tiempo mexicano* (Mexican Time) (1971) also directly contribute to the articulation of *Terra Nostra*'s engagement with Mexico's past.

Fuentes's works published after *Terra Nostra*, such as *Burnt Water* (1981), *Christopher Unborn* (1987), *The Campaign* (1991), *The Orange Tree* (1993), and the essays *Cervantes; or, The Critique of Reading* (1976), *Valiant New World* (1990), and *The Buried Mirror* (1992), further his inquiry into Mexico's and Latin America's cultural legacies. During the 1980s Fuentes began to rethink the trajectory of his more than twenty works of narrative fiction and organized them in a series of fourteen cycles he calls "La Edad del Tiempo" (The age of time). *Terra Nostra* is placed near the beginning and stands alone in a privileged position that Fuentes calls the "Time of Foundations"; *Terra Nostra* is the text that attempts to deconstruct and reconfigure Latin America's foundational myths.[7] It also takes a critical view of Spain's role in those myths.

---

6. Gertel, "El discurso transformacional en *Aura*," 31; Fuentes, *Aura*, 64–65.
7. For a full description of the cycles and the project of "La Edad del Tiempo," see Raymond L. Williams, *The Writings of Carlos Fuentes* (109–59). Included in the appendixes to Williams's study is an interview with Fuentes about "La Edad del Tiempo."

In his prologue to *Cervantes; or, The Critique of Reading,* Fuentes explains the importance of Spain's legacy in Mexico: "In its self-recognition, Mexico accepted its authentic Spanish heritage and defended it with the passion with which one rescues his father from misunderstanding and hatred" (México, al reconocerse, acabó por reconocer su auténtica herencia española y defenderla con la pasión de quien ha rescatado a su padre de la incomprensión y del odio, *CCL,* 9). This recognition reaffirms Mexico's and Spain's heterogeneous character against the homogeneous and normalizing legacy of Spanish absolutism. The displacement of the preexisting cultures of both Spain and the Americas forced the Indian, the Jew, and the Muslim to assimilate to a singular conception of the universe, or to perish. In the nineteenth century the Spanish American romanticists and modernists began to question the legacy of this displacement. They were inspired not only by romanticism in Europe but also by the revolutions in France and the United States, as well as their own Wars of Independence. They began to question the traditional legacy of "New Spain" and to seek a more autochthonous definition of their nations and cultures. Nonetheless, it was mainly in the twentieth century that Latin America produced writers willing to confront this historical-cultural dispossession as an immediate concern of the present.

In this respect, Zunilda Gertel has characterized *Terra Nostra*'s treatment of Mexico's diverse heritage as a "critical consciousness of history's use in contemporary Spanish American reality." *Terra Nostra* returns to history not simply to judge, interpret, or reconstruct it, but to reclaim it as the "cultural heritage of the present." This, of course, is reminiscent of Walter Benjamin's conception of history and the role of the historian: the necessity of rescuing history, "for every image of the past that is not recognized by the present as one of its own concerns threatens to disappear irretrievably." Although this view can be interpreted as "conservative in an eminent sense" as Jürgen Habermas does, Fuentes's approach to history and tradition is a critical reappraisal that does not simply restore the history and tradition, but rather questions them while rewriting them. In this sense, it is in *Terra Nostra* that Fuentes undertakes his most extensive deconstruction of the foundational myths of Latin America's cultural history.[8]

---

8. Gertel, "Semiótica, historia y ficción en *Terra Nostra,*" 63; Benjamin, *Illuminations,* 255; Habermas, *Philosophical-Political Profiles,* 138. For other crucial discussions of Fuentes's treatment of history in *Terra Nostra,* see Jaime Alazraki, "*Terra Nostra:* Coming to Grips with

Baroque, Modernist, or Postmodernist

According to Raymond Williams, *Terra Nostra* has been called a "metafictional" as well as a "metahistorical" novel, the first characteristic underscoring its modernist technique and the second its postmodern architecture and inquiry. As a novel, then, it also seeks to question the role of fictional writing itself in this process of deconstruction. It also questions the role of literature in modernity. There is an ongoing debate regarding whether Fuentes's *Terra Nostra* is a modernist or a postmodernist novel. The three most useful overviews of this debate are found in Raymond Williams's article "Fuentes the Modern, Fuentes the Postmodern" (2002), Maartin van Delden's *Carlos Fuentes, Mexico, and Modernity* (1998), and José Pablo Villalobos's review essay "Carlos Fuentes: Caught in the Modern/Postmodern Crossfire" (2000). All three authors seem to concur that Fuentes's approach to history and politics "goes beyond Postmodern interests in reducing historiography to just another text," as Williams puts it, and that the overall project of Fuentes's fiction is essentially a "Modernist enterprise." Van Delden asserts that the label of postmodernist does not sit well with Fuentes and that "given the persistence of Fuentes's affiliation with modernity, as well as the paucity of his references to postmodernism, it makes more sense to think of him as somebody engaged in the self-critique of an incomplete modernity—even when he appears to incorporate postmodern themes into his reflections."[9] Though I must agree with these critics, I do so hesitantly and only at a distance: my own position is that Fuentes, especially in *Terra Nostra,* was engaged in a poststructuralist critique of Latin American cultural history in the particular light of the European conquest of the Americas. Much of the discussion in this debate is often decontextualized in one extreme or another; either the critics neglect Fuentes's relationship to Latin American cultural traditions and its contemporary political conditions or they ignore the author's relationship to poststructuralist thought. For this reason, I will address these contexts.

History"; Verónica Cortínez, "Crónica, épica y novela: *La historia verdadera de la conquista de la Nueva España* y 'El Mundo Nuevo' de *Terra Nostra*"; van Delden, *Fuentes, Mexico, and Modernity;* Goytisolo, *"Terra Nostra";* Djelal Kadir, "Fuentes and the Profane Sublime"; Marta Paley Francescato, "Re/creación y des/construcción de la historia en *Terra Nostra* de Felipe Montero"; Lois Parkinson Zamora, *Writing the Apocalypse: Historical Vision in Contemporary U.S. and Latin American Fiction;* R. L. Williams, *Writings of Fuentes;* and Shirley Williams, "Mito e historia en *Terra Nostra* de Carlos Fuentes."

9. Williams, "Fuentes the Modern, Fuentes the Postmodern," 212; van Delden, *Fuentes, Mexico, and Modernity,* 144–47.

Terra Nostra's deconstruction of authoritarianism in the Hispanic tradition is also a profound commentary on the present. During the early 1970s when Fuentes was writing *Terra Nostra* the political panorama of Spain and Latin America was fairly bleak. Francisco Franco died the year the novel was published, leaving behind a legacy of repression, dictatorship, and censorship. Latin America was plagued by hunger, exploitation, illiteracy, and a series of dictatorships. Repression, torture, and political execution or "disappearances" were frequent in Chile, Argentina, Paraguay, Bolivia, Guatemala, and the Dominican Republic. Even in countries such as Peru and Mexico, political repression and corruption were prevalent. These dictatorships and corrupt governments also carried out neoliberal reforms that were to have devastating social and economic consequences, namely, the subsequent debt crises of the eighties and nineties and the current financial instability that have increased marginalization, urban crime, and impoverishment. The neoliberal reforms were a result of the dictatorships' willingness to abandon nationalist development and be minor players in multinational capitalism and the United States' economic and political hegemony in the region.[10] *Terra Nostra,* while examining the origins of authoritarianism in Latin America, also scrutinizes the curious alliance between absolutism in the seventeenth century and early capitalism. Although it is true that Fuentes's writings during the fifties and sixties have a modernizing pretension, shared by most of the boom writers, Fuentes has always been critical of the United States' hegemony and its form of modernity. *Terra Nostra,* in particular, and many of his writings after the midseventies show a profound concern for Latin American tradition as an alternative basis for the future "modernization" of the region.

In this vein, while Fuentes's narrative techniques can definitely be associated with the avant-garde, or modernism,[11] his vindication of Latin American culture as a baroque culture suggests a different kind of "modernity" that comes out of Hispanic and Latin American culture. Ortega y Gasset, Unamuno, Americo Castro, and José Antonio Maravall are very important precursors to Fuentes in this sense, all affirming, though not uncritically,

---

10. See Idelber Avelar, *The Untimely Present: Postdictatorial Latin American Fiction and the Task of Mourning,* 22–38. Avelar offers intriguing insights into the transformations of Latin American literature in the seventies and afterward, especially regarding postdictatorial fiction. In his observations on Fuentes, however, he deals only with Fuentes's writings from the sixties, those that demonstrate a more "modernizing" pretension. He does not discuss *Terra Nostra* or its deconstruction of authoritarianism in the Hispanic tradition.

11. Much has been written on Fuentes's relationship with North American writers, in particular, William Faulkner, John Dos Passos, and William Styron. See Fuentes's own essays on these writers in *Casa con dos puertas* (House with Two Doors).

"modern" or democratic values in Renaissance and baroque Spain that prefigure the Enlightenment. Most important, however, is Fuentes's relationship to Jorge Luis Borges, and to other writers from the fifties and sixties, mainly those of the so-called boom generation: Juan Rulfo, Alejo Carpentier, Julio Cortázar, Gabriel García Márquez, José Donoso, Mario Vargas Llosa, and others. Fuentes is also familiar with the thought of the French poststructuralists Jacques Derrida, Gilles Deleuze, and Michel Foucault, all of whom claim Borges as a precursor to some extent or another. What Borges, Fuentes, and the poststructuralists share in common is precisely a deep skepticism regarding the truth claims of "history" and the universalizing discourse of Western modernity.

Raymond Williams's tactful approach to Fuentes criticism helps us to observe potential pitfalls in the representation of Fuentes's treatment of history and politics. That some critics arguing for a "modernist" Fuentes can come to the conclusion that his writing "goes beyond postmodern interests in reducing historiography *to just another text*" reveals two major problems in much Fuentes criticism: on the one hand, the lack of understanding and rigor when it comes to the poststructuralist concepts of *writing* and *text*, particularly in relation to history,[12] and, on the other hand, the postmodernist critics' efforts to extract Fuentes from the very traditions he de/reconstructs. But to be fair to Raymond Williams we must respect the range of his commentary, for he attempts to reconcile the discrepancies in Fuentes criticism. In the following statement Williams describes what appears to be a moral imperative in Fuentes's writing:

> A commitment to an understanding of history and culture is essential to most of Fuentes's writing, including his texts with Postmodern tendencies. History and culture undergird the concept of identity in much of Fuentes's fiction. For this writer, writing implies an in-depth engagement with history, culture and identity. The foundations of Latin American history are to be found primarily in *Terra Nostra*, but are then elaborated in *The Campaign* and *The Orange Tree*.

12. Nelly Richard has commented on this problem in relation to Latin American studies in the U.S. in general: "Latin American Studies in the United States generally tends to deemphasize the problem of theory and writing, by either displacing its discussion outside of the sphere of Latin Americanism, reserving it for those departments that enjoy the recognized authority to speak—in English—about philosophies of deconstruction, literary theory or poststructuralism" ("Un debate latinoamericano sobre práctica intelectual y discurso crítico," 846–47). This is also the case within the realm of Latin American literary studies, and in particular Fuentes criticism, even though writers such as Fuentes often engage such theories.

When discussing Fuentes's relationship to postmodernism, however, Williams goes on to note that

> Fuentes's awareness of historical discourse and, above all, his questioning of the very assumptions of Western historiography, align *Terra Nostra* with the Postmodern described by [Linda] Hutcheon. In this sense, *Terra Nostra* is more deeply historical and political than many Modernist novels, including such overtly historical and political Latin American novels as García Márquez's *One Hundred Years of Solitude*, Vargas Llosa's *Conversations in the Cathedral*, and Fuentes's own *The Death of Artemio Cruz*.[13]

Williams points to an evolution of sorts in Fuentes's writing: in *Terra Nostra*, Fuentes's position is more critical and antifoundationalist in the sense that the novel deconstructs the mythical and historical "foundations" of Latin America. It is for this very reason that one cannot ignore his reading, and rewriting, of the poststructuralists. Nor can one examine such a reading without taking into account Fuentes's own references to Latin American cultural history; this is the problem with some of the critics who assert that Fuentes is "postmodernist." To extract Fuentes from the very tradition he engages implies yet another neocolonial reappropriation of a Latin American writer. Having said that, what is the problem with the "text"?

For Derrida, "there is no outside to the text" (il n'ya pas de hors-texte, "there is no outside-text"), a phrase grossly misunderstood and mistranslated in much criticism: what he does in his reconfiguration of the concept of writing is to recomprehend and deconstruct the classical opposition between speech and writing (signifier and signified, form and content, outside and inside, and so forth) in order to produce a new concept. In the classical opposition speech is associated with truth and the logos, whereas writing is subordinated as artifice, as fiction, as untruth, as "just texts" unable to represent "reality." Commenting on Rousseau's autobiographical writing, Derrida makes us aware of the impossibility of recalling the "so-called real existence" of Rousseau's family and acquaintances:

> What we have tried to show by following the guiding line of the "dangerous supplement," is that in what one calls the real life of these existences "of flesh and bone," beyond and behind what one believes can be

13. Williams, "Fuentes the Modern, the Postmodern," 212–15.

circumscribed as Rousseau's text, there has never been anything but writing; there have never been anything but supplements, substitutive significations which could only come forth in a chain of differential references, the "real" supervening, and being added only while taking on meaning from a trace and from an invocation of the supplement, etc. And thus to infinity, for we have read, *in the text*, that the absolute present, Nature, that which words like "real mother" name, have always already escaped, have never existed; that what opens meaning and language is writing as the disappearance of natural presence.

Hence the increased importance of letters and other autobiographical writings, not to mention legal documents, in historical studies. In recent times, Latin American historiography, particularly in Latin American colonial and cultural studies, has placed enormous emphasis on different modes of representation, media, and discursive strategies. Writing that is no longer subordinate to the logos and to "truth," that is, to realism and the metaphysics of presence, often emerges as deeply historical. As writing in this way becomes more concrete, it abandons the universalistic pretensions of the Enlightenment, of "progress" as a historical concept, of "modernity," and even of the "end of history."[14] "To reduce historiography to just another text" implies that the classical oppositions of form and content, speech and writing, are still in vigor in Fuentes criticism, in spite of Fuentes's own writing on the matter. In this book we will see just how important "texts" are in Fuentes's de/reconstruction of Latin American culture and history. Indeed, Fuentes's *writing* on the gift reexamines the history of discourses generated about the gift in its relationship to art and economy.

Furthermore, history and historiography make truth claims about the origins of peoples, present myths that often mask or justify very real power relationships, and in this way they repress the very history they purport to represent. Latin American *fiction* in the twentieth century has largely rejected the truth claims of the continent's history, opting to rewrite it as fiction—this is why Alejo Carpentier urgently called for Latin American writers to become the new "chroniclers of the New World" (cronistas de Indias), and why he and Fuentes have rewritten the *crónicas* (chronicles, historical texts).[15] Such texts need to be undermined and critiqued in order to produce a new

14. Derrida, *Of Grammatology*, 158–59. See also Kadir, "Fuentes and the Profane Sublime," 74–75; and Arkady Plotnitsky, *Reconfigurations: Critical Theory and General Economy*, 160.
15. Carpentier, "La novela latinoamericana en vísperas de un nuevo siglo," 47–48.

approach to the history. For Foucault, on the other hand, "texts" interact in what he calls discursive formations. Such formations are systems of rules for discursive practices that are inseparable from institutional and political practices. The terms *mezquita* ("mosque" for temple), *Indian, Spaniard, Indigen, Aztec, Mexican,* and *Nahua* are inseparable from specific past and present political and institutional practices that have had very real consequences in colonial and postcolonial society. Such terms have been used to create bodies of knowledge that ultimately determine how individuals are to be categorized and treated within social organizations and political regimes. For both Foucault and Derrida, and for Paul Ricoeur and Gilles Deleuze, texts are inseparable from the world of practice. (In Chapter 4 I will go into some detail regarding Deleuze and Guattari's conception of writing in relation to Fuentes's treatment of it in "The New World.") In general terms, poststructuralist criticism comprises a plurality of critical styles and forms of analysis, but not a program or a type of society; it is a radical, multidisciplinary strategy of reading and writing that undermines received meanings and truths, while it paradoxically leads to possible new reconfigurations of the past and the present. In Fuentes's writing, however, his dialogue with the poststructuralists must be considered in relation to his own reading of the Hispanic and Latin American traditions.

The postmodernist critics who desire to appropriate Fuentes's name for their program are also to blame for the confusion in Fuentes criticism. Many postmodernist readings reduce the specificity of Borgesian, baroque, and syncretic Latin American modes of thinking and expression within a fundamentally Anglo-European, modernist-postmodernist, or "late capitalist" theoretical frame. Several of the characteristics of *Terra Nostra* that Chalene Helmuth in *The Postmodernist Fuentes* associates with postmodernism, in fact, pertain to the neobaroque as conceived by Latin American writers since at least the 1940s: in particular, the novel's openness, indeterminacy, intertextuality, temporal and spatial distortions, and so on. The feeling that Latin American intellectuals had when such concepts defining postmodernism began to circulate in the 1980s was that it was not something new: fragmentation, decentralization, the coexistence of incommensurable realities were felt to be a part of their cultural reality. Moreover, I have seen few studies on Fuentes that address how he relates to Latin American discussions of postmodernism. For example, Brian McHale labels *Terra Nostra* "a paradigmatic text of postmodernist writing, literally an anthology of postmodernist themes and devices." His claim that postmodern narrations are characterized by an "ontological dominant" in reality only renames something that was already given in the tradition: Theodor Adorno had already recognized this literary phenomenon, but in regard to traditional fantastic art: "Fantastic art in romanticism, mannerism and baroque depicts something non-existent as though it had being. These invented entities are modifications of empirical reality, the effect being the presentation of the unreal as real."[16] McHale is right to highlight Fuentes's use of fantastic literary conventions to undermine the traditional conventions of the historical novel, but he largely ignores Borges's and Fuentes's sources for this type of inversion, namely, Cervantes and *his* contemporaries (among others as well).

To categorize *Terra Nostra* as postmodernist without tracing its baroque and Latin American precursors runs the risk of simply "reprogramming" it as just another reified commodity, and thus reintegrating it into late capitalism. Although this might be inevitable and postmodern writers often take on themes and issues that are not specific to their national cultures, it is my belief that the critic must keep in mind those traces to specific cultures if he or she is to understand the author's relation, or nonrelation, to that culture. (Often the novel's resistance is precisely this cultural difference.) To not do so, particularly with Latin American writers, is to risk turning a peripheral, decentralizing text into one that affirms the center, the metropolis. Jean Franco points to the innovations of the literary canon found in the essays of Mario Vargas Llosa, Carlos Fuentes, José Lezama Lima, and Severo Sarduy, in particular those essays that studied Cervantes and the baroque. She affirms that they "inverted the metropolis-periphery relationship in which it had traditionally been the metropolis which read, researched, observed, and recovered information about the periphery."[17] One intriguing aspect of *Terra Nostra* and *Cervantes; or, The Critique of Reading* is Fuentes's engagement with European philosophers and anthropologists who researched and studied Mexico and the Americas. Fuentes researches not only the "metropolis" in this sense but also how it in turn researched and constructed the image of itself through its "other," the Americas.

If the plurality of Fuentes's styles and approaches to history is poststructuralist and baroque, as I am suggesting, his project in *Terra Nostra* is also fundamentally postcolonial. To the extent that a postcolonial enterprise could

---

16. Helmuth, *The Postmodernist Fuentes*, 44–53; Mary Louise Pratt, "La modernidad desde las Américas," 831; McHale, *Postmodernist Fiction*, 15–18; Adorno, *Aesthetic Theory*, 28.

17. Franco, *Critical Passions: Selected Essays*, 504–5.

be considered "modernist," this term would have to be stripped of any northern, Anglo-American, or European centricity. Perhaps the most intriguing approach to the problem of Fuentes's "modernity" comes from Sang-Kee Song who, basing his study in Bolívar Echeverría's *Modernidad, mestizaje cultural, Ethos Barroco*, sees in Fuentes's writing a "baroque ethos" that operates as the privileged tool of his critique of modernity and that he posits as a possible alternative.[18] This corresponds with my own reading of Fuentes's neobaroque as an art of resistance to capitalist modernity. But what would this imply for the baroque's relationship to capitalist modernization, and the novel's traditional role in that process?

In *The Political Unconsciousness: Narrative as a Socially Symbolic Act*, Fredric Jameson describes the role of the nineteenth-century realist novel as the

> *systematic undermining and demystification, the secular "decoding," of those preexisting inherited traditional or sacred narrative paradigms* which are its initial givens. In this sense, the novel plays a significant role in what can be called a properly bourgeois cultural revolution—that immense process of transformation whereby populations whose life habits were formed by other, now archaic, modes of production are effectively reprogrammed for life and work in the new world of market capitalism.

It is my contention that *Terra Nostra* takes on this very problem: how can the Latin American novel recover and recodify the rich, syncretic heritage that distinguishes Latin America without reducing its cultural artifacts, values, and practices to mere commodities to be fetishized, consumed, and "reprogrammed" for a new massified global culture? At issue is the auratic function of gift giving and artistic creation: is Fuentes's treatment of the work of art and the gift an attempt to restore the cult or sacred dimension of art, or is it a profanation? For Idelber Avelar, the Latin American boom "strove to restore the auratic against the grain of a secular, modernized world. The impossibility of such a restoration would trigger the economy of mourning." And this mourning is intimately tied to the allegorical, and to the baroque.[19] In a way, *Terra Nostra* already mourns the boom novel, the new Spanish American novel, and the catastrophes of Latin American history, but it does

---

18. Song, "La sombra precolombina en el *ethos* barroco en las obras de Carlos Fuentes, Octavio Paz y Rufino Tamayo," 257. See also Echeverría, *La modernidad de lo barroco*, 38–41.

19. Jameson, *Political Unconsciousness*, 152 (emphasis added); Avelar, *Untimely Present*, 3, 32–33.

not do so out of nostalgia or to produce a forgetting. Fuentes's metafictional novel confronts the question of what was the function of these "traditional or sacred narrative paradigms"; it also investigates the very nature of the work of art and its ability to resist or adapt to commodification. This is where the work of art, fiction in particular, enters into relation with the gift economy, the sacred, and the question of sacrifice.

The Baroque Contamination: Language, Thought, Culture

Fuentes's revitalization of the baroque does not take place in a vacuum, nor is it really anything "new," even though it might seem strange or anachronistic to readers unfamiliar with Latin American culture. Iris Zavala points out that for the *modernistas* (Spanish American modernists) of the nineteenth century the baroque served as a mode of questioning authority, of countering U.S. neocolonialism, and of delineating the "inherent limitations of the Liberal political ethic and its paradoxes." This reintegration of the baroque is felt especially in José Martí's writings, but also in those of many of his contemporaries. Throughout Latin America, though especially in Mexico and the Caribbean, the baroque has been an important agent in the transmission of cultural difference, and "has fought against the imperial ideology's negation of the possibility that the colonized world had its own cultures and could create its own destiny."[20]

Zavala describes a third stage of the baroque, the "neobaroque," that dates from the 1940s and in which Severo Sarduy has been a pivotal influence, as we shall see in relation to Fuentes's take on the baroque. As a postcolonial discourse, the neobaroque relies on different artistic techniques and textual strategies, but two imaginaries intersect simultaneously: "One is the poetical/political utopia; the other, the creation of entropy of the Colonial through a baroque poetics. What is important is that each neobaroque text provides the reader with imaginative materials that provoke reactions and force objection into flux, always circling back to make words now true now false, echoing with the ambivalence and undecidability of a permanent uncertainty." Baroque writing integrates many different language types associated with ethnicities or cultural practices that resist colonialization and the established "truths" that it imposes—for example, Afro-Caribbean music and rhythms in Cuban

20. Zavala, "The Three Faces of the Baroque in Mexico and the Caribbean," 176–77.

poetry and fiction. For Zavala, "writing in Latin America (certainly in the Caribbean) has been a Baroque emancipatory expression of an independent cultural imaginary," and a will to action that counters the monological discourse of colonization.[21] Zavala's outline of the neobaroque echoes Fuentes's own writing on the baroque in *The New Spanish American Novel, Cervantes; or, The Critique of Reading,* and *Valiant New World.* Although not all of Fuentes's writings can be considered neobaroque, *Terra Nostra* establishes a direct relationship with the neobaroque, particularly in its critical relation with the Spanish and colonial legacies.

As metahistorical fiction, *Terra Nostra*'s reconfiguration of history involves a renewed interest in the chronicles of the conquest, as well as the integration of the indigenous and African cultural legacies through the revitalization of the Spanish baroque. Indeed, in *Terra Nostra* the baroque expands a critical conscience that abhors the void left by absolutism and inquisition. The Spanish American baroque is recast as a potential art of resistance, designed to counter the legacy of Cortés, the conquistador, portrayed in the novel through the character Guzmán. In a passage late in the novel, Felipe, El Señor, regrets having sent Guzmán to the Americas due to his servant's violent adherence to both seigniorial power and the rising mercantilist opportunism. To remedy this he has sent the priest and court painter Julián to the New World. He asks Ludovico about Julián's activity in the New World:

> "Did he construct his churches, paint his pictures, speak in behalf of the oppressed?" asked Felipe in an increasingly anguished voice.
>
> "Yes." Now Ludovico nodded. "Yes, he did the things you speak of: he did them in the name of a unique creation capable, according to him, of transposing to art and to life the total vision of the universe born of the new science . . ."
>
> "What creation?, what does he call it?"
>
> "It is called Baroque, and it is an instantaneous flowering; its bloom so full that its youth is its maturity, and its magnificence its cancer. An art, Felipe, which, like nature itself, abhors a vacuum: it fills all voids offered by reality."[22]

The void produced by the conquest, both in the fictional world of the novel and in relation to the present, is opposed by a cultural tendency that affirms

21. Ibid., 176–78.
22. Fuentes, *Terra Nostra,* 739; hereafter cited as *TN.*

the plenitude of life and nature and abhors the vacuum. José Miguel Oviedo has also commented on this passage and the *horror vacui* that it professes. According to Oviedo, Fuentes's writing is a baroque assemblage of the most heterogeneous and fragmentary elements that take on meaning only in their accumulation. He also points out that mythic thought in *Terra Nostra* relies on three cultural traditions—the heretical, the hermetic, and the revolutionary—that combine in a prophetic vision. *Terra Nostra,* in this sense, is a profound study of universal myth and eschatology that attempts a grand unification of myth and time. Oviedo concludes that the horror of the vacuum "is only satisfied by constructing a new cosmology that absorbs, usurps and loots all of the others."[23] One of the great achievements of *Terra Nostra* is the immediacy with which it renews and revitalizes Mexico's syncretic heritage; in this way the novel successfully reclaims the exuberance of the baroque as a critical conscience.

Following his conception of a new revitalized language, in this novel Fuentes seeks to renovate the literary language of the baroque. According to Fuentes, the contemporary Latin American novel engages the Americas' Spanish heritage with a critical view and seeks to reinvent a language that had maintained the hierarchical order inherited from the conquest and colonization of the continent. Fuentes elaborates on this point as a central concern of the so-called new Spanish American novel:

> Our language has been the product of uninterrupted conquest and colonization; a conquest and colonization whose language revealed a hierarchical and oppressive order. The Counter Reformation destroyed the hopes of modernity not only for Spain, but also for its colonies. The new Spanish American novel emerges as a new foundation of language opposed to the calcified protraction of our false and feudal foundation of origin and its equally false and anachronistic language. (*NNH,* 31)

This critical renovation of language creates a critical discourse that seeks to rewrite and profane the "calcified" and "sacred" rhetoric that was inherited from the colonial legacy and the Counter Reformation. Baroque culture in Spain was both the continuation of and the reaction against the modernizing trends of the Renaissance and the Reformation in Europe. Fuentes's critical renewal of the baroque, moreover, is in large part a reconsideration of the key

---

23. José Miguel Oviedo, "Fuentes: Sinfonía del Nuevo Mundo," 20–22.

issue of reference in language. The figurative devices Columbus, Cortés, and Bernal Díaz used to describe a world foreign to their own are not far removed from Don Quixote's use of catachreses to make sense of the world according to his own utopian idea of what it should be. Thus, it is no surprise that Fuentes begins *Cervantes; or, The Critique of Reading* with an appeal for the vindication of Mexico's Spanish and Indian heritage and ends it appreciating literature's desire to reduce the separation between words and things. When literature obscures the divide, according to Fuentes, it does so in the epic, and when it reveals the separation, it does so through poetry or in the novel (*CCL*, 110).

Fuentes takes up this theme again in his essay on Bernal Díaz de Castillo in *Valiant New World*, in which he compares the different interpretations of epic by G. W. F. Hegel and Simone Weil, on the one hand, and José Ortega y Gasset and M. M. Bakhtin, on the other, to corroborate his own reading of Bernal Díaz. Whereas for Ortega y Gasset and Bakhtin the epic treats what is already concluded, past, and known by an audience, for Hegel and Weil the epic is more dynamic, dealing with events in progress. Fuentes places Díaz's *True History of the Conquest of New Spain* somewhere in between, suggesting that his epic wavers between epic and novel: while Díaz laments the destruction of the city and culture that marveled the conquistadores, he portrays the tragic realities of the conquest with ambiguity and uncertainty. Similarly, for Michel Foucault, the divide between words and things is a determining factor in his assessment of Cervantes's great novel: "*Don Quixote* is the first modern work of literature, because in it we see the cruel reason of identities and differences make endless sport of signs and similitudes; because in it language breaks off its old kinship with things and enters into that lonely sovereignty from which it will reappear, in its separated state, only as literature."[24] The novels of Fuentes and of other contemporary Mexican writers often share in a critical rewriting of this divide between language and reality with regard to a specific context: the encounter of the Spanish imagination with the indigenous reality of the Americas, and the indigenous imagination with the Spanish conquistadores. These authors expose the fictitious nature of Mexico's history and are sensitive to hidden contemporary realities that, from time to time, oblige them to reinterpret the present according to the indigenous heritage masked by the conquest.

The Mexican historian Edmundo O'Gorman is widely credited with ex-

---

24. Foucault, *The Order of Things: An Archeology of the Human Sciences*, 48–49.

pressing the idea that the Americas were not discovered, but invented by the European imagination to satisfy the desire for a utopian space. In a similar vein, when Octavio Paz in *Posdata* places the 1968 massacre at Tlatelolco in the context of Mexican history, he notes that "to live history as a ritual is our way of accepting it; while for the Spaniards the conquest was a heroic deed, for the Indians it was a ritual, the human representation of a cosmic catastrophe."[25] For Paz, the massacre revealed that the history of a people is the visible manifestation of another history, an underlying history that needs to be deciphered. *Terra Nostra* demands of the reader a similar decipherment.

Terra Nostra is composed of three parts, "The Old World," "The New World," and "The Next World." After his return from the New World, the character Pilgrim relates to the king of Spain the story of his journey. His narration constitutes the entire second part of the novel. "The New World" borrows from several different chroniclers of the conquest: Bernal Díaz, Bernardino de Sahagún, and Francisco López de Gómara, to mention the most important. The reading experience of "The New World" itself has been compared to reading a pre-Columbian codex. According to Alice Gericke Springer, "The New World" is like a codex due to its spatial orientation and its use of imagery:

> The pictograms, the graphic images of a codex, are "read" the same way that a narrative is read, with the complete story being apprehended only after the reading is completed. Graphic images in general conform to an inherent spatially oriented logic since all aspects and component parts of the picture are apprehended by the viewer in an instant of time.... [T]hose constituent units do not necessarily conform to a linear temporal alignment. Pilgrim's mind corresponds to the screenfold of a codex, since that narrative is his recollection of his experience, and as such, is the *tabula rasa* on which are inscribed the images of the New World.[26]

"The New World," for its stylistic and cosmological integration of chronicle and codex, is one of the most innovative narrations that Fuentes has produced. Pilgrim is also reminiscent of the shipwrecked narrator of *The Solitudes* by Luis de Góngora and shares not only the same textual identity as his

25. Fuentes, *The Buried Mirror: Reflections on Spain and the New World,* 124–25; Paz, *El Laberinto de la soledad,* 291.

26. Springer, "An Iconological Study of the New World in Carlos Fuentes' *Terra Nostra,*" 3–4.

opposite, Guzmán, Fuentes's portrayal of Hernán Cortés, but also the identity of the god Quetzalcóatl, Plumed Serpent, and his opposite, Tezcatlipoca, Smoking Mirror. Throughout "The New World" Pilgrim is associated with Plumed Serpent, and although he must confront his adversary, Smoking Mirror, he finds out that he shares his adversary's destiny when he is told that he is "the Plumed Serpent in what you remember. The Smoking Mirror in what you forget" (*TN,* 445). While Pilgrim is still in the New World, he finds signs that in his capacity as Smoking Mirror he has been laying waste to the land (486–87, 491).

In "The Next World" Guzmán takes up this destructive destiny as a conquistador who sends "long chronicles of the discovery" (cartas de relación) to the king of Spain, which clearly alludes to Cortés (*TN,* 509, 708–10). Furthermore, scenes that occur in El Escorial mysteriously correspond to scenes in the palaces and temples of Tenochtitlán. Last, as Fuentes is particularly concerned with reviving Spain's multivalent cultural legacy in contemporary Spanish American reality, in *Terra Nostra* he seeks to renew this legacy mainly through the critical reintegration of Spanish and Spanish American baroque figures and tropes in a new heterogeneous writing.

With respect to this new writing, the present book has a threefold purpose. First, it will analyze the deconstructive functions of figural language at several levels of *Terra Nostra*'s narrative discourse in order to show how the revival of baroque style integrates European and Nahuatl figural strategies and how this renewal of baroque figural language complements the representation of general economies. Second, while engaging in this analysis I discern *Terra Nostra*'s relevance to current discussions in literary theory about the relationship between art and the question of the gift. And third, this book examines Fuentes's baroque in relation to *Terra Nostra*'s reconfiguration of Latin American cultural history.

When using the term *figural language* I refer primarily to rhetorical figures and tropes: catachresis, metaphor, and metonymy but also oxymoron and certain parallel structures that produce signifying excesses such as chiasmus. A common baroque figure, chiasmus will occupy much of my initial analysis, for its particular functions have a crucial importance in *Terra Nostra*'s language and design. Zunilda Gertel asserts the importance of the chiastic relationship between reading and writing in *Terra Nostra:* "The fragmentary accumulation of writings is the novel's defect, but also its virtue, since the superimposition of texts masks the void and at the same time refuses it. Any approach to *Terra Nostra* must begin with the understanding that the novel is a true chiasmus of reading and writing, or better yet, that its writing is the apotheosis of its reading."[27] In other words, the fragmentation and accumulation of "writings" demand of the reader an active participation in the novel's rewriting.

Because chiasmus is often used to describe social and economic reciprocity, its extended forms in the novel will complicate these relations. When the chiastic forms are condensed into oxymoronic structures, they will at times intensify such reciprocal relations, and in other instances annul them. Chiasmus and figural language in general will undermine closed structures and restrictive meanings, tending toward greater ambiguity and complexity in the discourse. When I use the adjective *figural* with other nouns besides *language*, or by itself, *the figural*, my usage includes nonlinguistic visual imagery that, nevertheless, shares the combinatory and transgressive force of the rhetorical figures I analyze. These may be complex iconic images that Fuentes recreates from baroque painting or from Aztec pictographic writing, or they may refer to the form and arrangement of letters and spaces on the written page that the reader experiences as visual figures.

The dynamism of baroque literary style can be traced, in part, to its excessive use of figural language to subvert the limits of rational discourse. The function of this is to produce obscurities, nuances, ambiguities of meaning that incite the readers to speculation, that engage them in solving a mystery. This intention of motivating the reader to go beyond literal meaning in baroque poetics also pertains to baroque art. As Umberto Eco notes, baroque poetics seeks to establish an inventive role for the reader or spectator who can no longer rely on the canon or authorized responses when faced "with a world in a fluid state which requires corresponding creativity on his part."[28]

Although this represents a modernizing turn in Western culture, the dynamism and indeterminacy of the baroque have a conservative character. According to José Antonio Maravall, the spectator is indeed guided to exercise a certain amount of freedom and invention, but within a given hierarchical social structure and in a manner that does not threaten that order. By motivating the spectators and readers to participate, the baroque work, in effect, makes them its accomplices; as the spectator becomes a coauthor, the work of art itself changes as well as the spectator's perspective. The manner

27. Gertel, "Semiótica," 64–65. See also Wendy Faris, "The Return of the Past: Chiasmus in the Texts of Carlos Fuentes."

28. Eco, *The Role of the Reader: Explorations in the Semiotics of Texts*, 52.

in which the baroque motivates the spectator is direct and immediate; it seeks to stir the passions. Maravall insists on this point: "The efficacy in affecting, in awakening and moving the affections, was the great motive of the baroque."[29]

In the first paragraph of *Cervantes; or, The Critique of Reading*'s foreword, in which Fuentes discusses Mexico's conflictive relation to Spain and Spain's equally conflictive relation to itself, his description is indicative of certain baroque concerns with the passions. Spain's history for Fuentes is "unresolved, masked and often Manichean. Sun and shadow, as in the Iberian bullring. The measure of hate is the measure of love. One word says it all: *passion*" (*CCL,* 9). With the contrasts of light and dark, a common technique in baroque art, and the appeal to the hidden and the unfinished to describe the tension, Fuentes not only takes a typically baroque posture but also recalls the Aztec sense of duality with its underlying passion.[30] Shaped by these conflicting legacies, Fuentes's interest in this history of passion offers insight into the character of Latin America and Spain, and complements his desire to move his audience to a passionate response comparable to his own. Often the baroque writer will employ figures of speech, such as metaphor and oxymoron, to create an image or a pictorial effect, not to provoke an intellectual response in the reader such as an abstract concept would require, but to stir emotions through sensorial stimuli. To produce these effects the baroque writer will borrow techniques from the visual and plastic arts, techniques such as the stark contrasts of light and dark, or chiaroscuro; the play of solid and void, surface and depth; and anamorphosis, or the optical distortion of an image.

In *Terra Nostra* both of these strategies, the use of visual images and the production of excess meanings, also have the effect of activating memory. Moreover, the functions of chiaroscuro on the visual plane and oxymoron at a rhetorical level are correlative to the visual punning in Aztec pictographic writing. According to Gordon Brotherston, the *tlacuilolli* was highly flexible in its layout, conforming "by turns to a chronicled narrative, an icon or map, or a mathematical table."[31] What most interests us in Brotherston's analysis is his description of the visual pun. The images painted in this visual lan-

29. Maravall, *Culture of the Baroque,* 75–78, 126–45, 171–2.

30. Aztec "duality" is almost a misnomer due to the complementary and simultaneous relationship between the opposite forces involved. See Miguel León-Portilla, *Aztec Thought and Culture: A Study of the Ancient Nahuatl Mind,* 83.

31. Brotherston, *Book of the Fourth World: Reading the Native Americas through Their Literature,* 50.

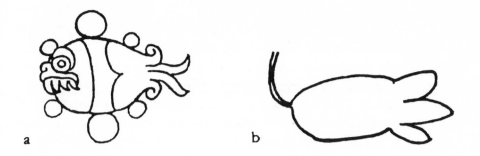

Figure 1. Doubled images of the heart: (a) fish (Boone, *Magliabechiano*, fol. 3v); (b) flower (Cruz, *Libellus*, fol. 53v). Reprinted with the permission of Cambridge University Press.

guage could be combined and superimposed as in the image of a swimming fish (fig. 1a) that has the shape and characteristic features of the symbol for the human heart (fig. 1b).

The image of the fish-heart that Brotherston uses to make this point comes from *The Codex Magliabechiano* and the *Libellus de medicinalibus;* examples of both images, figures 1a and 1b, are also found in *The Codex Borgia.* The common image of the heart (b) allows for a greater appreciation of the modification to the combined image (a). Generally in Aztec art, the heart image is also superimposed with the image of a flower or a prickly pear or both.[32] In *Terra Nostra* the combinatory potential of such visual puns, including metaphorical or oxymoronic images, produces images, landscapes, and motifs that integrate baroque and Aztec elements. The combination of ideogram, phoneticism, and pictography, the iconic script used in Aztec and Mixtec codices, or *tlacuilolli* as it is designated in Nahuatl, produces images that require interpretation somewhat analogous to that required by the complex figures found in baroque poetry, emblems, and imagery in general.

The visual image formed through a rhetorical figure maintains, moreover, a difference with respect to literal and abstract meaning. The figural blocks together two heterogeneous spaces in discourse, the visible and the textual, and thus produces opacity in language. By injecting the figural into abstract discourse, the writer gives to discourse the same "flesh" as that of the sensible.

32. See Elizabeth Hill Boone, *The Codex Magliabechiano and the Lost Prototype of the Magliabechiano Group;* and Gisele Díaz and Alan Roberts, eds., *The Codex Borgia: A Full-Color Restoration of the Ancient Mexican Manuscript.*

This standpoint coincides with José Lezama Lima's reading of the famous first verse of Góngora's "Capture of Larache" (La toma de Larache): "the swift serpent in crystalline swirls" (en roscas de cristal serpiente breve). In his essay "Sierpe de Don Luis de Góngora" (The Serpent of Don Luis de Góngora), Lezama Lima takes advantage of Paul Valéry's misreading of the line, in which he confuses *roscas* (twists, spirals) with *rocas* (rocks), to make the point that Góngora is not forming a contrast between fluid and fixed matter, but instead gives a diminishing image of movement. Furthermore, Valéry takes the word *cristal* (crystal or crystalline) literally, whereas in Góngora's poetry it is a consistent metaphor for water. Lezama Lima argues for a reading of the line that does not reduce the image to literal or abstract meaning: "In Góngora we are dealing with an impulsion, with a constant allusion to a movement that is integrated metallically, a metaphor that advances like a shot, and then autodestructs in a painterly light, rather than in an abstract meaning." The concrete image or metaphor destroys itself in its extension; the baroque object here is occulted not through shadow, but in the excessive radiance of the metaphor. The purpose of this, as Lezama Lima goes on to suggest, is a desire to transgress the limits of meaning so as to give the verse corporality. Góngora had a secret desire to bring into his verse another kind of radiance that would sensualize it, as in Arabic poetry. This other element in discourse, that which gives it body, is the figural.[33]

Nevertheless, the "radical heterogeneity" of the figural in discourse is not exclusively the blocking together of the figurative and the literal, or the visual and the textual; in all discourse the figural also corresponds to the relations of the letter to the line, and of meaning to the event of its inscription. In this light the figural deconstructs discourse by making us aware of something in it that cannot be reduced to a meaning, that cannot be represented, but it does not annihilate discourse. Jean François Lyotard is careful to show that the opposition he postulates between "the figural" and discourse, in which the figural appears to enjoy some primacy, can also be deconstructed to the advantage of discourse. Lyotard's book *Discours, figure* opens with the visible attributed more to the figural, and the textual more to discourse. However, the titling of a late chapter "Fiscourse Digure" "marks the extent to which the book has worked to deconstruct the opposition on which it is based, to find the discursive in the figural ('Digure') as well as the figural in the discursive ('Fiscourse')."[34]

33. Bill Readings, *Introducing Lyotard: Art and Politics,* 22; Lyotard, *Discours, figure,* 58; Lezama Lima, "Sierpe de Don Luis de Góngora," 202.
34. Readings, *Introducing Lyotard,* 36; Lyotard, *Discours, figure,* 7.

The Excess of the Baroque and the Logics of the Gift

The play of these transgressions and excesses over discourse functions at several levels of *Terra Nostra*'s complex narrative structure, and is characteristic of the baroque work of art. In this sense the novel deliberately exhausts its possibilities, and thus verges on caricature. Borges once wrote that in the final stage of all art, when it exhibits and squanders its media, it could be considered baroque. *Terra Nostra*, in a sense, also marks the end and exhaustion of the Latin American boom novel, but at the same time it reaffirms the subversion of the neobaroque. The renewal of the baroque in Latin America during the twentieth century has a particular tenor: the exuberance of the baroque opposes itself to the ethics of the capitalist economy. According to Severo Sarduy,

> To be baroque today means to threaten, to fool and to parody bourgeois economy, to attack the stingy management of wealth at its very core: the space of signs, of language, the symbolic base of society and the guarantee of its functioning, of its communication. To overspend, to waste, to squander language only for pleasure—and not for information, as in domestic use—is an attack on common sense, on morality and on what is "natural"—like Galileo's circle—the basis of all ideology of consumerism and the accumulation of wealth.[35]

The "economy" of the baroque, then, would be an economy of expenditure wherein nothing is held in reserve and where language transgresses its useful function as communication. I place "economy" in quotation marks because what Sarduy is describing is really a practice more akin to Georges Bataille's "general economy" than to classical political economy. At the semiotic level of values and practices, what the baroque does is oppose the capitalist political economy with a whole realm of practices that are not economical, that are not "practical" in a utilitarian sense. In this sense, the baroque places cultural values over economic values. But can we be content with Sarduy's assertion that pleasure is the only function? In Fuentes there are ethical and political dimensions to the practice of the baroque that go beyond pleasure and are associated with gift giving.

Fuentes's renewal of baroque figural language is intimately tied to this economy of expenditure and to the question of the gift. In *Cervantes; or, The*

---

35. Sarduy, *Barroco*, 99.

Critique of Reading, Fuentes describes the gift's disruption of exchange, and, from this, one can deduce the natural affinity between the baroque and the gift: they upset balance, destroy reciprocity, and pose a challenge to their recipients. Fuentes's commentary on the gift prefaces his observations on the role of expenditure and potlatch in James Joyce. He observes that the critique of writing in Joyce's works is a critique of individual writing: the author as a single subject is annulled; the novels are written by everyone and by Joyce, who are one and the same (*CCL*, 107–8).[36] This implies that the reader must also be the author of the text. As in baroque works, the exuberance of Joyce's writing is designed to challenge the reader and to thus break the normal, hedonistic exchange between reader and writer. Fuentes compares Joyce's writing to a potlatch, which is an ostentatious gift designed to challenge the receiver to come up with a superior gift. In this way the gift leads not to reciprocal exchange, but rather to a wasteful or luxurious expenditure on the part of the giver, and to an obligation, a future of indebtedness, for the receiver. An exchange, then, does not take place; there is only the challenge that does not allow any illusion of reciprocity or symmetry.

Fuentes cites Georges Bataille as the source of this conception of the potlatch, but the term is a Chinook word that appears in Marcel Mauss's book *The Gift: Forms and Functions of Exchange in Archaic Societies*, an anthropological study of "gift exchange" among several cultures, including the Indians of the Pacific Northwest. According to Mauss, the term *potlatch* translates as "to feed" or "to consume" and refers to the continual winter festival of "feasts, fairs and markets, which also constitute the solemn assembly of the tribe." But in these festivals there is a "principle of rivalry and hostility" between chiefs who are in constant power struggles. Referring to these practices as described in Mauss, Bataille points out that often potlatch was the "solemn giving of considerable riches, offered by a chief to his rival for the purpose of humiliating, challenging and obligating him."[37]

Bataille emphasizes, moreover, that in gift giving, as in the potlatch, the giver appropriates a power over the receiver when the latter accepts the challenge to reciprocate with a better gift and that this acquisition cannot work without the dissipation of useful wealth. Although Mauss argues that in the

36. Fuentes makes these observations based on the interpretations of Hélène Cixous and C. G. Jung.

37. Mauss, *Gift*, 6; Bataille, *Accursed Share*, 67–69. For an overview of the history of potlatch and its conceptualization, see Lewis Hyde, *The Gift: Imagination and the Erotic Life of Property*, 28–39.

giving of gifts, such gifts were often interested, invested, with an obligation to reciprocate, he also conflates gift giving with reciprocal exchange and the general circulation of goods. In Bataille, the logic of the gift is not so much its reciprocation as the acquisition of the power to surpass the receiver, and the expenditure or loss that comes with the gain. Furthermore, once a gift is reciprocated with a return or countergift, the original gift and the debt incurred are annulled. Bataille goes on to add, however:

> In reality, this absurdly contradictory aspect of potlatch is misleading. The first giver *suffers* the apparent gain resulting from the difference between his presents and those given to him in return. The one who repays only has the feeling of acquiring—a power—and of outdoing. Actually, as I have said, the ideal would be that a potlatch could not be repaid. The benefit in no way corresponds to the desire for gain. On the contrary, receiving prompts one—and obliges one—to give more, for it is necessary to remove the resulting obligation.[38]

Both Georges Bataille and Jacques Derrida, who expands on Bataille's reading of Mauss, distinguish the gift from reciprocal exchange, or "gift exchange," and Derrida in particular defines the gift as annulling all exchange economy. (This will have significant consequences for any reading of *Terra Nostra*.) For Derrida, once the gift has been conceived of as a gift, once it is recognized, it implies a return (or the expectation of a return), a countergift, and an interest, and that is why it becomes an exchange or falls back into the circle of debt. But Derrida does not stop there. Whereas for Bataille the gift is annulled as soon as the giver receives the countergift, Derrida has taken the question further; he points out that Mauss was too comfortable in describing the gift as "gift exchange," with no concern for whether the gift could still be considered a gift once it has been "exchanged." According to Derrida:

> Mauss does not worry enough about this incompatibility between gift and exchange or about the fact that an exchanged gift is only a tit for tat, that is, an annulment of the gift. By underscoring this, we do not mean to say that there is no exchanged gift. One cannot deny the phenomenon, nor that which presents this precisely phenomenal aspect of

---

38. Bataille, *Accursed Share*, 70–71. For further reading on the gift in this respect, see Jacques Derrida, *Given Time: I. Counterfeit Money*, 1–70; Marshall Sahlins, *Stone Age Economics*, 149–83; and Alan D. Schrift, ed., *The Logic of the Gift: Toward an Ethic of Generosity*.

exchanged gifts. But the apparent, visible contradiction of these two values—gift and exchange—must be problematized. What must be interrogated, it seems, is precisely this being-together, the at-the-same-time, the synthesis, the symmetry, the syntax, or the system, the *syn* that joins together two processes that are by rights as incompatible as that of the gift and that of exchange.

Derrida deconstructs the totalization of Mauss's definition of the gift; as Mauss describes the gift as a "total social phenomenon" he confuses giving and exchanging.[39] This point is very important for our reading of *Terra Nostra* because the tendency in criticism on Fuentes's writing has also been to confuse his conception of potlatch and gift economy with reciprocity and exchange. This represents an easy, totalizing critique that implies a metanarrative and utopian vision that does not correspond with Fuentes's narrative and that obscures his position on the question of the gift and its function in his writing.

One of the most direct examples of this tendency is found in Roberto González-Echevarría's article "*Terra Nostra:* Theory and Practice," an otherwise excellent critique of the novel. When González-Echevarría comments on Fuentes's discussion of potlatch in *Cervantes; or, The Critique of Reading,* he states that in Fuentes, "the return to a basic set of figures and events is a demolition prior to a reconstruction that reader and writer will accomplish through a ritualistic exchange."[40] González-Echevarría is not accurate in his interpretation of the concept of potlatch: by equating the potlatch in Fuentes and Joyce with a "ritualistic exchange," he repeats the same error as Mauss when he confuses gift and exchange, the part for the whole (see also Claude Lévi-Strauss's critique of Mauss in his introduction to the works of Marcel Mauss). To reduce the potlatch in Fuentes's conception of the narrative process to a "ritualistic exchange" is to lose all the rich nuances that are produced in the temporal separations between the act of giving, the obligation to reciprocate, and the receiving implied in narration.

Another important example of this type of misreading is found in Wendy Faris's study of "narrative expenditure" in Fuentes's *Death of Artemio Cruz* and Faulkner's *As I Lay Dying,* "Southern Economies of Excess: Narrative Expenditure in William Faulkner and Carlos Fuentes." Faris rightly characterizes the excesses of Fuentes's and Faulkner's narratives as "narrative potlatches," and bases her analysis on Bataille's notions of expenditure, excess,

---

39. Derrida, *Given Time,* 24, 37–38.
40. González-Echevarría, "*Terra Nostra:* Theory and Practice," 137.

and potlatch. Faris is also correct in assuming that the reader is in some ways obligated by the readings, but her attempt to explain this obligation in Fuentes's novel falls flat:

> In performing these rites, by animating the voices of the participants, the reader repays the obligations incurred by the narrative potlatch she has been offered. In a sense, it is true that the dead cannot be repaid by actual gifts in life as potlatch tradition requires, but since their voices are ceremonial, textual voices, perhaps in a textual sense they can; one re-pays them by reading more words in these narrative expenditures than humans are normally accorded in recounting events.[41]

Faris falls into a quasi-quantitative explanation for the obligation that for me is more qualitative, despite her insight on the reading of dead voices. In this sense, it is not so much a question of "more words"—indeed, the excess of words is designed to challenge the reader to go beyond a passive reading. The *more* of the excess implies a jump to another level or plane. But what does that mean? Here the important issue is the nature of the *challenge*.

In *Terra Nostra*, and from what is implied in *Cervantes; or, The Critique of Reading*, the reader "repays" not by reading, but by *rewriting*, which suggests an open-endedness in the encounter with the novel. This is the sense of Fuentes's reading of James Joyce; Fuentes challenges the reader to reconsider or reconfigure Latin American culture and history, to come up with his or her own version, but there is no "ritualistic exchange." Furthermore, although Faris's essay contains many crucial insights, its scope is often narrow; her use of Bataille's notion of excess is too limited in its application to "primitive tex-tual economy." Bataille's reading of Mauss is *critical*; for Bataille, the potlatch is not a closed exchange, as Faris reads it, but rather a temporalized, open-ended challenge. This is why Bataille emphasizes an idea that Mauss hid away in a footnote to his essay on the gift: "'The ideal,' indicates Mauss, 'would be to give a potlatch and not have it returned.' This ideal is realized in certain forms of destruction to which custom allows no possible response. . . . It is only through loss that glory and honor are linked to wealth."[42] Bataille emphasizes the principle of loss in the acquisition of power. Fuentes's narra-tives, if we see them as potlatches, as challenges, are very aggressive and are not so easily repaid as Faris would have us believe. And this is precisely why

41. Faris, "Southern Economies of Excess," 345.
42. Mauss, *Gift*, 42, 122n201; Bataille, *Visions of Excess: Selected Writings, 1927–1939*, 122.

Fuentes irritates so many of his readers, on the one hand, but on the other hand receives from just as many almost unreserved devotion and respect. Moreover, one of the often misunderstood consequences of Bataille's writing is precisely the deconstruction, or undermining, of the "primitive" versus "modern" dichotomy.

Perhaps the main problem with González-Echevarría's and Faris's critical readings of Fuentes's "narrative potlatch" is that they look for a closure; in this sense it is the critic who imposes a totalization, a completed circle, in a word, an exchange. This is why González-Echevarría is led to see *Terra Nostra* as a closed text. My position is that the reading makes the reader aware of the debt, of the obligation, but this condition is permanent or indefinite at best. How can we "repay" *Terra Nostra*, or for that matter *The Death of Artemio Cruz*? Is it even possible? And if it were, who would bother to read Carlos Fuentes?

According to Pierre Bourdieu, who also discusses the problem of gift giving, this type of totalization or objectification of gift giving denies and annuls the temporal lapse that allows the interpretation of the gift as an act of generosity; it destroys the reality of all practices that, like the gift, suspend the laws of calculation and self-interest. These practices are primarily symbolic labor that hides calculation, and for that reason they are related to fiction and storytelling in general. Throughout this study it must be remembered that the exchanges and gift giving that we examine in *Terra Nostra* should not be automatically interpreted as signifying reciprocity; in other words, they should not be totalized or detemporalized. For this reason we must adhere to Bourdieu's warning against the tendency to detemporalize and totalize the practice of giving:

> To be truly objective, an analysis of exchange of gifts, words, or challenges must allow for the fact that, far from unfolding mechanically, the series of acts which, apprehended from outside and after the event, appears as a cycle of reciprocity, presupposes a continuous creation and may be interrupted at any stage; and that each of the inaugural acts that sets it up is always liable to fall flat and so, for lack of a response, to be stripped retrospectively of its intentional meaning (the subjective truth of the gift can, as has been seen, only be realized in the counter-gift which consecrates it as such).[43]

43. Bourdieu, *The Logic of Practice*, 112, 105.

Whereas Derrida would probably question the statement in parentheses (for him, the gift is annulled in a countergift), what precedes it is a very important guiding precaution, not only for our approach to the general economies in Fuentes's novel but to any approach to narration as well. As we will see in this study, the creative and disruptive play between "gift economy" and exchange in *Terra Nostra,* and the temporalizing practices of gift giving, potlatch, and challenge, determines to a great extent the heterology and metafiction of Fuentes's writing.

Following Bataille's conception of potlatch, Fuentes dismantles the traditional ritual of reading by provoking a critical rewriting and rereading of cultural history. This is a challenge to the reader, not a completed exchange. In Fuentes's observation, the potlatch not only breaks the economy of exchange but also disrupts the conservative status quo and "erects in its place a principle that is contrary to that of conservation: parties and spectacles, games, prolonged funerary ceremonies, wars, cults, the arts and perverse sexual acts" (*CCL,* 108). This is what Fuentes means by an economy of excess: celebration is valued over work, and wealth is neither exchanged, circulated, nor simply accumulated. Instead, it is consumed, destroyed, wasted—an economy of loss and expenditure. Sacrifice functions in a similar fashion; it is both a sumptuary consumption, as in the case of burnt offerings, and also the temporary fulfillment of an obligation, a debt. Potlatch, the very expression of exuberance and excess, represents a challenge with disruptive consequences for traditional narrative writing, and for the exchange that takes place between reader and writer. Fuentes points to this when he discusses Joyce's economy of writing:

> Party, spectacle, duel, battle, ceremony, perverse literary activity, an assault against all previous culture, against the traditional subject, against the distinctions between exteriority and interiority, . . . Joyce's writing is a potlatch that breaks the traditional regime of narration and modifies the miserly norm of the truck between writer and reader, the Columbian norm of you-read-me and I-read-you. You-read-me, you-read-yourself, you-read-us, Joyce says to the reader: I offer you a potlatch, an excremental discharge of words, I melt your verbal gold ingots and I throw them to the sea, I challenge you to give me a gift superior to my own, which is *the gift assimilated in the loss.*

> (Fiesta, espectáculo, duelo, batalla, ceremonia, actividad literaria pervertida, atentado contra toda la cultura previa, contra el sujeto tradicional,

contra las distinciones entre exterioridad e interioridad, . . . la escritura de Joyce es un potlach, que rompe el régimen tradicional de la narración y modifica la norma avara del trueque entre escritor y lector, la norma colombiana [*sic*] del melés y teleo. Melés, telés y noslés, le dice Joyce al lector, te ofrezco un potlach, una propiedad excrementicia de las palabras, derrito tus lingotes de oro verbal y los arrojo al mar y te desafío a hacerme un regalo superior al mío, que es *el don asimilado a la pérdida*.) (*CCL*, 108–9; emphasis added)

According to Fuentes, Joyce defies the reader to give up the "lazy, passive and linear reading" and to participate in the rewriting of narration. As can be seen, the exchange between reader and writer, "you-read-me and I-read-you" (melés y teleo), which is disrupted by the potlatch, is here expressed as both a chiastic and a reciprocal relation. (When Fuentes combines the pronouns in "you-read-me, you-read-yourself, you-read-us" [melés, telés y noslés], he is playing on Joyce's writing in which the latter combines words to form new ones that in turn require a more active reading on the part of the reader.) The form of Joyce's challenge, the potlatch, is an excremental discharge of words in one direction, involving a dispersive neobaroque rhetoric that goes beyond obscuration. An assault on literal meanings, this rhetoric produces ambiguities and double meanings that challenge the reader to reconstruct multiple identities and cultural values in a countergift—a countergift, however, that has yet to consecrated. "You-read-me, you-read-yourself, you-read-us" implies an elliptic, uneven challenge in a discourse where identities and subject positions are not simply exchanged, but enter into contiguous relations; self and other are obliged to occupy the same cultural space, the critical "rewriting of all the codes of your culture" (la re-escritura de todos los códigos de tu cultura) (*CCL*, 109).

This rewriting of Latin America's cultural heritage traces back to the initial encounter between the Old World and the New: the reader of *Terra Nostra* must confront the same dilemmas as the character Pilgrim, who is faced with his contradictory identities as Bartolomé de Las Casas and Hernán Cortés, Plumed Serpent and Smoking Mirror. This immense novel is not only a countergift, a gesture of gratitude that recognizes Mexico's diverse heritage, but also an ostentatious gift that challenges its readers in a particular way: *Terra Nostra* functions as a gift that does not seek to close an exchange, but seeks to oblige the readers to rethink Latin America's and Spain's mutual history, to confront its silences, and to reinvent themselves in the process.

*   *   *

A few words on the organization of this book: Fuentes's approach to the question of the gift, and its relation to the work of art and culture in general, is quite complex. The novel is vast, and because it is an experimental space where he confronts different aspects of literary theory and aesthetics, there is indeterminacy and a plurality in the way he addresses the question of the gift. Fuentes seems to vacillate in a range that extends from Mauss's conflation of gift giving as exchange to Bataille's gift of rivalry, and there are even passages that prefigure Derrida's notion of the gift as the annulment of all exchange. In this book we will look at the full range of these notions and how Fuentes appropriates them and transfigures them through his "peripheral" reading. This requires an examination at different levels and through different lenses.

Chapter 1 begins with an outline of the theoretical relationship between writing and economy that Fuentes's establishes in *Cervantes; or, The Critique of Reading*. It then takes a historical view of the tension between gift economy and exchange economy in Fuentes's depiction of the decline of feudal absolutism in Spain during the time of the conquest. Chapter 2 explores the relation between gift giving and the act of narrating, with special attention given to "The New World" and its narrative time. This chapter also examines Fuentes's depiction of myth in relation to the gift and narrative time. Chapter 3 examines the neobaroque integration of Mesoamerican and European textual strategies in Fuentes's deconstruction of the utopian image of the Americas in "The New World." Chapter 4 deals specifically with the general economies of writing (inscriptions, carvings, tattoos, and so on) in "The New World." This chapter looks at Fuentes's idea of a collective, literary utopia. Chapter 5 takes up Fuentes's treatment of history and memory through his re-creation of traditional literary characters and historical figures. In this chapter we pay special attention to his notion of *herencia*, or "inheritance" and "heritage."

1

The Old World Meets the New

Money, Usury, and the Decline of Feudal Absolutism

A T THE CONCLUSION of *Cervantes; or, The Critique of Reading* Carlos Fuentes refers not only to Georges Bataille's conception of general economy but also to Jacques Derrida's deconstruction of "white mythology" as sources for his own conception of economy's relationship to writing. Traditionally, the study of economy in literature has focused on questions of production, the distribution of elements within a literary work, and the relationship between signs and literary tropes. Because literary works are composed of tropic exchanges, metaphor, and other literary tropes involving the exchange of meaning and qualities, some of these exchanges can be analyzed in terms of economic form. For Marc Shell, "the economy of literature seeks to understand the relationship between literary exchanges and the exchanges that constitute a political economy."[1] In this context, Fuentes's treatment of Bataille and Derrida serves as a road map for the study of literary economy in *Terra Nostra*. Nevertheless, while Fuentes does indeed use economic metaphors to represent political and economic power in *Terra Nostra*, his discussion of Bataille's theory of "general economy" and Derrida's

1. Shell, *The Economy of Literature*, 152.

"white mythology" requires a critical approach that goes beyond a study of "political economy" in the novel. For example, in *Terra Nostra* the tension between, on the one hand, the general economies of gift giving, excess, and expenditure and, on the other, those restricted economies of accumulation and exchange is instrumental to the novel's historical representation of the decline of feudal power and the rise of the capitalist economy. Thus, in this chapter we will not only study the political and economic history that Fuentes re-creates, that is, the conflicts between the nobility, the king, and the merchant of sixteenth-century Spain and the impact of usury and mercantilism on the king's power, but also study the general economies of social relationships based on noneconomic allegiances, the visual and artistic representation of power, and the role of abstraction at the level of metaphor and figuration. To understand the representation of power and economy through metaphor and writing, we first need to examine Derrida's deconstruction of white mythology, also a form of general economic analysis, and then look at how Fuentes uses it to characterize James Joyce's "critique of writing."

Derrida's deconstruction of "white mythology" traces the general economic play of metaphor in philosophical discourse. In particular, he employs the metaphor of usury to describe a process of abstraction in philosophical discourse, wherein figures, signs, and metaphors become abstracted through "a progressive erosion, a regular semantic loss, an uninterrupted exhausting of the primitive meaning." The rhetorical figures lose the sensorial and material opacity of their original meaning. In this way, the ruining of a figure implies a definite loss, but this loss in philosophical discourse has the motive, the interest, of producing abstract concepts; philosophers prefer the most worn-out words because they have the greater potential for precision and abstraction, for producing a surplus of meaning. Out of a semantic loss, there is the promise of a gain in abstracted meaning. Derrida, of course, finds this assumption very amusing. In more concrete terms, Derrida likens usury in metaphor to the "active erosion of an exergue," that is, the wearing down of the inscriptions, numerical values, and portraits on coinage (and these are images that Fuentes exploits in his deconstruction of absolutist authority, as we shall see). This erosion of the figure or word though abstraction signifies the metaphorical process Derrida calls "white mythology."[2] Derrida's decon-

2. Derrida, *Margins of Philosophy*, 211–15. Theodor Adorno comes to a similar conclusion, but adds his critique of the ideology behind this tendency in philosophy: "The apologia for dearth is not merely one for a thinking that has once more shrunk to a point. It has its precise ideological function. . . . The concept, purified as it rejects its content, functions in secret as

struction of white mythology coincides with Bataille's general economic study of gains and losses at the level of metaphorization, and can be considered as a practical application of Bataille's insight. In more general terms, this is also the theoretical framework for my study of *Terra Nostra*.

In *Cervantes; or, The Critique of Reading*, Fuentes discusses white mythology in terms of what he calls James Joyce's "critique of writing," particularly the idea that writing is exhausted, that words have lost their meaning. For Fuentes, the discourse of Europe and the West is the rational, individualistic, and ultimately absolutist discourse of the universal subject, a discourse in which language has suffered increased abstraction and distance from what would be, for Fuentes, Europe's true reality: the radical heterogeneity of its peoples and cultures. And while this divorce between words and things is most pronounced in the devastation of World War II, Fuentes traces the separation back to the moment of the encounter between Spain and the Americas, which includes the expulsion of the Jews and Muslims alongside the fanatical drive for a unified Spain and the purity of the Spanish race, *el casticismo*. In his discussion of Joyce's "critique of writing" Fuentes employs heliotropic and economic metaphors similar to those that Derrida deconstructs in his essay "White Mythology: Metaphor in the Text of Philosophy." According to Fuentes:

> Joyce is not satisfied with dictionaries; he takes the whole of Western discourse, reads it and doesn't understand it: the time, the usage and the epic adventure of a society in conflict with itself has exhausted each and every one of its words: the field of writing is sown with rotted cadavers, with semantic coins weakened to extinction, its verbal bones bleached by the sun of habit; secretly inscribed on the wall of Western writing is what Jacques Derrida calls *white mythology:* an invisible writing, with white ink, from white men, faded by history.

> (Joyce no se contenta con los diccionarios; toma el discurso total de Occidente, lo lee y no lo entiende: el tiempo y el uso y las aventuras de la épica de una sociedad en lucha consigo misma han gastado todas y cada una de las palabras: el campo de la escritura está sembrado de cadáveres corruptos, de monedas semánticas adelgazadas hasta la extinción, los huesos verbales blanqueados por el sol de la costumbre; en el muro de la

---

the model of a life that is arranged so no measure of mechanical progress—the equivalent of the concept—may ever, under any circumstances, do away with poverty" (*Negative Dialectics*, 121).

escritura occidental se inscribe secretamente lo que Jacques Derrida llama *la mitología blanca:* una escritura invisible, de tinta blanca, del hombre blanco, deslavada por la historia.) (*CCL,* 102–3)

In the apparent exhaustion of words, Fuentes finds, nevertheless, the seeds for a renewal of language's collective and pluralistic function; the deciphering of "white mythology" also implies the rewriting of all values and the recuperation of the West's multivalent heritage. This, of course, implies a general economic relation: in the exhaustion of writing, there is the promise of renewal. For this reason Fuentes revisits the initial encounter with the New World, in which Europe was confronted with a completely unknown other, for it is in this encounter that Spain confronts a new heterogeneity at the moment it tries to suppress its own cultural plurality. The encounter of the Old and New Worlds also marks the abrupt expansion of the market economy to regions where gift economies were still predominant. In *Terra Nostra* the tension between usury and the gift in the transition from a gift economy to an exchange economy also plays out at the level of signification. The resulting process of metaphorization is the same that takes place in white mythology.

Fuentes activates or reemploys Bataille's and Derrida's general economies of writing in *Terra Nostra* within the specific cultural and historical context of Spain's relationship to the Americas. Much of the first part of the novel, "The Old World," deals with Spain in the moment prior to the conquest of Mexico, the moment when Spain's nobility begins to lose the last vestiges of feudal power in the face of expanding market forces. Fuentes uses the main characters in the novel to portray and reflect on the complex economic and social relations of that era. One of the most significant political economic relationships is the vassalage between Felipe, El Señor, the king of Spain, and his servant Guzmán, a displaced lesser noble. Felipe's and Guzmán's association with Don Gonzalo de Ulloa, merchant and usurer, also demonstrates how the tension between political and general economies frames the narration of "The New World." For example, in "The Old World" the practice of ostentatious consumption by the king and the nobility is juxtaposed by the economy of exchange. In "The New World" the law of barter *(trueque)* and reciprocal exchange is suspended by potlatch, or the economy of the gift. In economic anthropology it has long been recognized that "reciprocal exchanges" in societies not dominated by market economies are embedded in noneconomic institutions such as kinship relations, marriage, age groups, secret societies, totemic associations, and public solemnities.[3] When the gift or potlatch appears in Fuentes's writing, however, reciprocity is suspended and exchange disrupted. (What Fuentes does in his study and depiction of such relationships is to temporalize them in the sense that both Derrida and Bourdieu describe, and as I discussed in the Introduction.) Throughout *Terra Nostra*, moreover, these types of economic and social intercourse imply relations of power that are negotiated and represented at the level of figuration, that is, through rhetorical figures such as metaphor, metonymy, oxymoron, and chiasmus.

The Displacement of the Land as the Visible Referent of Power

In "The New World" the protagonist named Pilgrim, a wanderer with no memory of his origins who flees the Old World and its tyrants, narrates the story of the encounter of the two worlds. He embarks on a journey with another refugee named Pedro, the peasant who once led an aborted uprising and now seeks a new life and a place to call his own. Later, when Pilgrim has returned to the Old World, he is called upon to narrate his adventure in the New World to Felipe, El Señor. This narration that consists of the entire second part of the three-part novel has an immense impact on the rest of the novel. It implies a change at various levels, most important because the knowledge of the New World undermines Felipe's power. The knowledge of the New World changes the identity of the Old, subverting the old paradigms of the world's order (hence the play among the section titles: the term *world* is exhausted in the encounter between Old and New, leading to a different conception that affirms the resulting heterogeneity—the *Other* World). In this respect, the king had discussed with Guzmán his anxiety over the rumor that there is more to the world than what is known to him, than what is known to Europe. He cannot accept that there would be another world beyond what he can see: "Look at that map on the wall: look at its limits, the Pillars of Hercules. . . . Guzmán, swear to me that there is nothing more; I would go mad if the world extended one inch beyond the confines we know; if it were so, I would have to learn everything again, begin everything again, and I would know no more than the usurer, the workman, you know. . . . Spain is

3. Karl Polanyi, *Primitive, Archaic and Modern Economies: Essays of Karl Polanyi*, 84.

contained within Spain, and Spain is this palace" (*TN*, 319). The map represents what is known to him, what he can measure and comprehend. In this sense, he lords over all that has been measured and contained in the map, which is inside his palace, El Escorial.[4] The palace becomes a necropolis where he has warehoused not only knowledge but also all the corpses of his ancestors, saints and sovereigns alike. It is an excessive image of death, and through its creation Felipe desires to control death, control Spain and all that is contained within. As Felipe desires to be the absolute ruler of all that is known, this new world challenges and undermines his power. Furthermore, Pilgrim's narration contains both general and restricted economic scenarios that mirror "The Old World," but with crucial differences that highlight the fundamental conflicts of the novel as a whole.

In this new land that Pilgrim describes to the king, he encounters sacrifices, gifts of rivalry, and a religious belief system based on the obligation to an originary debt. He also participates in potlatches, exchanges *(trueques),*[5] and observes a tributary economy that somewhat recalls the despotism of Felipe's reign. Moreover, it should be kept in mind that the exchanges the narrator refers to are not confined to the political economic relations presented in the novel, and that the representation of "reciprocal exchanges" in particular often depends on specific rhetorical figures, such as chiasmus. For this reason the analysis of exchange economy in *Terra Nostra* cannot be limited to representations of the distribution and circulation of wealth. Moreover, as I will demonstrate in Chapter 2, the apparent "exchanges" are actually temporalized and often open-ended, creating a series of potlatches that reinforce and reconfigure social bonds. In all discussions of "exchanges" we must keep in mind Bourdieu's warning against temporalizing and totalizing such events, a warning I addressed in the Introduction.

The tributary and exchange economies that Pilgrim describes in the New

---

4. I am reminded here of Raymond Williams's highly original study of Fuentes's reconstruction of El Escorial, a direct integration of architecture and writing. According to Williams, "Both El Escorial and *Terra Nostra* are architectural constructs that imagine the Americas from the space in the Guadarrama Mountains. The four towers and the imposing walls of El Escorial imagine the domination of the Americas." He also states that the "architectural object of El Escorial, like several of its predecessors, was conceived as orbus mundi—an architectural utopia designed to protect its inhabitants from the empirical world outside" (*Writings of Fuentes*, 78–79).

5. Because the terms *truck* and *barter* are rarely used in the plural in English, and because *exchange* has such a broader semantic field than the more restrictive *trueque*, which is more akin to *barter*, I retain the plural of *trueques*.

World are a powerful theme, a vertical axis that runs through his narrative. Nevertheless, we can already see the importance of figuration in the representation of such economic and social relations in "The Old World" when Guzmán, Felipe's servant and adviser, laments the displacement of the Spanish nobility. In the chapter "Guzmán Speaks," he depicts Spain's transformation from a feudal economy, wherein power is represented through the hereditary ownership of land, to one in which economic power shifts to the rising merchant classes:

> It is I, Guzmán, who tells you this, not some bastard son of a bitch, but a Lord like you, although broken by debts. . . . Not some lout from Guadarrama turned highway robber, but a nobleman incapable of understanding or of holding back an invisible movement in which the solid land, the base of all power, could be converted into insubstantial money, and where castle walls constructed for eternity would last a briefer time than winter's swallows, walls subjugated by a power that needs neither fortification nor cannons, the power of the usurers, merchants, and miserable clerks of the leprous cities. (*TN*, 141; translation modified)

> (Te lo digo yo, Guzmán, no un hijo de puta y padre desconocido, sino un señor como tú, pero quebrado por las deudas. . . . No un mozo acompañante de saqueadores de Guadarrama, sino un hidalgo incapaz de comprender o detener un movimiento invisible en el que la sólida tierra, base de todo poder, se convertiría en inasible dinero y las murallas de los castillos, construidas para la eternidad, durarían menos que las golondrinas en invierno, avasalladas por el poder sin murallas ni cañones de los usureros, los comerciantes y los cagatintas de las ciudades leprosas.) (*TN*, 147)

This passage demonstrates the transformation of land as a concrete economic source of power, which generates wealth through its use and the consumption of its products, into something intangible that can be abstracted and exchanged. Land is inherited within a feudal economy, and with it power, which is lost when land is commodified and becomes mobile within an exchange economy. This is the way that Fuentes represents the exhaustion, the ruining of the term *land*. According to Karl Polanyi, a commodity is a thing that is produced to be bought and sold, and therefore land, labor, and money cannot be true commodities for they are not products. Nevertheless, the "commodity fiction" is a necessary organizing principle for them to function, to be bought and sold within a market economy. Guzmán's reference to usurers, merchants, and clerks emphasizes that power is shifting from those that inherit and amass lands and wealth for tributary distribution and consumption to those who control markets where gains and profits are made through exchange and interest.[6]

In Guzmán's complaint about the breakdown of seigneurial privilege, Fuentes re-creates the nobility's sense of crisis during that era. Moreover, the transition involving a shift from a concrete referent, the solid land *(la sólida tierra),* as the base of all power to one dependent on an abstracted and "insubstantial" *(inasible)* symbolic form of money manifests one of the fundamental problems that *Terra Nostra* addresses: the separation between "the representational *usage* of language" and the *"experience* of the being of language" (*CCL,* 110). The divorce between *words* and *things* has a parallel trajectory with the rise of capitalist exchange. The power of the merchants and usurers is invisible in contrast to the visible image of the land that Guzmán describes—the metaphorical image of castle walls representing the solidity and power of seigneurial lands. In the comparison of the walls to the swallows, the semantic quality of solidity is diminished in a metaphoric shift brought on not simply by the comparison, but also by the inversion in the term *subjugated (avasalladas,* made a vassal, referring to the walls). The walls are enslaved by the invisible power of the merchants. Consequently, they become as transitory as the swallows—in other words, as fleeting as capital. Thus, the economic process has a corresponding figuration in which the metaphor experiences a semantic loss—in this way Fuentes links Derrida's deconstruction of white mythology to the rise of capitalism as he depicts it. At this point we should revisit Fuentes's manner of describing white mythology in *Cervantes; or, The Critique of Reading* because it corresponds directly with the analysis of the novel: "Secretly inscribed on the wall of Western writing is what Jacques Derrida calls *white mythology:* an invisible writing, with white ink, from white men, faded by history" (*CCL,* 102–3). Is not the "wall of Western writing" referring back to his own deconstruction/reconstruction of white mythology in *Terra Nostra?* Is not the "invisible writing" this very process of abstraction, usury, commodification, exhaustion, and separation

6. Polanyi, *Primitive, Archaic and Modern Economies,* 30–31. This novel, *Our Land,* as well as most of the novels of the boom generation, is a deconstruction and reconfiguration of the "novel of the land," the genre most associated with the formation of national identities in Latin America. The passage is also very reminiscent of Maravall's depiction of the shift of economic power to the city (*Culture of the Baroque,* 107–8).

of words and things in nascent capitalist modernization? The play between the visible and the invisible, moreover, is also reminiscent of Bataille's and Derrida's general economic studies of gains and losses.

Instead of representing power, the castle walls, a concrete, *visible* referent, become defined by their servitude to the *invisible* power of money. The visible become subordinated and redefined by the invisible. The opposition of money as an invisible power and land as a visible one corresponds to a belief that traces back to the ancient Greeks. Visibility and invisibility were associated with money and were directly related to questions of power among the Greeks. According to Marc Shell in *The Economy of Literature:* "The tyrant depends upon money for his material or economic base, and it is money that precipitated in the Greek world changes in the organization and understanding of visible and invisible estates. The distinction between visible and invisible things in Greek thought includes the opposition of *ousia phanera* (visible substance) to *ousia aphanēs* (invisible substance)." Shell further explains that there are two meanings to this opposition: on the one hand, with relation to witnesses, *ousia phanera* is property "whose transfer was seen by others, and *ousia aphanēs* is property whose transfer was not seen"; on the other hand, in terms of money "*ousia phanera* is a non-monetary commodity (such as land or 'real' estate) and *ousia aphanēs* is money (such as coin)."[7]

In *Terra Nostra*, the opposition of the visible and the invisible forms of wealth, or substance, is also evident in an earlier example of Guzmán's commentary on the growing power of the cities and the usurers who inhabit them. He says to Felipe that the usury of the cities pays homage to the king, but also mentions the destruction and deception of the cities' power. Guzmán points out that money even characterizes the king's relations with the workers building his palace: "The shepherds and laborers of these lands today are workers at the palace; El Señor has left them with no sustenance but their daily wage. And it is easier to take money from a wage than to collect bushels from a harvest, for the harvest can be seen in measurable fields, while wages are manipulated invisibly" (*TN*, 105). Not only is the contrast of the invisible movements of money to the visible products of the land evident in this passage, but Guzmán's attitude itself is a partial deception that parallels the opposition of what is seen and not seen. When he speaks to the king he must hide his true feelings, whereas when he addresses his falcon, his observations on the same matter take a different tone altogether. The play between the

7. Shell, *The Economy of Literature*, 31–32.

visible and the invisible, between appearances and what is hidden in deceit, is a fundamental aspect of Guzmán's relationship with Felipe, his liege. In a scene from early in the novel, Guzmán's outward deference covers the general annoyance he feels toward his physically weakened king, as indicated when Guzmán must help his liege in a simple task:

> El Señor shivered and his breviary fell to the ground; his impulse was to pick it up, he even bent forward slightly, but like a flash Guzmán was kneeling before his Lord; he picked up the book of devotions to hand to his master. From his kneeling position Guzmán ... for an instant looked directly at El Señor, and he must have arched an eyebrow in a manner that offended his Liege; but El Señor could find no fault in his servant's celerity in demonstrating his obedience and respect; the visible act was that of the perfect vassal, although the secret intent of that glance lent itself, and all the more for being ill-defined, to interpretations El Señor wished both to accept and to forget. (*TN*, 41)

On the surface Guzmán fulfills his duty as a vassal, even though his expression betrays his scorn. As the two men reach down, moreover, the wound on Guzmán's hand accidentally rubs against the wound on Felipe's hand; the accident further reveals the difference between the seen and the unseen: "Guzmán's wound grazed the wound on El Señor's hand; the handkerchiefs that bound them were of very different quality, but the scratches caused by a spiked collar were identical" (*TN*, 41). While the brushing of their wounds also gives cause for a mutual annoyance, the disparity in the material of the bandages testifies to the oppositions of visible and invisible, surface and depth. On the surface there is a hierarchical relation of lord and servant; underneath, however, they are both of the same vulnerable flesh. What is more, although Felipe's physical weakness corresponds to his waning feudal power, at the level of appearances his authority is still acknowledged by those who truly wield power—the usurers.

The invisible movement of money also parallels the shift between metaphorical discourse, primarily representational, and metonymic discourse, which involves relations of combination, contiguity, and contexture.[8] At first it would appear that this metonymization of the commodity structure (fiction) might disrupt reciprocal relations at other levels. The political and economic

---

8. See also Becky Boling, "A Literary Vision of History: Marxism and Positivism in *Terra Nostra* by Fuentes," 129–30.

relations between the nobility and the king, as Guzmán describes them, depend on a social pact involving reciprocity. In the following passage this is expressed with the figure of chiasmus:

> My fathers and grandfathers, Sire, fulfilled before your ancestors the ceremony of homage and thus entered a pact: our service in exchange for your protection. In this way, we would all maintain the fundamental principle of our society; *no Lord without land and no land without a Lord.* . . . Our service continued but not your protection. You allowed the debilitation of power based on the land, confronted with the power of commerce based on money. (*TN*, 141–42; emphasis added)

> (Señor, cumplieron ante los tuyos la ceremonia de homenaje y así concluyeron un pacto: nuestro servicio a cambio de vuestra protección. De esta manera, manteníamos todos el principio fundamental de nuestra sociedad: *ningún señor sin tierra y ninguna tierra sin señor.* . . . No cumpliste el trato. Continuó nuestro servicio pero no tu protección. Permitiste que se debilitara nuestro poder, basado en la tierra, frente a los poderes del comercio, basado en el dinero.) (*TN*, 147; emphasis added)

If the chiastic play of the words *land (tierra)* and *Lord (señor)* are compared to the earlier reference to *solid land (sólida tierra)*, it becomes evident not only that the king, El Señor, and the lords are interdependent but also that their power depends on the solidity of the land, whose concreteness in representation depends on its hereditary distribution. There is also a mutual dependence between the nobles and the king: the nobles support the king's power through their service, which is possible due the economic power of the land, while the king protects their seigneurial privilege from the pressures of mercantilism and ensures their superior position in the social hierarchy.

Money, Power, and the Metaphor of Usury

The theme of mercantilism in the novel is crucial in that it intensifies the conflicts between different social classes. In his discussion of baroque culture, José Antonio Maravall defines and describes the role and the values of mercantilism in the conflicts between new and traditional social forces during the fifteenth and sixteenth centuries in the following way:

What was new is the zeal for gaining power, growing larger, for wealth and expansion; this zeal has served as an impetus for European sovereigns and for particular realms since the technical, economic, and demographic boom at the beginning of the modern age. It is this desire for wealth and power that inspires this repertory of concrete measures—not always coinciding in content, but much more so in their declared finality—that we call *mercantilism*.

He later adds, "If people are stimulated to strive toward possessing more and, at the same time, believe that the volume of available goods does not alter as a whole, they have no option left but to direct themselves toward others so as to succeed in augmenting their own share at the expense of others."[9]

Although this depiction will help to clarify Fuentes's treatment of mercantilism in *Terra Nostra*, it does not give a full picture. As we have seen, Fuentes presents the usurers and merchants as undermining the feudal ties to the land and labor as well. According to Karl Polanyi, however, "Mercantilism, with all its tendency toward commercialization, never attacked the safeguards that protected these two basic elements of production—labor and land—from becoming the objects of commerce." Although Polanyi was writing mainly about England and France, not Spain, this quote might point to a possible anachronism in Fuentes's depiction of the disgruntled Guzmán who complains about the merchants' and usurers' conversion of the land into commodity form.[10] As we shall see, however, the character of the usurer will waiver between his desire for material gain, on the one hand, and his desire for social rank within the nobility, on the other. What is important here is the transition from mercantilism, represented mainly by the usurer, to the rapacious capitalism of Guzmán and later the United States.

Felipe, nonetheless, is responsible for the breakdown in the reciprocal social contract that ties the lords to the land and their allegiance to the king in exchange for his protection. With respect to Spain's waning feudalism in the face of rising mercantilism, Maravall portrays the baroque society of sixteenth- and seventeenth-century Spain as one in which an absolutist monarchy was converted into the principle or, rather, the keystone of the social system. In the absolutist regime of the baroque, moreover, "the monarchy capped off a complex of restored seigniorial interests, supporting itself on the predominance of land ownership that became the base of the system."

9. Maravall, *Culture of the Baroque*, 166.
10. Polanyi, *Primitive, Archaic and Modern Economies*, 29.

Though recognizing that there were remnants of feudalism, the restored rank and interests of the nobility, Maravall nevertheless argues against the classification of baroque Spain's monarchical-nobiliary society as feudal.[11] In *Terra Nostra*, Guzmán explains that Felipe has ruined the social contract between the monarchy and the nobility. As well, the king's expensive campaigns against heresy and his construction of a costly and inaccessible monument to God and death have led the general population to identify power with luxury as opposed to death, or religion, which delegitimates the monarchy (*TN*, 141–42). More important, for Guzmán these and other excesses put the nobility at the mercy of the merchants and usurers in the cities: "You left your noble vassals undefended; . . . we had to sell our lands, assume debts, close the workshops that could not compete with the city merchants, and sell our serfs their freedom. . . . You have destroyed the grades of nobiliary authority between the Liege and the cities" (*TN*, 142). Seeing himself reduced to a rogue as a result of Felipe's inability to protect the lesser nobles (*hidalgos*) from the market forces of the cities, Guzmán marks his time in anticipation of the moment in which he can take advantage of the monarchy's weakness before the rising power of the merchants. Although Guzmán at first regrets the loss of the monarch's protection guaranteed to the nobility, he later joins forces with the usurers and highway robbers (also the conquistadores) to help Felipe maintain his waning economic power. In fact, it is Guzmán who introduces Felipe to the usurer who helps the king pay off his debts. Finally, what is most disconcerting for Guzmán is the fact that the breakdown in the social contract is due to the king's religious ostentation and wasteful expenditure.

Felipe becomes perturbed by the intervention of the usurer and the subordination that his help implies. This is evident when he complains about the usurer: "Who is that old man, who is he really? Is he the Devil, a homunculus come here to humiliate me, to offer me money in exchange for my life; but that is the most horrible sin of simony, does he want my soul in exchange for my money?" (*TN*, 315–16). Before the king becomes indebted to the usurer, he is offended by the offer. The loan, and the resulting debtor relationship, as compared to that which he maintained with the nobility, accentuates the further divorce between language and its representational use. The reciprocity between the power and protection of the king, on the one hand, and the nobility's service and homage, on the other, is represented as a con-

11. Maravall, *Culture of the Baroque*, 27, 271n23.

crete social relation. Seigneurial privilege—as articulated by Guzmán, "no Lord without land and no land without a Lord"—represents the fundamental principle of the society, the concrete relations upon which rested the pact between king and nobility. As Felipe ironically suggests, the usurer puts a price on the king's soul, and thus the king will suffer the same metaphoric erosion and abstraction as we saw with the land. This later becomes represented through the decay of his body and wasting away of his image on coin, reminiscent of the semantic loss in white mythology.

This pricing has a violent and destabilizing effect similar to that of the destabilization of value generally implied in pricing. According to Foucault, "Money, like words, has the role of designating, yet never ceases to fluctuate around that vertical axis: variations of price are to the initial establishment of the relation between metal and wealth what rhetorical displacements are to the original value of verbal signs." Money in this sense has the figurative ability to shift values, to cause a sign to shift in relation to what it designates. Moreover, the nature of exchange involves a "reciprocal relation between utilities"; while creating and augmenting utilities, or use values, the exchange diminishes the original value.[12] In the case of Felipe, the circulation of his image on coin, its representation, falls within the domain of the merchants who control its movement. Felipe's usefulness as a symbol of stability correlates with the decline of his economic and political power, with his inability to guarantee seigneurial privilege. In the scene in which Felipe signs the loan contract with the usurer, the latter explains the symbolic value of the crown when he defers before the king's annoyance:

> El Señor, numb in body and soul, took the pen. But first, narrowing his glassy eyes, he asked: "If I may, I would like to pose a question to this gentleman: If your powers as a merchant and moneylender are so extensive, why do you accept mine?"
>
> The aged moneylender bowed his head. "Unity, Sire, unity. Without a visible head, bodies are wont to be dispersed. Without a supreme power to which to appeal, we would devour each other like wolves. Thank you, Sire." (*TN*, 315)

> (El Señor, entumecido de cuerpo y alma, tomó la pluma. Pero antes, angostando la vidriosa mirada preguntó:

---

12. Foucault, *Order of Things*, 198–203. Karl Marx also recognized that money has the tendency to turn the concrete, the sensual, or the spiritual into something abstract (*Economic and Philosophic Manuscripts of 1844*, 105).

—Siento una curiosidad, caballero. Si tantos son vuestros poderes de mercaderes y usureros, ¿por qué aceptáis el mío?

El viejo prestamista inclinó la cabeza:—La unidad, Sire, la unidad. Sin cabeza visible, los cuerpos se disgregan. Sin suprema instancia, todos nos devoraríamos como lobos. Gracias, Sire.) (*TN,* 323)

Felipe's unusual usage of the Spanish second-person plural in the question Why do *you accept* mine? (¿por qué *aceptáis* el mío?) displays a hostile irony: while he recognizes the need to agree to the loan, he resents it, and he disdains the usurer for his moralizing justification of usury and exchanging. When the usurer inclines his head in deference before the sovereign's anger, his response is no less ironic and demonstrates his belief that the king's power is mainly symbolic. The usurer's use of metaphor and analogy is also no coincidence; it is he who defines the king's power through the turn of a trope: the metaphor "visible head" corresponds to the frequent play between visible and invisible manifestations of power. In a similar vein, the anaphoric "without a supreme power" (sin suprema instancia) is also a further abstraction from the more concrete comparison to "wolves" for the usurers. Likewise, the use of two reflexive verbs in Spanish, "are wont to be dispersed" (se disgregan) and "would devour each other" (nos devoraríamos), enhances the sense that economic exchanges take place among the merchants; they separate and come together. Whereas in the hypothesis the king is a passive object that remains above, or statically distant, the merchants are active.[13]

The "visible head" also corresponds to a general usury that functions through metaphor in the novel, much in the way that Derrida describes usury in "White Mythology." The image of the king's head appears on coins that are circulated and that become worn and faded with time, like the words and numbers in an exergue. This usury becomes more pronounced toward the end of the novel, as is evinced in a scene from "The Next World." When the monk Simón and Ludovico, two companions from Felipe's youth, reunite, they discuss their estranged friend, Felipe, and also Celestina. The latter had asked Simón to give Ludovico some coins on her behalf. As Simón hands the coins to Ludovico, he contemplates Felipe's image stamped on the coinage:

---

13. This image is also reminiscent of the general division in baroque painting, and in the Neoplatonic tradition, between two floors or levels: the lower representing the mundane, chaotic world weighted down by gravity, while the upper is characterized by weightlessness and souls are governed by reason. An example of this is El Greco's *Burial of Count Orgaz.* See Gilles Deleuze, *The Fold: Leibniz and the Baroque,* 29–30.

But first she gave me these coins for you. It was her last generous gesture. She wept as she gave them to me. She had laughed as she took
them.

Look carefully at the profile minted on these coins, Ludovico.

The salient jaw.

The heavy, protuberant lip.

The dead gaze.

It is El Señor. (*TN*, 540–41)

The image is of a man aging and fading, a spirit in decay—the transition
from a youthful "Felipe" to an aging and weakened El Señor. Nonetheless, a
more direct image of the wearing of the coin can be found in the last chapter
of the novel. The young man who witnesses the apocalypse at the end is associated with the series of reincarnated souls that trace back to Felipe and his
doubles, and that includes Polo Febo. (Throughout *Terra Nostra* characters
are interrelated through reincarnation and the sharing or exchanging of destinies.) In his hotel room he contemplates the residues of his past lives: "You
open, often, the long case of Cordovan leather that houses in beds of white
silk the ancient coins you love to caress, effacing even more the blurred effi-
gies of forgotten Kings and Queens" (*TN*, 764). The wearing away of the
image in these and other passages also relates to the fading of documents, letters, calligraphy, with emphasis on their materiality in time. Moreover, in the
preservation and fading of letter, paper, and minted image there is a simultaneity of memory and forgetting that parallels the gain in abstraction and
the loss of "primitive" meaning in white mythology. Despite all his angst and
despite the specificity of his life experiences, Felipe, El Señor, becomes just
another "forgotten king," abstracted and exhausted in the same way as the
"land" he represented as the sovereign.

The metaphor of usury in the images of the coins follows a pattern of
wearing and thus suggests a principle of loss that corresponds to the decay
not only of Felipe's power but also of his body. On the other hand, the
usurer's actions and self-interest are based on a principle of accumulation, as
can be determined in his conversations with Felipe and Guzmán. In this
sense the usury is symbolic of the decline of absolutism and feudal power,
and is symptomatic of the shift from the gift economy to the profit economy
in Western civilization.

During the meetings between Felipe and the usurer, which occur shortly
before and after Pilgrim's narration of his journey in the New World, the

usurer's observations on Pilgrim's narration are key to understanding the differences between general economic relations in both "The Old World" and
"The New World." Moreover, their comparison will reveal a change in which
latent tensions within the power relations between the usurer and Guzmán,
on one side, and Felipe, on the other, lead to conflict and subversion. In the
first meeting, the usurer tries to convince the monarch that his motives in
loaning the money are honorable. His comments are reflective of mercantilists' attitudes toward monarchy during the baroque era, for they accepted
the traditional organization of land and labor, the system of seigneurial privilege, and supported their absolutist despots.[14] In *Terra Nostra* the usurer ex-
emplifies this position when he recognizes that although his values differ
from those of the landed nobility, he can still serve the king and seigneurial
privilege. The usurer contrasts his values with those of the old order:

> Times have changed, the codes of yesteryear no longer have their old
> following, their old value; it used to be that illness and hunger caused
> men to cherish hopes of the world beyond, but now a man can work,
> Señor, dedicate his life to hard labor, and harvest his fruits right here on
> earth. . . . I live, Exalted Señor, from what I earn and from the money I
> change; that will not impede me from serving you and from sustaining
> with my tired old bones a power based on inherited rank. (*TN*, 314)

The expression of the values of work and self-motivation, along with the
image of scarcity, is very much in tune with Maravall's depiction of the
consciousness of crisis in the baroque and the belief in the need to motivate
oneself to survive.[15] Moreover, as I have shown above, the usurer clearly distinguishes his own dynamic values as the necessary response to an immobile
and stagnant society. And while the usurer does contrast his own values of
self-sufficiency, earning, and profit with those of inherited wealth, he nevertheless hopes to gain some of the noneconomic vestiges of seigneurial privilege. On the usurer's behalf Guzmán has recommended to Felipe that he
offer the usurer the title of knight commander *(comendador)*.

The usurer himself, however, alludes to his own desire to gain in prestige

---

14. Polanyi, *Primitive, Archaic and Modern Economies*, 29–30.

15. According to Maravall, the belief in the human potential to improve reality was height-
ened during the Spanish Renaissance, in part due to the stabilizing policies of the Catholic
kings and the monarchs who followed. The sense of crisis, however, was most acute beginning
with the last decades of the sixteenth century and continuing into the seventeenth when
Spanish society experienced a general decline. See Maravall, *Culture of the Baroque*, 19–79.

at the same time that he subtly implicates Felipe in reciprocal obligations involving the sovereign's illicit relations with the usurer's daughter, who is a
novice. When the usurer explains the conditions of his loan, which include
payment at 20 percent interest, he tries to ensnare the king with the suggestion that the money will return to the king through his relations with the
usurer's daughter: "My money, thanks to Inesilla, will revert to El Señor's for-
tune." Of course, the usurer does expect something in return as Inés's father:
"As the girl—whom from the chapel I watched leave your bedchamber this
night—will again demonstrate her devotion to El Señor, in the same way El
Señor demonstrates his devotion to her father in a thousand little ways" (*TN*,
314–15).

The usurer manipulates the situation with the ambiguous line "in the same
way El Señor demonstrates his devotion to her father," which can be taken in
two ways: First, the usurer diplomatically recognizes that by being the sovereign the king implicitly gives to the father; this follows the literal use of the
present tense. The idea of a return, moreover, is reinforced in the chiasmus
(Inés—devotion to El Señor; El Señor—devotion to the father of Inés).
Second, in what follows, the usurer implies that he should receive something
more in return for what he sees as his daughter's service:

> for in dealing with El Señor a man will not have to come many times to
> the well, and anyone who comes to the aid of El Señor must surely re-
> ceive something more than the ordinary moneylender's interest, for El
> Señor can make a gentleman of a flea, and permit me in December to
> enjoy the pleasures of May, and add honor to riches. (*TN*, 315)

> (pues seguramente, en esta ocasión, quien dineros ha de cobrar muchas
> vueltas no ha de dar, y quien así acude en ayuda del Señor algo más que
> el interés de un préstamo ha de recibir, pues el Señor puede hacer de una
> pulga un caballero y permitirme, en mi vejez, gozar de mayo y añadir
> honra a riqueza.) (*TN*, 322)

The second part of this chiasmus, "and anyone who comes to the aid of El
Señor," could refer either to Felipe receiving the money or to the father pro-
viding a service through his daughter. In this respect, the manipulation implies that the king has dishonored the usurer and that he also has and should
exercise the power to restore that honor by granting the old usurer the status
of a knight or gentleman. The usurer's hypocrisy goes even further: in the implied prostitution of Inés—the usurer essentially tries to buy honor with his

daughter—love is commodified and therefore profaned, its meaning exhausted. Moreover the term *devotion* also becomes thoroughly corrupted by self-interest, and therefore devoid of spiritual and primitive meaning.

At this juncture in the novel the usurer is knighted, and thereafter referred to as "El Comendador" (The Knight Commander). This character, moreover, takes on yet another nominal transformation when he is later identified as "Don Gonzalo de Ulloa," modeled after the character of the same name from Tirso de Molina's *Joker of Seville*. This nominal transformation represents both a gain and a loss in meaning: as his name moves from the general to the particular, the character loses the specificity of his identity and of his role in the novel as he comes to be associated with a previously existing literary archetype.

But here the main interest in the usurer has to do with what he says in his conversations with Felipe, the king, and with Guzmán, the king's vassal. Toward the end of "The Old World," the first part of the novel, Guzmán introduces the usurer to the king. And although at first Guzmán had decried the dissolution of the nobility's power at the hand of usurers and merchants, who were buying up the land, he finds in the usurer an ally in his own efforts to advance himself.

Expenditure and Exchange

Once Pilgrim, the protagonist of "The New World," has finished his narration, Guzmán and El Comendador discuss Pilgrim's narration and the possibilities and limits that the existence of a different world might present. The attitudes of the usurer and Guzmán become much more aggressive; they see in the New World the possibility of gaining power at Felipe's expense. They also see the monarchy as an obstacle to progress. El Comendador decries the lack of productivity in monarchy and religion, the absence of utilitarian values, and in particular the principle of wasteful expenditure that underpins Felipe's power. According to El Comendador, "Nonproductivity; for as the monks do not propagate sons, El Señor does not propagate riches; he cannot, it is contrary to his most profound reason for being; if what I know of him . . . is true, then it is also true that his rank, his power, his cult, depend upon loss, not acquisition. El Señor's dynasty confuses honor with loss, glory with loss, rank with loss, power with loss" (*TN*, 499). Clearly, El Comendador favors productivity and acquisition, and relates the noneconomic aspects of Felipe's absolutist monarchy—honor, glory, rank, and power—*with a principle of loss, or wasteful expenditure,* that benefits no one.

This is not the first time El Comendador complains of this type of wasteful expenditure: during his initial meeting with Felipe, El Comendador mentions several instances of ostentatious display among the nobility that he had witnessed, most notably the planting of freshly plowed fields with silver instead of seed and the wanton burning of thirty horses at the end of a party (*TN,* 313–14). For El Comendador, this squandering is a spectacle designed to impress and to give the nobles a sense of superiority. (Bataille emphasized, moreover, the importance of witnesses to such wasteful destruction, of the spectacle as a condition for the appropriation of power.) El Comendador emphasizes the image and appearance of wealth and power, which he later contrasts with the productive acquisition of wealth that will be possible in the conquest and expeditions he proposes for the New World.

The noble's rank, as well as Felipe's power, then, is related to the principle of potlatch that is *the wasteful expenditure of wealth designed to produce obligation and power.* On the one hand, there is the ostentatious display of the palace, but on the other hand, the analogy of the magpie that steals and hoards implies that the expenditure is neither distributed nor circulated (*TN,* 499). Therefore, the ostentatious consumption of the sovereign and his nobility cannot be associated with the practice of feudal largesse, for in the Middle Ages largesse was not only a manifestation of power but also an exercise in generosity and the redistribution of wealth.

Fuentes seems to be exploring and parodying the questions of ostentatious consumption and potlatch from a variety of standpoints, El Comendador representing what potlatch looks like from a capitalist's point of view. In *The Accursed Share,* Georges Bataille discusses the problem of generosity in the potlatch, and also what is gained in such conspicuous consumption. When a surplus is produced, there arises a need to give away, lose, or destroy the surplus; however, the gift, or the wasteful consumption of the surplus, takes on the "meaning of an acquisition." *The giving becomes the acquiring of power.* And the consumption must be a spectacle, must be viewed by others in order for the lord, the chief, the ruler to gain anything from the destruction or gift.[16] El Comendador, on the other hand, does not recognize this form of acquisition precisely because it is something that is not quantifiable, measurable, or material for that matter. His observation is based on the appreciation

16. Bataille, *Accursed Share,* 64–69.

of commercial values and measures power only according to the acquisition and amount of wealth. Therefore, it is natural that the squandering appears to him a total loss, regardless of his own desire for honor and status. El Comendador's comparison of Felipe's ostentatious consumption with the potlatches in Pilgrim's narration, moreover, further clarifies the stakes in the transition from a gift economy to a profit economy:

> Power is a challenge based upon offering something for which there is no possible counteroffering. A challenge, I say, for greatest is the power of the one who ends by having something that is nothing; in the end, loss; in the end, death; in the end, sacrifice: sacrifice, death and loss for others, as long as it is possible, and when it is no longer so, then sacrifice, death and loss for oneself. My solution is very simple; to these negative practices I oppose the very positive proposition of exchanging in order to acquire; to loss, I oppose acquisition. (*TN*, 499)

The challenge of such an offering that can have no counteroffering, or of a consumption that cannot be matched, implies for El Comendador a useless and meaningless sacrifice. Nevertheless, as will be seen, his interpretation of the potlatches of the New World does not do them justice: the death and loss of oneself will lead to a kind of power other than what Felipe and the nobles hope to gain through their ostentatious displays. In a novel in which characters' souls transmigrate into other characters and are reincarnated, this loss leads to freedom from the previous destiny and to renewal.

As El Comendador opposes his own "positive" principle of acquisition to the "negative" practices of the monarch, he also details the relation of dependence that the king has with him. Not only is Felipe dependent on merchants, entrepreneurs, and producers to prepare for the exploration and conquest of this new land, but he will also need the men of action like Guzmán, the dispossessed who themselves are in need of some way to deal with their own material crisis. This implies a potential alliance between the merchants and the conquistadores, one that allows El Comendador and the men like Guzmán the opportunity for their own material acquisition of power. El Comendador spells out the deceptive nature of this new alliance. "Does he wish to colonize the new lands? He will have to come to men like you, Don Guzmán, and to every last ordinary man in this palace, . . . and we shall be repaid for our efforts with the gold and pearls that will flow from the hands of the natives into ours, though we will take care to reserve the royal fifth part for El Señor, and to collect payment for his debts in advance, and to make him content, and deceive him" (*TN*, 499). This represents a key moment in the transition from gift economy to profit economy—the moment when mercantilism begins to take advantage of the absolutist monarchy's economic dependence, to wrest control of the circulation of wealth. Moreover, the novel alludes to Spain's future debt and decline when El Comendador decides to defy Felipe's decree that the New World does not exist, by spreading the rumor of it to his associates in Genoa, Porto, Antwerp, and Danzig (*TN*, 500).

Guzmán is won over by El Comendador's arguments and also takes on a subversive attitude in response to Felipe's inaction regarding the news of the New World. His response, furthermore, reinforces the binary oppositions that El Comendador postulated, while at the same time giving the reader a clear idea of his association with the historical figure Hernán Cortés. While speaking to his hawk Guzmán declares, "The new world, if it exists, hawk, how can I not play a part in it?, oh, hawk, I am beginning to believe not only that it exists but that actually it exists for me, for men like me to demonstrate there in those jungles and seas and rivers and plains and mountains and temples that the universe will belong to action and not contemplation, to strength and not inheritance, to chance and not fatality, to progress and not stasis" (*TN*, 502). The dynamic values that Guzmán opposes to the feudal remnants of Felipe's absolutism are products of the Renaissance and Reformation. They also represent the self-interest that marked not only the general character of the mercantilists and conquistadores but also the voracious energy behind future capitalist expansion into the Americas. His assertion that he will write "long chronicles of the discovery" (cartas de relación) (*TN*, 502) is a clear allusion to Hernán Cortés's infamous letters to the emperor Carlos V, in which he tries to convince the king that he, Cortés, is the only one who can ensure the king's sovereignty over New Spain. After "The New World" Guzmán and El Comendador conspire to deceive Felipe into believing that they act in his interests. Nonetheless, while El Comendador will secretly use the epistle to counteract Felipe's decree and spread the news of the New World, Guzmán will address it directly to Felipe in order to mask the nature of his actions there.

The Dissolution of the Commune

In *Terra Nostra*, on the eve of the discovery of the New World, Spain witnesses the decay of seigneurial power due to the king's extravagant expenditures of national wealth in "costly and distant" wars against the infidels, and the construction of a "useless mausoleum" that leads the population to identify his power not with death but with luxury (*TN*, 142). The sacred but ostentatious deeds and offerings of the king lose their symbolic force in a world now ruled by "interest" and calculation. As we have seen, according to Guzmán, Felipe's obsessions and costly behavior are what left the nobility vulnerable to the mercantilists in the first place. In addition, the construction of El Escorial displaces the pastors who lived there beforehand and were then forced to become the very workers who built it. The workers themselves are keenly aware of the reason for the king's extravagance; they see the palace as the king's effort to guarantee his acceptance into heaven (*TN*, 80). Furthermore, not only have the workers been displaced from their lands but they also receive very little for their labor. The peasants, much like Guzmán, complain of the king's failure to protect them from the lords (*TN*, 80–83). Whereas Felipe cannot protect the nobles from the usurers, neither can he protect the serfs and peasants from the taxation and debt incurred under the seigneurs.

Martín, one of the workers building the palace, describes the severity of the seigneurs' wrath toward those who try to escape such debts. When his brother tries to flee, he is captured and sentenced to death by hunger, thirst, and cold. Martín cites the punishment as the reason for his own flight: "From a distance, we watched him die, and there was nothing we could do. He became like the earth, hungry, thirsty, and cold; he became one with the earth. I fled" (*TN*, 82) (Le veíamos morir desde lejos. Nada podíamos hacer por él. Se convirtió en tierra: hambrienta, sedienta, fría; y a la tierra se unió. Yo huí) (*TN*, 88). His brother's consubstantiation with the earth—he is both converted to earth and united to the land—suggests a metaphorization in which the thing represented, Martín's brother, is substituted yet also combined with a concrete, sensual referent—the hungry, thirsty, and cold land. This metaphoric transformation is opposite to what takes place with Martín, who enters a metonymic process as he flees. According to Martín:

> I came to Castile. I hired out my hands for this work. No one asked me where I came from. No one cared to know the name of my land. They urgently needed hands for this construction. The Liege of my land orders death for all who flee. I made myself one of you, exactly like you, and hoped no one would recognize me here. (*TN*, 82; translation modified)

> (Llegué a Castilla. Alquilé mis brazos para esta obra. Nadie me preguntó mi origen. Nadie quiso saber el nombre de mi tierra. Urgían bra-

zos para esta construcción. El señor de mi tierra ordena la muerte de quienes se fugan. Confundíme entre ustedes, a ustedes idéntico, y espero que nadie me reconozca aquí.) (*TN*, 88)

While "hired out my hands" (alquilé mis brazos) suggests a metaphoric relationship, that no one asks of his origin or the name of his homeland implies that he is now safely and anonymously defined by his *function* as laborer. As a peasant who sells his arms and his labor he is further alienated from the land, a process that began with the indebtedness to the seigneur. The repetitions of "no one" (nadie) also give a sense of distance and absence between himself and his past and his new environs. The images of the two brothers are allegorical: whereas one brother becomes combined with the land and the other more separated from it, there is never in either case any mention of ownership or the desire to appropriate land; they are either tied to it or separated from it. Implied in the allegory is the loss of the auratic value or force of the land, as well as the mourning implied in the separation of human beings from the intimate relation of the land lost in alienated labor. Ultimately, this is a baroque allegory for deterritorialization.

This is not the case with the peasant named Pedro, the unfortunate leader of a rebel commune who is arrested by his comrades, only to watch them compromise the commune's independence by allying with one seigneur to protect themselves from another (*TN*, 117–19).[17] As the young Felipe narrates Pedro's dream, the story of the commune, he describes the communal life as an almost utopian existence where everything is shared: "You are living in your happy commune, old man; the harvests belong to everyone and every person takes and receives from his neighbor. The commune is a great island of freedom surrounded by the seas of serfdom" (*TN*, 117). Pedro flees the commune and subsequently decides to leave the Old World. In "The New World," when he embarks on his journey with Pilgrim, he abandons the principle of sharing he upheld in the commune. Instead, he seeks a plot of land that he can call his own. When he and Pilgrim land on the coasts of the New World, Pedro fences off a portion of the beach for himself. The local natives, who follow a communal lifestyle similar to the one Pedro abandoned, do not recognize his claim, and Pedro dies by their hands.

17. Citing José Antonio Maravall, among other historians, Fuentes points to the *comuneros* revolts of the early sixteenth century as one of the signs of nascent democracy and modernity in Spain. The *comuneros* were peasants who formed autonomous communes that rejected the authority of the seigneurs. He also argues that their repression was one of the factors that limited the future viability of Spanish America's political systems (*CCL*, 56–61).

In "The Old World" the land as the representation and site of power suffers two fundamental transformations: First, the rise of mercantilism and the invisible power of money have displaced the land as the visible representation of power. Consequently, the social alliances between sovereign and noble are weakened, and new alliances are formed with those who wield increasing power, namely, the moneylenders and entrepreneurs. The latter, nevertheless, must still defer and recognize the central authority of the monarch, even as they guarantee his demise. Second, the peasants find themselves indebted to the seigneurs, and the only alternative to their servitude and arrearage is compromised when the communes fail. Moreover, the displacement the peasants face when transformed into workers further separates them from the land and from each other. "The Old World" depicts a world in crisis, where the peasants are dispossessed and where the power of the sovereign, Felipe, is weakened and dispersed. Neither the old order nor the forces of progress offer a positive vision of the future.

In this chapter I have shown that these sociohistorical processes correspond to the usury in white mythology as a fundamental correlation to capitalist modernization. We have also seen that the abstraction and exhaustion of words, following Fuentes's readings of Joyce, Derrida, and Bataille, is also played out at the level of metaphor in the novel, that is, through the debilitation of land, the king's power, and the wearing down of those images that represent his power. Furthermore, the land as an exhausted metaphor implies a utopian negation; linked to its demise is the loss of the communal principle of mutual interest, this loss implying a critique of the present as well as the past. This seems to raise a paradox in that "reciprocity" has traditionally been associated with "primitive economy" and utopia, but also with *exchange*, whereas potlatch seems to breakdown reciprocal relations, having an apparently negative function, yet it too has a utopian impulse. In the following chapters we will see how *Terra Nostra* deals with this paradox.

2

The Gift of (the) Story

Gift Giving as Narrative Time,
Act, and Death

As we saw in Chapter 1 the ostentation and the wasteful consumption that Guzmán and the usurer complain of in "The Old World" function as potlatches that destabilize the reciprocal relations guaranteeing seigneurial privilege. Felipe's El Escorial is a form of wasteful expenditure that pays homage to death and to God, at the same time that it signifies his abandonment of the nobility. In this chapter I will show that the apparent "reciprocal exchanges" in "The New World" are actually temporalized and often open-ended, creating a series of potlatches that reinforce and reconfigure social bonds. In all discussions of "exchanges" we must keep in mind Bourdieu's warning against temporalizing and totalizing such events, a warning I addressed at the end of the Introduction. In "The New World" the gift, at times in the form of a potlatch, thwarts reciprocity and functions at different levels of the narration: it disrupts exchange; starts and stops the flows of narrative time and discourse; and the characters themselves both refer to gifts to explain their relations of obligation with other characters and use gifts to attain power. What Fuentes calls "the gift economy" is, perhaps, what most defines that novel's overall structure and determines the relationship between reader and author. How Fuentes writes the gift into his texts is largely determined by his readings of Georges Bataille.

That Fuentes sets loose the strange logics of the gift in *Terra Nostra*'s writing, understood as both writing and rewriting, is not so far-fetched if we take into account what he says about the gift in *Cervantes; or, The Critique of Reading*. As we have seen, Fuentes compares James Joyce's writing to a potlatch, that is, to a gift of rivalry that breaks the traditional patterns of narration. Moreover, he refers to Bataille to explain the sense and function of potlatch in the disruption of the exchange economy: "Georges Bataille tells of the breakup of exchange economy by that of the potlatch or gift that creates an economy of expenditure or of loss in order to destabilize wealth within totemic economy. . . . *Potlatch* breaks the conservative status quo and erects in its place a principle that is contrary to conservation" (*CCL*, 108). Fuentes follows Bataille's definition of the gift, and potlatch, which emphasizes that through the gift the donor appropriates a power when the receiver of the gift accepts the challenge of returning the gift, of giving a superior countergift. What is important here is that the return is delayed. In this sense, the logic of the gift annuls reciprocity; what is acquired, the appropriation of a power, is achieved through loss and wasteful expenditure, the useless destruction or consumption of what has been given. As Fuentes points out, this alters the "conservative" status quo, thus breaking and reconfiguring hierarchical relations, and erects a principle that is contrary to conservation or accumulation.

Much as the potlatch breaks reciprocity, the gift disrupts exchange in general. The tension between a gift and an exchange economy is one of the fundamental conflicts running through the novel, determining in large part its narrative discourse. (Often, this tension is expressed in the distance between the time of the narrator and that of the story or *legend* narrated.) Although exchange and reciprocity often appear to be the ordering principal of the narration, in fact they are not necessarily "exchanges" per se, even though the narrator characterizes them as such. Rather, the events narrated present a series of potlatches, or gifts and countergifts, that occur in an open, ongoing cycle. Throughout "The New World," for example, the "exchanges" that take place between the characters seem to form a predominant pattern in the narration. This is confirmed in the chapter titled "The Ancient's Legend," in which Pilgrim breaks off his narration to address the king directly:

> Oh, Sire, as you hear me today, tell me, after listening to all I have recounted and without knowing what is still to tell, you who understand as I the truest truth of that world into which my misfortunes had cast

me: tell me—for what I have still to tell will only serve as corrobora-
tion—of how here all things were an exchange: exchange of life for death
and death for life, endless exchanges of looks, objects, existences, memories, with the proposition of placating a predicted fury, of temporizing
against the subsequent threat, of sacrificing one thing in order to save
another, of feeling indebted to every existing thing, of dedication both
life and death to a perpetual renovating devotion. (*TN,* 396–97)

(Oh Señor que hoy me escuchas, dime si después de oír cuanto aquí he
contado, y sin saber aún lo que me falta por contar, entiendes como yo la
verdad más verdadera de ese mundo al que mis desventuras me arro-
jaron, dime, pues cuanto me falta por decir no hará sino fortalecerla: que
aquí todo era un trueque de vida por muerte y muerte por vida, cambio
de miradas, de objetos, de existencias, de memorias, sin cesar, y con el
propósito de aplacar una furia anunciada, aplazar la siguiente amenaza,
sacrificar una cosa para salvar a las demás, sentirse en deuda con cuanto
existe y dedicar vida y muerte a una perpetua devoción renovadora.)
(*TN,* 402–3)

This is a crucial moment just after "the ancient of memories" reveals Pilgrim's
destiny in the New World as "Plumed Serpent," the Giver of Life. After his
shipwreck, Pilgrim lands on a strange shore and becomes a member of the
local community of Indians. Once he has learned their language he meets the
ancient. Pilgrim refers to the mysterious old man as "the old man" (el viejo),
"the ancient" (el anciano), "the Lord of Memory" (el Señor de la Memoria),
and "the guardian of the pact" (el guardián del pacto). The ancient serves as
the keeper of the collective memory of the people of the New World. When
he relates the legend of the world's creation to Pilgrim, he gives the castaway
a role in that history. In the passage above, Pilgrim characterizes the "exchanges" he has witnessed and participated in as the rule of the land. Nevertheless, the system Pilgrim describes here is questionable: when he declares
this economy of exchange to be "the truest truth of that world," this hyper-
bole has an ironic ring (perhaps a pun on Bernal Díaz's work *The True History*) and leads the reader to suspect that this truth will not be absolute. By
characterizing the "exchanges" as such, Pilgrim as narrator detemporalizes
the actions from a future present. This commentary represents an important
distancing that ultimately limits his version of the events as it accentuates the
paradox of narrative time. Pilgrim detemporalizes the legend when he comments on it, reinforcing the idea of legendary or mythic time as static, eternal.

Yet the story is also the testimony of his own personal adventure that, when he is narrating the action, has a rhythm and pace that is accentuated and punctuated through the encounters he has. This tension between narrative time and the time of the narrative act plays out at several levels.

The passage also serves to demonstrate at several levels the general economic relation between the reciprocity of the exchange *(trueque)* and its figuration in the chiasmus: "life for death and death for life." The apparent reciprocity of the exchange between life and death is deceptive: the chiastic structure allows the exchange to appear equal when in fact it is generally imbalanced because the two do not occur simultaneously. In this light, the exchange of life for death and death for life has the sacrificial function of delaying the inevitable "announced fury"—the threat of death. According to Georges Bataille, sacrifice preserves and unites the commonality; in order for the community to survive the impending doom, it must placate death by offering the victim over to violence.[1] In Fuentes's *Terra Nostra,* as in Nahua cosmology, this consumption of life in sacrifice celebrates the abundance of life and represents a "perpetual devotion" to renewal. One thing is sacrificed to save everything else. In addition, the violence of sacrifice is similar to the semantic violence of a catachresis, or a synecdoche: one term is deliberately mistaken for another; a particular life is sacrificed as the symbolic payment for a debt that all must eventually pay. This delaying action prevents the completion of the exchange, the *trueque,* and therefore prolongs the debt as the binding obligation.

In the novel this obligation is evident just before Pilgrim's comment on the exchanges in the New World. After telling Pilgrim the legend of the world's creation, the ancient challenges Pilgrim to give him something in return to renew the alliance and continue the cycle of "exchanges." The initial question also comes after the enumeration of the gifts given up to this moment:

> For a long time he looked at me with his sad eyes as black and decayed as the jungle, as etched and hard as the temple, as brilliant and precious as the gold. He raised the scissors and worked the blades. He said he thanked me for them. I had given him the scissors. They had given me gold. I had given my labor. He had given me memory. When he asked, finally, the light in his eyes was as implacable and as cruel as the eyes of the mother goddess must have been: "What will you give us now?" (*TN,* 396)

1. Bataille, *Accursed Share,* 59.

(Me miró largo tiempo con sus ojos de tristeza, negros y podridos como la selva, duros y labrados como el templo, brillantes y atesorados como el oro. Mostró mis tijeras y las movió. Dijo que me las agradecía. Yo di las tijeras. Ellos me dieron el oro. Yo di mi trabajo. El me dió la memoria.

Los ojos del anciano lanzaron una luz implacable, tan cruel como debía ser la de los ojos de la diosa madre, cuando al cabo me preguntó: "¿Qué nos darás tú ahora?") (*TN*, 402)

During Pilgrim's first encounter with the people of the coast, he gave them the scissors as a peace offering; this in turn led them to respond with the gold and to accept him into the community. As a member of the community Pilgrim gave his labor. The ancient responded by giving Pilgrim the memory of the creation of the world, and thus his role in that legend. The tension between reciprocal exchange and potlatch plays a subtle role in the passage. The series of reciprocal exchanges follows a chiastic pattern of first- and third-person positions: I (to them) / he, they (to me) (Yo [a ellos] / él, ellos [a mí]). The second-person "you" (tú) breaks that chain and refocalizes the discourse in a dialogic question that is repeated through various voices at different moments in the narration.

The old man's question converts the legend into a potlatch, into a challenge to counter with an equal or greater gift. In this sense the legend, as myth, is temporalized, made actual and unconcluded. The fact of giving Pilgrim the memory demands that the latter either counter with a gift superior to that legend or subordinate himself by remaining in the old man's debt. To this end, the question binds Pilgrim to the legend: "Everything the ancient had spoken until now seemed pure fantasy and legend until these words made me a participant in that fantasy and a prisoner of that legend: 'What will you give us now?'" (*TN*, 397).

In the novel, Pilgrim, literally "Pilgrim," receives his name from Pedro, his fellow castaway, who names him thus because Pilgrim has no recollection of his own origins and is a wanderer. When Pilgrim arrives in the New World, the ancient Lord of Memory identifies him as "Plumed Serpent." This ties him to the Toltec god Quetzalcóatl, one of the most venerated gods of Mesoamerica before the arrival of Christianity. Historically, Quetzalcóatl was a priest-ruler at Tula who preached against human sacrifice, and was thus consider a benevolent figure. The god is associated with Venus, the morning star and the evening star. Legend has it that Quetzalcóatl was deceived by his brother, Tezcatlipoca, "Smoking Mirror," who had tricked Quetzalcóatl into becoming inebriated and then convinced him to sleep with his own sister. Ashamed by what he had done, Quetzalcóatl fled, but was prophesied to return from the East in the year Ce Acatl, 1519, which corresponded with Cortés's arrival, allowing the latter to exploit the prophesy. Tezcatlipoca, the god of night, is associated with death and destruction, is the patron saint of sorcerers and robbers, and was widely respected due to his mischievous intervention in human affairs.[2] While Pilgrim is mainly associated with Plumed Serpent, he escapes the destiny of Smoking Mirror. Guzmán will become associated with Smoking Mirror when he takes on his role as conquistador.

The ancient's question "What will you give us now?" turns the legend of creation into a challenge similar to the potlatch described in *Cervantes; or, The Critique of Reading:* "you-read-me, you-read-yourself, you-read-us" (melés, telés y noslés). By including Pilgrim in the tale, the ancient also incites him to see "The New World" and to retell it from an insider-outsider perspective: the legend of a different people (you-read-me), himself as part of the legend (you-read-yourself), and his own transformative role in their history (you-read-us). The question turns the initiative over to Pilgrim, forcing him to shift from a passive to an active role. Furthermore, the first pair of terms, *fantasy* and *legend,* implies something inconsequential, distant, a doubt cast upon the ancient's tale. Their repetition, however, is metastatic: Pilgrim finds himself intimately involved in the fantasy and the legend. The ancient's words, the memory, and the legend become superior to Pilgrim's life by placing him in the ancient's debt.

The challenge in the form of a question, "What will you give us now?" is a veritable speech act that disrupts the flow of the narrative prose and binds Pilgrim to the legend. The repetition of the question frames and suspends Pilgrim's reflection on the potlatch. At the same time, it accentuates the transformation and temporalization he experiences in that moment. Thus, between the narrative time of one story and the corresponding gift in return, time is suspended by the question. (This suspense is both an effect of the challenge of giving and a result of narrative strategy.) The challenge disrupts narrative time because it applies to both forms of time: the telling and the action in the story. Moreover, the use of the future tense is reminiscent of the second-person fragments of *The Death of Artemio Cruz,* for the question in the future tense can apply at multiple levels and times: it is as if Pilgrim were

2. For a critique of Fuentes's reconstruction of the myth of Quetzalcóatl, see Santiago Juan-Navarro's study "Sobre dioses, héroes y novelistas: La reinvención de Quetzalcóatl de Carlos Fuentes."

not only relating what had happened but also still feeling its effect. He is also, by uttering the question, in the position of directing it toward his narratee, Felipe.

In general, the reiteration of this question throughout "The New World" has the effect, like a sacrifice, of stalling and restarting narrative time. It is also of no coincidence that the question "What will you give us now?" which provokes and clarifies the potlatch, would be followed by a description of the future exchange in the figure of a chiasmus: "The old man was asking that I renew our alliance—for him so clear, for me so obscure—with a new offering, something of greater value than his words, as his words had held more value than my life—which I owed to him" (*TN*, 397). In this case the language recalls Bataille's description of the potlatch; the chiasmus describes an exchange that is unfulfilled, that hasn't been completed. Not only does the question suspend the exchange, by both anticipating a response and producing a suspension by its severity, but it also integrates Pilgrim with other identities and destinies by making him a party to the debt cycle of the Earth Goddess's sacrifice. Furthermore, it should also be remembered that as the ancient recounts his legend, he constantly answers the questions Pilgrim has about it, much as in a Socratic dialogue.

The inversions and displacements of narrator and narratee, moreover, are not chiastic, nor are they reciprocal. As the narrator-protagonist of "The New World," Pilgrim in turn becomes the narratee of the ancient's tale. While Pilgrim listens he becomes aware of his own role as Plumed Serpent in that legend. In a Borgesian twist the old man's legend absorbs Pilgrim as its hero. Furthermore, the old man displaces Pilgrim as narrator, but does not become the receiver of a tale. Rather, when Pilgrim gives him the mirror, the old man sees an unexpected image of himself; he had not been aware of the passage of time. Instead of an exchange in which Pilgrim reciprocates by offering an equal or superior narration to the ancient, he gives him the mirror. While the mirror does have the effect of making the ancient see himself differently, much as he had made Pilgrim see himself in a different destiny, this does not occur as a narrative potlatch. Perhaps one could argue for a "reciprocal exchange" expressed through a chiasmus, yet this would happen between two different but complementary levels of narration: the story as a challenge is answered with its opposite, the silence of a glance *(una mirada)* not exchanged, but turned inward.

When the old man looks into the mirror, Pilgrim sees in his face the terror of infinite time condensed into an instant (*TN*, 397). The ancient realizes that his time is up. At first, Pilgrim does not comprehend the nature of the gift's effect, the cause of the old man's terror. Shortly thereafter, he turns his own gaze into the mirror and recognizes the true terror the ancient experienced: "I held the mirror to my face, fearing to see in its reflection the image of my own decrepitude, magically acquired in the swift exchange of glances between the ancient and myself. . . . I looked. And then, only then, as the mercury returned to me my own youthful semblance, I understood that the ancient had not been aware of his own age" (*TN,* 400). Pilgrim recognizes that the old man believed that he was eternally young, which is confirmed when the ancient dies and his warriors learn of his death. One of them kneels beside the old man, caresses his head, and says, "Young chieftain . . . youthful founder . . . first man" (*TN,* 398). As the timeless "first man," the ancient must ignore how time passes for himself in order to preserve the memory of his people, of Pilgrim, and of himself. Thus, when Pilgrim looks into the mirror expecting to see an old face, and sees instead his own image of youth, he realizes that the old man believed himself to have lived according to a different temporality.

In the Nahua tradition of the "wise men" *(tlamatinime),* who show their students who they are, they are said to give their students a face, a personality. The idea of the face that never ages lies at the heart of Plumed Serpent's (Quetzalcóatl's) role as the bearer of truth. According to Miguel León-Portilla:

> No one among the Nahuas could symbolize the yearning for a metaphysical investigation of truth more suitably than Quetzalcóatl. Evoker of myths, Quetzalcóatl's name is synonymous with his wisdom and his quest for a beyond, where, unlike the earth, there would be no sin and faces would never age. In Tula, Quetzalcóatl had discovered the existence of sin on earth and the fact that faces must grow old. He had then fled to the East, to the land of the black and the red colors, the region of knowledge.[3]

By this, the gift of the mirror's reflection alters time as the ancient understands it; Pilgrim, an unwitting Quetzalcóatl, reveals to the old man a truth about the latter's temporal existence. What this implies for the ancient, in the most simple of terms, is that he was subject to the sins on earth and the limits of time as humans experience them, but did not realize it until he looked

3. León-Portilla, *Aztec Thought and Culture,* 31.

at himself in the mirror. Furthermore, any reciprocity between the old man and Pilgrim is asymmetrical in that the countergift of the mirror corresponds to a level outside of the narrative time of the old man. Instead of another narration to counter the old man's legend, Pilgrim gives a gift that annuls the narrative time in which the ancient lives, the gift of death. By doing this he repeats Smoking Mirror's treachery, and thus transforms the narrative time of the ancient into a concluded mythic time.

The time and the law of the ancient follow the economy of the exchange *(trueque)*, of gift-countergift, in which a challenge is posed by the giving of a gift with the expectation that the challenged will respond with a greater gift, thus renewing the alliance sought. In this way the "pact" and the allegiance are temporalized because they must be continuously renewed. In the chapter "The Ancient's Legend," the old man explains to Pilgrim how the two of them are different from others. After Pilgrim declares that in nature everything fades and dies, the ancient explains that "some lives are like arrows. They are shot into the air, they fly, and they fall. My friend's life was like these. But there are other lives that are like circles. Where they seem to end, they in truth begin again. They are renewable lives" (*TN*, 388). The old man's view of his and Pilgrim's destinies is circular, a circularity that also corresponds to the circulation of things in reciprocal exchanges.[4] Yet the old man goes on to mention that sacrifice is the only way to ensure such a renewal. In this sense, Pilgrim's journey to the interior of the New World, as the beginning of a new destiny for him, also marks the end of the ancient's life. Instead of an exchange of existences, Pilgrim's countergift, the mirror, has the effect of a sacrificial displacement.

As a potlatch, Pilgrim's countergift is not so much the mirror, which Pilgrim takes back, but the mirror's effect. The mirror breaks the circularity of the exchanges between Pilgrim and the ancient, making any further exchange between the two impossible. So it would seem at that point; the ancient, however, does return at another crucial moment in the chapter "Day of Flight," although Pilgrim thinks the old man may have returned in a dream (*TN*, 482–85). In a similar vein, Zunilda Gertel notes that historical facts are cyclically recodified in the novel's text as the intertextuality between the narrative voice and the reader, as cultural memory: "This cyclical operation does

4. For a discussion of the centrality of the figure of the circle in exchange and reciprocity, in economy in general, and also how these disrupt and are disrupted by the gift, see Derrida, *Given Time*, 6–31. Also see Rodolphe Gasché's "Heliocentric Exchange" cited in Schrift, *Logic of the Gift*, 106–9.

not simply offer the form of a circle, but rather the spiral, as an open and alternating disjunction, in a transformative process of memory and forgetting." Lois Parkinson Zamora also examines Fuentes integration of the historical and literary past into the narrative present, and the rejection of linear time that this implies. She traces the figure of the spiral in this integration to Vico's theory of *corsi e ricorsi,* which she affirms is consonant with Fuentes's historical vision "precisely because it combines progression and retrogression in its spiraling form. The image of historical movement presented in Vico's *New Science* is in fact a spiral. . . . The process of ricorsi, the discussion of which occupies the final section of the *New Science,* implies the constant recovery and rendering of the past as present and available in the structure of current and more complex forms."[5]

The spiraling and cyclical flows of memory and forgetting correspond at several layers of the narration: from the alternations of existences, the disruptions of gifts, to the reiterations of historical events in the mnemonic collaboration of reader and narrator. While the law of the *trueque* implies circularity and a cyclical alternation of existences, of life and death, throughout the novel sacrifices and gifts disrupt the circular flow of such cycles. A new cycle may begin, but the renewal implies that it cannot begin or end in the same place or time. Consequently, the figure of the circle gives way to that of the spiral.

The Stories, the Gifts of the New World

At the end of "The New World," when Pilgrim is preparing to leave the New World, the twenty Spanish-speaking natives he rescues from the land of the dead recount the series of gifts and challenges he had to give and face. This account, considered in both its economic and its narrative meanings, is largely organized around an implied allegiance to the land, in particular to the "New World" as it is re-created by Pilgrim's arrival.

The twenty youths Pilgrim rescues from the land of the dead are in a sense created from his *mestizaje;* the love and desire from which the twenty youths are born are clearly associated with the passion of a nomad who has no homeland, a sailor who has no singular port of origin. This love shifts the allegiances of the natives and allows for the emergence of a "New

5. Gertel, "Semiótica," 71–72; Zamora, *Writing the Apocalypse,* 162.

World." The twenty youths begotten of Pilgrim's love will give themselves to a different New World other than the land prior to the encounter. The youths make this clear once they have recounted the gifts given, and once Pilgrim asks what they will do with the gift he has given them: "'To whom will you give your lives?' I asked. 'To the new land that gave life to Pedro'" (*TN*, 483). Pilgrim is now the one asking the question of who will give what to whom. In a sense, he has earned the right to pose questions because he has himself given, though perhaps most important because he is now outside of the debt cycle as indicated by the response to the question. Pilgrim does not ask, however, what the twenty youths will give to him, but rather to whom they will give their lives. This implies that Pilgrim no longer has anything left to give to them. Nonetheless, while the cycle of debt in the New World appears to close with the twenty youths' offering of their lives to the new earth, Pilgrim follows a different time due to the fact that he did not have an affiliation to any land, because of his unique situation as an outsider, as a nomad. The recounting of the series of gifts given, furthermore, offers an insight into the relationship between gift giving and narration. While following the trajectory of Pilgrim's journeys as a mythological hero figure, the narration also follows the trajectory of the gifts given and received. Yet it can be interpreted as well in terms of things not given, rejected, or even stolen. The recounting serves as a ritual speech act that justifies the potlatch, *the giving of a gift that cannot be surpassed*. It also releases Pilgrim from the bond of allegiance, from the bond of his destiny:

> "Pedro gave his life for you."
> "You gave the scissors."
> "They gave you gold."
> "You gave your labor."
> "They gave you memory."
> "You gave them a mirror."
> "They gave you the gift of their deaths."
> "You responded with love: to them, already dead; to a woman,
>   still living."
> "She gave you your days."
> "The five days of the sun offered you twenty days of shadows."
> "The twenty days of smoking mirror offered you your double."
> "Your double offered you his kingdom."
> "You exchanged power for the woman."
> "The woman gave you wisdom." (*TN*, 483)

According to the youths, the narrative cycle begins with Pedro's gift from the earth: "The new land gave life to Pedro; in that life your friend culminated his entire existence, his dreams, his sufferings, and his labors. His life was worthwhile. The new world gave him his life, completed" (*TN*, 483). The cycle ends with an unsurpassable gift from the youths to Pilgrim; the latter is freed from the debt cycle:

> "You gave us our lives."
> "We give you your freedom."
> "Can you make a greater offering?"
> "You cannot."
> "The story has ended." (*TN*, 483)

The unsurpassable gift of freedom terminates the story *(historia);* Pilgrim's role as the "Giver of Life" has been fulfilled, and the youths free him from fulfilling the dark days of his destiny, from his role as Smoking Mirror in the debt cycle. He then is able to return to Spain to relate the story as the narrator character Pilgrim. Although at first the account might appear to be a series of exchanges, there are several reasons this cannot be so, some of which I have already entertained. The very question and answer, "Can you make a greater offering?" "You cannot," belie the idea of an exchangist relation and affirm the culmination of a concatenation of potlatches, of gifts and counter-gifts. Some of the gifts have a contradictory and imbalanced nature not unlike the give-and-take involved in potlatch (giving an ostentatious gift to appropriate a power over the receiver). Moreover, the scissors and the mirror, the two items that come to designate Pilgrim's multiple identities in the New World, are objects that Pilgrim had originally *stolen* in the Old World (*TN*, 388).

The scissors and the mirror, as stolen items, have a function in the narration that can clarify the general economic relations between narration and destiny. When Pilgrim steals and then later gives away these two items, in each case he alters the path of his destiny. At the beginning of "The New World" the theft of the two items corresponds to his desire to link his destiny to Pedro's, but when he gives the scissors to the coastal natives on the beach he does so to avoid Pedro's fate, his death at the hands of the coastal natives (*TN*, 378–79). By presenting the scissors as a gift he forces an allegiance with the natives, and therefore ties himself to their destinies and to those of the ancient. In her analysis of "The New World," Alice Gericke Springer notes that "the scissors are an item that [Pilgrim] uses for trade, giving them in exchange for his life to the chieftain of the jungle tribe as required according to the cultural codes of the 'New World.' His possession of the scissors also indicates his new status in the indigenous society when they are returned to him after the ancient dies."[6] Pilgrim's offering of the scissors to the men on the beach undoubtedly spares his life; Pilgrim confirms this when he revisits the scene with the ancient of memories: "'Your friend wished only to take. He wished to offer nothing.' I looked at the scissors in the hands of the ancient and was again convinced that it was to them I owed my life" (*TN*, 388). That he gave them in "exchange for his life," though accurate in a general sense, misses the nuances of gift giving; the "cultural code" required a countergift and therefore the initiation of a series: "You gave the scissors." "They gave you gold." The image of Pilgrim holding the scissors and the mirror once the ancient has died does more than confirm his status in the "New World": "They placed the scissors in my hands. I still held the weapon of the crime: my mirror. My cross and orb. The warrior from the beach clasped the belt of black feathers about his waist, the sign of ritual confrontation" (*TN*, 399).

Alice Gericke Springer considers the scissors to be a sign that distinguishes Pilgrim the Old World sailor from his other identities as Plumed Serpent, Smoking Mirror, or the ancient. The scissors and the mirror, however, also come to designate Pilgrim as a composite of these destines, and have their functions in the initiation and closure of his role within the legend. The scissors are also a sign of Pilgrim's syncretism. As Springer suggests, moreover, the items as insignia combine in a way to designate a particular character or concept, as in a pictogram.[7]

When he gives the mirror to the ancient, Pilgrim's destiny is multiplied; the gift's effects of reflection and doubling, and of the revelation of the passage of time, coincide with this transformation. Within the frame of Pilgrim's gifts, the mirror corresponds to the multiple times that are lived in the same space: Pilgrim as Plumed Serpent in what he remembers and Smoking Mirror in what he forgets. In his final confrontation with his double, Smoking Mirror in his guise as Lord of the Great Voice, Pilgrim tries to use the mirror to free himself of his shared destiny with his double, expecting that his nemesis will be destroyed by his own image much as the ancient had died

---

6. Springer, "Iconological Study," 9.
7. Ibid., 8–9.

when he stared into the mirror (*TN,* 397–98, 471–72). The strategy back-fires, however, because Smoking Mirror is not afraid of that which is similar to him—what he fears is difference: "I do not fear what resembles me. I feared you in the forest, when you chose your desire over my heart. Today I ceased to fear you when you converted the power I gave you into desire" (*TN,* 471). Smoking Mirror feared Pilgrim during their first encounter because Pilgrim rejected his gift, his heart, and the obligation that it implied (*TN,* 418). In the final confrontation, however, Smoking Mirror does not fear Pilgrim because the latter has succumbed to temptation, thus affirming the mythic cycle of Quetzalcóatl and Pilgrim's conformity to that myth/destiny. Smoking Mirror turns the mirror back against Pilgrim, entrapping him in a circular destiny in which he would never have left the basket where he had killed the ancient; Pilgrim would become imprisoned in the destiny of the one he displaced. Nevertheless, Pilgrim escapes his double and the destiny of the ancient by killing Smoking Mirror with the scissors. This allows him to alter and leave the cycle of the legend.[8]

As gifts, the scissors and mirror alter the direction of Pilgrim's multiple destinies. The series of moments involving these gifts conforms to a chiastic A-B-B-A pattern in "The New World": Pilgrim gives the scissors to the coastal natives, delaying an inevitable violence, then gives the mirror displacing the ancient as a possible twin in another time; when faced with Smoking Mirror he tries to destroy him with the mirror, but fails; and last, he uses the scissors to destroy his double, closing a cycle of violence that began with Pedro's death. Yet the violence and debt cycles begin previous to Pilgrim's first encounter with the coastal natives; they begin when Pilgrim encounters the turtles on the beach. They end with the twenty youths. Therefore, the narrative flow follows the gifts' disruptions of the cycles of debt, which alter the circular movements of Pilgrim's multiple destinies as a castaway, and as both Plumed Serpent and Smoking Mirror.

The initial encounter between Pilgrim and the coastal natives, in particular, the moment he presents the scissors to the natives, is very significant and points to one of the fundamental conflicts of the novel. The tension between potlatch and exchange economy *(trueque)* is so pronounced in *Terra Nostra* that Fuentes titles a chapter "The Exchange" (El trueque), demonstrating its complexity as a social phenomenon, a complexity that affects the relation between the reader and the text through the rhetorical figures it employs. The

8. Ibid., 75.

scene is important because it marks Pilgrim's first encounter with the people of the New World. After Pilgrim and Pedro are reunited on the beach and become aware of the arrival of the coastal inhabitants, the reciprocal exchange of glances between the two groups is reinforced through a chiastic formation: "Then thirty or more men leaped from the trunks into the water. . . . And other men like them, similarly armed and naked except for the cloth that concealed their shame, erupted from the jungle. They looked at us. We looked at them" (*TN*, 377). The positioning of the two sentences "They looked at us. We looked at them" on separate parallel lines accentuates the visibility of the textual chiasmus in the reading. Furthermore, the shifting positions of grammatical person and pronouns emphasize the chiasmus as a visual figure:

> THEY looked at US   first-person plural third-person plural
> WE looked at THEM   third-person plural first-person plural

The placement is designed to produce a momentary shift in the phenomenal experience of the reader. The visuality of the chiasmus strengthens the feeling of wonderment the reader experiences as he or she reads of the similar feeling between Pilgrim and the coastal inhabitants. In this way, the chiasmus's visuality on the page provokes a momentary disruption of the reading, and the awareness of a difference—the awareness of one's reading as a gaze.

The initial moment of the encounter is, like the question that the ancient asks, filled with potential violence as the two groups seek alliance or simply an exchange. As a protagonist, at this stage of his journey into the New World Pilgrim still has not learned of the sacred debt the coastal inhabitants owe to the earth, which the ancient later explains to him. Yet when he and Pedro encounter the coastal inhabitants, he realizes that the giving of a gift might prevent violence. Pilgrim detects an imbalance due to his and Pedro's inability to respond verbally to the leader of the band. This produces a dangerous confusion. According to Pilgrim, violence is imminent:

> I searched desperately for an escape, for some response, . . . and at that instant, born from some miraculously recovered instinct, came an idea born of the exchange—the simple fact that first we'd exchanged looks and then been unable to exchange words, and from the mutual looks had been born an original and duplicated amazement, but only violence had come from the unanswered words. I shouted to Pedro without

thinking, as if someone else were speaking through me, using my voice: "Old man! Offer them your house! Offer them something quickly!" (*TN*, 378)

Pedro, nonetheless, refuses to give up his piece of land and consequently pays with his life, for his refusal is an offense. In *The Gift*, Marcel Mauss asserts that "to refuse to give, to fail to invite, just as to refuse to accept, is tantamount to declaring war; it is to reject the bond of alliance and communality." In this same vein, Claude Lévi-Strauss maintains that "there is a link, a continuity, between hostile relations and the provision of reciprocal prestations. Exchanges are peacefully resolved wars and wars are the result of unsuccessful transactions."[9] Pilgrim's survival points to a key ethical and existential disposition that becomes necessary for his survival: the willingness to share, to give away what one has unconditionally, the will to give oneself over to another. Moreover, as the ancient later explains, Pedro defied the land and the people when he refused to share; by doing so, he chose not to form an alliance with them.

In the moment after Pedro is killed, as Pilgrim mourns him, he closes his eyes and remembers the turtle he himself had killed: "And I could see upon a black background the cadaver and the blood of the ancient turtle I had killed with the same scissors I still grasped in my hand" (*TN*, 379). Pilgrim's memory of the turtle at the moment of Pedro's violent death would suggest an exchange of lives, a balancing of life and death between two figures that represent opposing relations to the land: on the one hand, the "ancient turtle" as a manifestation of the Earth Goddess, her sacrifice and sovereignty over the land; and the other hand, Pedro, who falsely believed he could own the land in contradiction with his previous communitarian principles. But this is not the case. Pedro suggests that he must die in order for Pilgrim to live before he and Pilgrim see the coastal natives approaching. As they discuss their shipwreck, Pedro recounts that Pilgrim murmured the following words in his sleep: "I'm living this the second time . . . it happened long ago . . . two shipwrecks . . . two survivors . . . two lives . . . only one can be saved . . . one must die . . . so the other may live" (*TN*, 375–76). Ultimately, both Pedro and the turtle are sacrificed so that Pilgrim may begin a new cycle of his destiny—his role as Plumed Serpent and Smoking Mirror.

When Pilgrim witnesses Pedro's death at the hands of the natives, at first he wields his scissors as a weapon. He then succumbs to his first insight and offers the scissors to the leader who is happy to accept the gift and the ges-

9. Mauss, *Gift*, 13; Lévi-Strauss, *The Elementary Structures of Kinship*, 67.

ture. The leader's reaction upon touching the scissors, however, suggests that he attributes an excess meaning to the scissors as a gift. Pilgrim describes the native's reaction:

> I held out my hand; I opened it. I offered the chieftain the scissors. He smiled. He accepted them. He flashed them in the sun. He did not know what they were. He manipulated them clumsily. He nicked a finger. He threw the scissors upon the sand. Uneasy, he looked at the blood. Uneasy, he looked at me. With great caution he picked up the scissors, as if fearing they had a life of their own. (*TN,* 379)

> (Alargué mi mano. Abrí mi puño. Ofrecí las tijeras. El jefe sonrió. Las tomó. Las hizo brillar contra el sol. No sabía manejarlas. Las manipuló con torpeza. Cortóse la carne de un dedo. Arrojó las tijeras a la arena. Miró con azoro su sangre. Me miró con azoro a mí. Recogió con gran cuidado las tijeras, como temiendo que tuviesen vida propia.) (*TN,* 386)

The observation Pilgrim makes allows for two possible explanations for the further drawing of blood. Pilgrim's own rational observation suggests simply that the man was clumsy with an instrument he had never handled before. His *interpretation* of the coastal native's response, however, is crucial. According to Pilgrim, to the Indian the scissors appear to be alive—they have a spirit. This corresponds to Marcel Mauss's fetishistic conception of "the spirit of the thing given," the magic of the gift, which binds the receiver to reciprocate with interest. It should also be noted that the spirit of the gift implies a supplementary relation in that it is often considered to be a detachable part of the soul of the person giving the gift. This, according to Mauss, implies a law: "In this system of ideas one clearly and logically realizes that one must give back to another person what is really part and parcel of his nature and substance." As we have discussed, Mauss was criticized by Derrida and Deleuze and Guattari for his inability to distinguish between the gift and exchange. Indeed, Derrida in *Given Time* insists that the gift disrupts exchange, whereas in *Anti-Oedipus* Deleuze and Guattari locate the fundamental problem of the primitive socious, "the problem of inscription, of coding, of marking," precisely in what they call the finite blocks of debt: the speaking voice, the marked body, and the enjoying eye.[10] In this sense, the shedding of blood corresponds to writing (this we will discuss in Chapter 4).

---

10. Mauss, *The Gift,* 12; Deleuze and Guattari, *Anti-Oedipus: Capitalism and Schizophrenia,* 190. For an in-depth critical treatment of Mauss's usage of the Maori term *hau* from which he

Following the fetishistic notion, the gift exerts "a magical or religious hold" over the receiver, the debtor. Thus, in "The Exchange" the spirit of the scissors appears to be alive and to carry a part of the giver. This can be deduced from the coastal native's "uneasy" glances from his blood to the scissors and ultimately to Pilgrim, the source of the spirit. Though *con azoro* (uneasy) can mean "frightened" or "disturbed," the word *azoro* alone can also mean "goblin or imp" *(duende),* "apparition" and "ghost," all words related to spirits and the effects they might produce. The action of the scissors and the spilling of the blood, moreover, are not necessarily one and the same; they form a composite, or parts of a process. The cutting reminds the coastal man of his obligation to reciprocate and corresponds to debt inscription. (The manner in which the cutting is described blurs the question of agency, for the phrase "He nicked a finger" [Cortóse la carne de un dedo] in the Spanish can be read both as active and passive voice.) The spilled blood, moreover, implies a certain metaphysical dimension in that blood is a sacred element in Aztec cosmology that serves as a nexus between the world and time of humans and those of their gods. This could provide another possible explanation of the leader's expression of fright *(azoro).* All of this points to a parody of Mauss's fetishism, or more important a highlighting of the distance and objectifying gaze of the Westerner who tries to interpret the other.

The sequence of actions that takes place between the two men at that instant is also characteristic of the potlatch: the verbs in first person, "I held out" *(alargué),* "I opened" *(abrí),* "I offered" *(ofrecí),* are followed by verbs in third person, "He took them" *(las tomó),* "He manipulated them" *(las manipuló),* thus indicating the direction of the gift as a challenge. To add to this, the coastal native's glances are marked by fear: "Uneasy, he looked at the blood. Uneasy, he looked at me" (Miró con azoro su sangre. Me miró con azoro a mí). The offering of the scissors is much more than the surrendering of a weapon; it is an offering of alliance and therefore imposes the laws of obligation and hospitality (in this case, the obligation is not a "spirit"). By the coastal native's own standards he must accept and counter the gift, and by doing so join his destiny with that of Pilgrim. To do otherwise is to risk losing his own destiny. This is the surplus meaning extracted from the shed blood: *the solemn and fearful bond of obligation in the face of death.* Pilgrim's description of the countergift he receives and the coastal leader's reciprocation confirms the ritual solemnity and conclusion of a pact.

---

deduces the fetishistic aspect of the gift, see Marshall Sahlins, "The Spirit of the Gift," in *Stone Age Economics,* 149–83, also cited in Schrift, *Logic of the Gift,* 70–99.

He ran back to the chieftain and handed him a coarse cloth similar to that of their loincloths. The cloth held something. The chieftain clutched the scissors in one hand. With the other he handed me the small parcel. I hefted its weight in my open hands. The rough, stiff cloth fell open. In my hands lay a brilliant treasure of golden grains. My gift had been reciprocated. (*TN*, 379)

(Corrieron de regreso hacia el jefe y le entregaron una burda tela, semejante a la de los taparrabos. La tela envolvía algo. El jefe apretó las tijeras con una mano. Con la otra pasóme el bultillo. Lo sopesé entre mis palmas abiertas. La rugosa y tiesa tela abrióse sola. Mis manos sostenían un brillante tesoro de pepitas doradas.) (*TN*, 386)

Along with the urgency of the men running to and from the canoes, the leader's gesture of squeezing the scissors in one hand while handing the countergift with the other accentuates the seriousness of Pilgrim's offering. Moreover, the ambiguity in Spanish of the expression "The rough, stiff cloth fell open" (La rugosa y tiesa tela abrióse sola) is also suggestive of an active thing impregnated with spirit. Most significantly, this countergift, itself a composite of cloth and golden seeds, or grains, implies a tension between two opposing economies: the fetishistic notion of the gift and the economy of reciprocal exchange. Yet the seeds also appear to be a form of money, and thus to have exchange value. In this light, the gift's value is measured to be of equal or greater value according to its weight: the coastal native holds the scissors tightly, while Pilgrim notices the weight of the cloth and its contents.

As Pilgrim becomes a member of the coastal village and later learns of their tributary relation with the people of the interior, reciprocal exchange seems at first to be the dominant economic principle, as opposed to the potlatches he experiences. He also encounters forms of writing that appear to complement these "reciprocal exchanges," but later he finds that this writing, and the "exchanges," functions within a tributary economy, as we shall examine in Chapter 4. What is most important here, however, is that the narration of Pilgrim's interaction with the people of "The New World" ends through the recounting of the series of gifts and countergifts, culminating with an unsurpassable gift.

"The True Gift" and the Gift of Death

Much earlier in the novel the Mad Lady (Juana La Loca) first discusses the idea of an insuperable gift and its effects. In the chapter "Monologue of the Lady Voyager," after rescuing the young castaway from a deserted beach the Mad Lady explains to him the motive and spectacle of her funerary procession: her public repossession of her late husband's body. Felipe the Fair (Felipe el Hermoso) had been unfaithful to her, had exercised his "right of first night" with many women, and had married her only for the purpose of producing heirs to the throne. Once he is dead she jealously flaunts her possession of her husband's corpse and plots to recompense herself for the neglect and suffering she endured. As she prepares to explain how the castaway will help her, she makes the following commentary on the nature of the gift: "A true gift does not admit equal recompense. An authentic offering rises above all comparison and all price. My honor and my rank, señor caballero, prevent my accepting anything in exchange which could be considered superior or even equal to my gift: a total, final, incomparable, and uncompensatable crown or body" (*TN*, 74). For the Mad Lady the "true gift" cannot be returned or reciprocated; it breaks the circulation and reciprocal exchange of things. No price can be put on it because nothing can be compared to it, this comparison being what would determine its value. In the case of commodity exchange, value is determined through the comparison of one commodity with another. Thus, an equivalent value can be determined through their difference.[11] But the gift cannot be an equivalent; no price or value can be placed upon the gift precisely because its condition of possibility is that it supersedes all comparison to anything else. The "true gift" cannot be equaled or surpassed; hence, it cannot take place in an exchange—indeed, it arrests and destroys exchange.

This impossibility of comparison and exchange implies not only the loss of value but also the loss of meaning. The gift (its "value") cannot be determined in the sense that it cannot be defined; it must be indeterminable. The Mad Lady's gift to Pilgrim shows how the gift breaks the circulation of meaning in the chiasmus when she says: "I am offering my life to death. Death offers me its true life. At first, being born, I believed I was dying, although unknowing I was born. Later, dying, and knowing, I have again been born. This is my gift. This is the unsurpassable offering of my cult" (*TN*, 74). A difference is already apparent between "life" and "true life" that is played out in the extended repetition of the chiasmus. The basic A-B-B-A chiasmus

---

11. See Hyde, *Gift*, 60. Lewis Hyde discusses the "worth" of the gift and the differential determinant of the value of a given commodity in Marx's *Capital*. The quotes from Marx can be found in chapter 1 of the first volume of *Capital*.

life-death/death-life expands in such a way that all terms are clearly different: A1 (being born), B1 (believed I was dying), C1 (unknowing I was born) / B2 (Later, dying), A2 (knowing), C2 (again being born). The chiasmus is divided into six terms to flesh out the differences; *creía morir* is not the same as *morir,* and likewise *nacer* is not the same as *volver a nacer* (*TN,* 80). Besides, in any basic A-B-B-A chiasmus A2 is never an identical repetition of A1 because of its inverted location, and also because for a sign to be a sign it must be to some extent different each time it is employed.[12]

What is clear in the following sentence, "This is my gift" (Tal es el regalo—also "*Such is* the gift"), is that the Mad Lady is defining not the gift, but how it operates, its effect. The gift frustrates the meaning of the "exchange" (between her and death) by its very nature as difference; it confounds the meaning of what is given. Life becomes "its true life," which is indeterminate, an undefined difference made so by its relation to death. Yet the gift also generates a new or different form of life. Not only is there a loss of meaning in these terms, but there is also an expansion, or multiplication, of their meaning: life and death both lose in the exchange, and gain in the abstraction. They have taken on contradictory nuances.

Through her distorted logic the Mad Lady affirms a fundamental characteristic of the gift, namely, its indeterminacy. She also affirms another trait: the gift disrupts time. The Mad Lady seems to imply in her use of the extended chiasmus that time now flows backward for her: "You will forget everything I have told you. All my words have been spoken tomorrow. This procession is moving in the opposite direction from that you know how to measure. We came from death: what kind of life could await us at the end of the procession?" (*TN,* 74). She can discuss her cult of the gift precisely because she is, feels, out of his time. Like the gift, time is immeasurable for her. She refers to the castaway as someone who counts or measures time, and because he will not remember anything, she can bestow a gift. (This is echoed later in "The New World" when the ancient narrates the creation myth.) She also declares that a gift cannot be bought, that is, appropriated through a monetary exchange. All this implies a definite power relation: only the giver can give, and the receiver must receive the gift passively. It should also not be forgotten that the Mad Lady is, in effect, casting a spell.

Yet there is a problem in the way the Mad Lady frames the question of her bestowing a gift (besides her insanity). Following a more radical definition of

12. Derrida, *Speech and Phenomena, and Other Essays on Husserl's Theory of Signs,* 50–51.

the gift, in order for a gift to be received, it cannot be seen as a gift at all. It must be forgotten not only by the receiver but by the giver as well. According to Derrida, "As the condition for a gift to be given, this forgetting must be radical not only on the part of the donee but first of all, . . . on the part of the donor." Not only must the gift not be repaid, it "must not be kept in memory, retained as symbol of a sacrifice, as symbolic in general." From the moment a gift appears as such, it implies and symbolizes a sacrifice or "economic structure that would annul the gift in the ritual circle of the debt." This applies as well to what Derrida refers to as "gift supplements": "potlatch, transgressions and excesses, surplus values, the necessity of give or give back more, returns with interest—in short the whole sacrificial bidding war."[13] That the Mad Lady is caught in a circle of debt, that she is recompensing herself for her martyrdom, becomes clear at the beginning of "Monologue of the Lady Voyager" when she states, "The mystery of other individuals, señor caballero, is ordinarily grief we neither share nor understand" (*TN,* 63). She wishes to share this suffering, to seek compensation for it through her gift. By all of this she contradicts herself and remains within the debt cycle because she does not forget the "gift" given to her, nor the "gift" she gives to the castaway: she expects something in return. Her motivation is a potlatch in which the castaway is subordinated to her through indebtedness, and thus is forced to participate.

The spell the Mad Lady casts makes him share with her the identical dreams that a couple should have, and not the separate, different dreams that she exchanged with her late husband, Felipe the Fair: "An exchange of dreams, señor caballero. Impossible! I shall dream of him. But he will dream of other women. We should be separate again" (*TN,* 71). But his love she cannot reproduce; her only recompense is to acquire power: "My husband's body is mine only in the realm of thought; I give it to you, señor caballero, for you to inhabit, not in the name of my love, but of our power. Such is my offering. You can neither reject it nor make an offering in return" (*TN,* 76). What the Mad Lady calls a "gift" is, in truth, a sacrifice and a potlatch; she forces a different identity on the castaway and attempts to appropriate his soul. The shared power, or the spectacle of power, can be seen as a recompense for his sacrifice. Perhaps it is not he who receives the "gift"; he is only the instrument of a more horrid potlatch: "This we who possess everything offer to those who have nothing: do you understand me, poor dispossessed soul?

13. Derrida, *Given Time,* 23–24.

Only one who can allow himself the luxury of this love and this spectacle, señor caballero, deserves power. There is no possible alternative. I bequeath to Spain what Spain cannot offer me: the image of death as an inexhaustible and consuming luxury" (*TN*, 74). She insists on framing the exchange as an insuperable gift, and thus claims an illusory power over those who would receive it. Regardless, she still remains within the economy of exchange *(trueque)* in that she gives the "gift" in the name of power; she exchanges the body of the king for power. In this sense, the potlatch is definitely interested and cannot be consider a "true gift," for this would have to go unrecognized if we follow the limits set by Derrida.

The Mad Lady believes the body and the image of death to be gifts that break the circle of exchange, thus freeing and empowering her. Nevertheless, they are limited by her inability to give love, to give away that which she never received: her husband's love. Her obsession over her husband becomes an obsession with power, neither of which she comes to acquire. As she attempts to gain power through the "gift" of the king's body, she forces a meaning on death—her own self-interest. In this sense, she attempts to appropriate the image of death, which in the process becomes inexhaustible and devastating, and thus appears excessive and luxurious: "Give us your lives, your sparse treasures, your strength, your dreams, your sweat, and your honor to keep our pantheon alive. Nothing, poor gentleman, can diminish the power based upon the meaninglessness of death, because only for men does the fatal certainty of death have meaning, and only the improbable illusion of immortality can be called madness" (*TN*, 74). Here the image of death is directly associated with the sacrifice and loss of the commoners, as well as a loss in meaning. The image of death, the cadaver, is an obsessive baroque image that was used in all forms of public spectacles and was most definitely associated with social controls; through the spectacle of terror the masses were more efficiently kept in their place.[14] In her attempt to master time and to regain power, the Mad Lady tries to arrest and appropriate death through representation, the spectacle of death, and through the subjugation of the castaway. She exaggerates its meaning, and its meaninglessness, to gain power and to master time—to be immortal. Her death, she implies, would be another life beyond that of the common death. In this way, as we have seen, death loses something of its meaning. In her representation of it, however, death does not lose meaning in a sovereign operation.

14. Maravall, *Culture of the Baroque,* 163–65.

This representation of death and the Mad Lady's subordination of the castaway are symptomatic of the dialectic of lordship: her dependence on the castaway's subordination for her to realize her designs is indicative of her own servitude. Moreover, a sovereign operation, as Bataille and Derrida understand it, would have to render death meaningless; the image of death would have to be one that sacrificed its meaning.[15] This implies not an absolute destruction of meaning in writing, but rather a relation to the loss of meaning, a figural effect not unlike that described by Lyotard, where the meaning of a figure becomes opaque.

Furthermore, the deconstructive moments of the gift and sovereignty are similar in that they must not be recognized as what they are. Nor can they have any conventional value as meaning in the case of sovereignty, or as symbol of sacrifice in the case of the gift. Both must be forgotten. Whereas sovereignty (and the sovereign "subject") must "expend itself without reserve, lose itself, lose consciousness, lose all memory of itself and all the interiority of itself," the gift too cannot be thought of as a gift, but must be forgotten and divorced of questions of debt or obligation. Any such expenditure cannot be "kept in memory." For death to lose meaning it needs not simply to create life, but also to be useless.[16] Although the image of death the Mad Lady elaborates is definitely excessive and ceremonious, it nevertheless turns out to be a minor farce, a laughable image that highlights her failed efforts to regain power and free herself from the circles of exchange and time.

Because the Mad Lady *conceptualizes* and premeditates the spectacle's usefulness as gift in her attempt to gain power, she falls into the servitude of lordship and into the circle of debt. Indeed, where the Mad Lady, Felipe, El Comendador, and Guzmán speak seriously of issues of power, of the gift and of exchange, we cannot help but notice a farcical tenor; each of these characters appears somewhat pathetic in the overall scheme of the novel. If we consider their dialogical relations, the combination and interaction of their voices, this farce would imply a sovereign writing precisely because Fuentes takes the seriousness of what each character is saying and makes it "appear as an abstraction inscribed in play." This follows Derrida's characterization of sovereign writing in his essay "From Restricted to General Economy: A Hegelianism without Reserve."[17] The Mad Lady's and Felipe's discussions of gifts are both serious in their execution but farcical in their futility.

15. Derrida, *Writing and Difference*, 261, 270.
16. Ibid., 265; Derrida, *Given Time*, 23.
17. Derrida, *Writing and Difference*, 256.

In "The Next World" Felipe also desires to exercise power with the unsurpassable gift of his own death. As with the ancient and the Mad Lady, for Felipe the greatest divine gift would be the ability to arrest the flow of time, to exercise mastery over history (*TN*, 104). He too falls into the cycle of debt, for his "gift" not only is predicated on the extinction of life on earth but would also condition the existence of heaven and hell. In other words, the attainment and confirmation of heaven and hell would depend on Felipe's sacrifice: "There will be only Heaven and Hell, without the accursed intermediary step of life on earth, and this will be so because no one can offer a gift surpassing that of the end of everything, the offering we make of everything that exists, exists for the last time, in order that it all end here with me, with us, and not in the broad and terrifying chance of a new world where everything can begin all over again . . . nononono" (*TN*, 493–94). For the sacrifice to work there cannot be another world, there cannot be anything that Felipe does not already see or know. Everything must culminate with his death. (And this does prefigure the apocalyptic ending of the novel in which Felipe's descendant ultimately must sacrifice his self, or what is left of it.) Whether in heaven or hell, Felipe's immortality will be the recompense for his sacrifice. Yet his desire to be "the only and the last" of his line, and to be recompensed for his death, is itself a desire for a return and a reaffirmation of the very circularity he wishes to avoid. Moreover, the announced intention of giving implies a return, a narcissistic gratitude owed and paid to oneself.

In this sense, Felipe's gift of death is a self-affirmation, an anxious gratitude that seeks to reassure the necessity of his lordship in the face of unknown dominions. But this gift is also an appropriation; in the sacrifice Felipe lays claim to all that is consummated, the preservation of which in death would depend on his memory, on his knowledge. Should there be a New World, Felipe would not be able to give or offer anything—he would be worthless. Guzmán, on the other hand, offers a different gift of death that implies an appropriation of power other than that of Felipe and the Mad Lady.

In "Ashes," Felipe reads Guzmán's letters relating his conquests in the New World. The letters and deeds resonate with Cortés's legacy; the events in the letter illustrate the cruelty in a manner not unlike the graphic depiction Fray Bartolomé de Las Casas gave of the conquest. Guzmán manifests his power and his will through violence and fear: "In each village he branded some, killed others, promised life to many more if they agreed to a life as beasts of burden, he gave license to his soldiers to take any woman who pleased them, and instilled fear in all" (*TN*, 704). Guzmán's rage against children in particular most reminds us of Las Casas's condemnation of the abuses against women and children.[18]

According to Guzmán's letter, even with those groups that did not resist, he would starve them into submission, and, as a lesson, "among those he took with him, chained and bound, he allowed many to die from hunger; actually, he preferred the death of very young children deprived of mother's milk, whom he left along the roads to be seen by all" (*TN,* 704–5). With each encounter and potential exchange with a new tribe Guzmán presents a counter-gift designed to instill fear in those who receive him:

> This rage against children culminates in a town of those called Puré-pechas, or Tarascans, where the inhabitants, as a gesture to demonstrate their peaceful intentions, delivered several pigs to Guzmán, and he, in appreciation for their gift, gave them a great sack filled with dead children. When he came to the next town, he repeated these exploits. (*TN,* 705; translation modified)

> (Esta saña contra los niños culminó en un pueblo de los llamados puré-pechas o tarascos, donde los habitantes, para manifestar su ánimo pací-fico, le entregaron varios puercos a Guzmán, y él para agradecer el regalo, les devolvió un costal lleno de niños muertos. Al llegar al siguiente pueblo, repetía estas hazañas.) (*TN,* 709)

The countergift of the dead children and the language used to describe the exchange, "and he, in appreciation for their gift" (y él para agradecer el regalo), suggest an atrocious irony, a mockery of the inhabitants' generosity and desire for allegiance. With such a countergift Guzmán defies the obligation implied in the villagers' gesture of peace and undermines any pretense of exchange, reciprocity, or alliance. They are to submit unconditionally.

The image contrasts, moreover, with the ostentatious images of death that Felipe and the Mad Lady impose on Spain; whereas the sovereigns make a spectacle of cadavers long dead (here I include Felipe's warehousing of the remains of ancestors and saints in his necropolis, El Escorial), Guzmán's spectacle is one that robs its viewers of their future promise—their children as the heirs to their cultural legacy. Felipe and the Mad Lady try to elevate the image of death by appropriating and displaying the already dead, by controlling their memory in such a way that the sovereigns themselves are empowered. Felipe wishes to be the last of his line, and the Mad Lady seeks to

---

18. Las Casas, *Brevísima relación de la destrucción de las Indias,* 104–32, esp. 123.

reclaim for herself the legacy of her unfaithful husband's body. Guzmán, however, extinguishes life, demonstrating a real power over life and death as opposed to the image of power. Indeed, throughout much of the novel it is Guzmán who ministers death on Felipe's behalf, but without regard to Felipe's wavering and uncertainty. In "The Old World" Guzmán and his henchmen are in control when they take the aging king out on a hunt. Guzmán also kills the peasant Martín when the latter becomes the queen's lover, and in "The Next World" it is Guzmán who crushes the rebellion of the peasants, tortures the survivors, and ambushes those who enter Felipe's palace. Guzmán's actions serve to ensure Felipe's tyranny despite Felipe—a farcical and ironic depiction of the Hegelian dialectic of master and slave, wherein the lord's power depends on the servant's exercise of it. In the New World Guzmán acts more for his own profit and empowerment.

In each case the gifts of death serve to alter both the past and the future; they also disrupt the present by redirecting the flows of time and debt. In the three cases of the Mad Lady, Felipe, and Guzmán, these manifest their power through the spectacular submission of other people's bodies: Felipe and the warehousing of the mummified relics of his ancestors, the Mad Lady and her possession and display of her husband's body, and Guzmán's torture, enslavement, and murder of *comuneros,* Jews, Muslims, and Indians. The bodies are offered as gifts much in the same way that sacrifices reaffirm allegiance to both a god and a center of power in the interaction between the executioner and the victim. In this respect, the marking of the body and the spectacle of such "gifts of death" also serve the purpose of reminding subjects who their rulers are and wherein lies their power.

In conclusion, we have seen that in *Terra Nostra* the gift and its many possible variations, or "supplements," appear to be a theme of enormous consequence in the novel's depiction of Spain at the moment of its encounter with the Americas, at the beginning of what is considered the modern age. Moreover, Fuentes entertains a broad range of possible interpretations of gift giving and of its plurality as a social phenomenon, with much irony directed at the Maussian and Hegelian totalization of the gift in its relation to humans' desire to master time and space. In the novel the narrations alongside the gifts are presented in such vast series that it is nearly impossible to conceive the whole without distorting the sense and importance of the gifts, potlatches, and sacrifices it depicts. This vastness, plurality, and accumulation of almost infinite series of heterogeneous gifts and stories points to a particular style: the neobaroque.

3

Ostentatious Offerings

The Neobaroque Economies
of "The New World"

IN THE INTRODUCTION I argued that Fuentes sought to recover
the heterogeneous legacy of Spain through the critical revival of baroque
style as a form of resistance and as an affirmation of Latin America's multi-
cultural identity. For both Carlos Fuentes and Severo Sarduy, the neobaroque
is designed to counter the more ruinous legacy of both colonialism and capitalism. One of the advantages of the neobaroque as a literary strategy is its
ability to resist homogenization, its capacity to integrate different cultural
values without synthesizing them, and thereby reducing them to the mere
reflection of preestablished Western values. In this respect, Fuentes's neobaroque scrutinizes and deconstructs one of the ideas that were first associated with the New World: paradise. Indeed, as part of Fuentes's deconstruction
of both utopia and power, or absolutist authority, he traces back to their origins in both Europe and the Americas, focusing on the discovery and conquest, but also on the early empires of both continents. At the time of the
European discovery of the Americas, the ideal of the golden age was a definite undercurrent in much of Western thinking and produced a wide body of
utopian thought. This utopian vision at first was used to explain the existence
of the Americas and then to explain the indigenous peoples: for some, the

"noble savages" were believed to be closer to God, and for others they were thought of as less than human.

Lois Parkingson Zamora also gives some insight into Fuentes's rejection of utopianism:

> The imposition of a European temporal mode on the mythic American realm began, Fuentes would have it, with the utopianism projected by the Old World upon the New World. America was immediately conceived by Europe as a utopia so that it could wash its sins there. This, Fuentes asserts, is the very meaning of the discovery of the New World. . . . If Fuentes rejects this utopianism, it is not because he rejects the possibility of a better world. What he does reject is the idea that a better world can be achieved by discarding the past in the name of the future.

Maarten van Delden takes a different position regarding Fuentes's attitude with respect to utopianism. He states, "In *Terra Nostra* Fuentes celebrates utopianism and condemns all forms of authority, including, of course, the authority of the state," whereas in his journalistic and essay writings he is more critical of utopianism. Van Delden suggests that Fuentes casts the millenarian movements of *Terra Nostra* in a positive light. Although this is partially true, in the novel these same movements become corrupted, are betrayed, and ultimately fail. I would agree more with Zamora's view that *Terra Nostra's* treatment of utopianism is fairly negative. Indeed, following Juan Goytisolo's and Juan Villoro's readings of Fuentes, his utopian vision is tragic and Goyaesque. Regarding the historical thought that imbues the novel, Goytisolo points out that it "seems to waiver . . . between two opposed ideas—the necessity and the failure of revolution—without fixing definitively on either." Writing about Fuentes's *Buried Mirror,* but also about *Terra Nostra,* Villoro declares: "Goyaesque and baroque, Fuentes erects a gallery of mirrors that partly restores the broken history of two worlds."[1]

Fuentes is critical of utopian thought in its application and expression in *practice.* For Fuentes, following Octavio Paz, the utopian *moment is located in time,* in the imagination: its spatiality exists only in the world of fiction, or may be glimpsed in the eternal instant, usually in the erotic encounter. In *Terra Nostra,* however, this corresponds to the negative function of utopian thought: it must serve as a critique of the present, of the mystification of

1. Zamora, *Writing the Apocalypse,* 150; van Delden, *Fuentes, Mexico, and Modernity,* 118; Goytisolo, *"Terra Nostra,"* 229; Villoro, "Goya y Fuentes: Los trabajos del sueño," 102.

modernity, and as a tragic revisiting of past errors (in history and tradition) in order to liberate thought and action from the past. This is projection toward a possible transformation of history in the present.[2] In *Terra Nostra* this implies a direct confrontation with and revitalization of the language and thought of the baroque.

In the novel Fuentes's neobaroque employs figural language not only to deconstruct the impositions of Western values and meanings on the interpretation of the Americas; it also integrates the rhetorical strategies of Nahuatl poetry and pictographic representation as part of the "contamination" of baroque rhetoric. This contamination generates primarily from "The New World," the second part of the novel that re-creates the encounter between the two worlds. Early in "The New World," the story of Pilgrim's journey through the New World, the castaway learns about the everyday life of the natives—a knowledge that proves crucial to his survival and protagonism in that land. Much like the chronicles of Bernal Díaz de Castillo and Hernán Cortés, his narration is designed to transmit to his audience, Felipe and by extension the reader, the wonderment that is experienced when one encounters a people and place for the first time. As a storyteller, however, Pilgrim has already learned to interpret and decipher the signs and events of the New World. His narration integrates baroque and Nahuatl figural strategies, at the same time that it deconstructs the utopian, golden-age vision of the New World.

One of the keys to interpreting "The New World" is found in the chapter "The Ancient's Legend." When Pilgrim is challenged to give a countergift, the ancient Lord of Memory's sad, hard stare can be seen as an emblem of a whole series of semiotic elements and complementary relations repeated throughout "The New World." Images such as the ancient's eyes, and the rhetorical figures used to elaborate them, interrelate within a semiotic series or chain. At a first reading, however, the meaning of such images, and their interrelation, is not at all clear; Fuentes introduces keys to their interpretation later in "The New World." Therefore, when they are first read, the inscription and enunciation of these images have a nonsemiotic effect—they might be startling, for example—a figural effect that transgresses any positioning within a signifying chain. This effect can be provocative, calling attention to the event of the enunciation, or to its inscription on the page. Therefore, my analysis of passages from *Terra Nostra* will address both the ef-

---

2. Fuentes, *Tiempo Mexicano*, 13–32; Paley Francescato, "Re/creación y des/construcción."

fects of the rhetorical figures employed as well as the semiotic elements that form signifying chains, that generate "meaning."

Most readers will discover at first that the image of the old man's eyes reproduces the same contrasts illustrated earlier in "The New World" when Pilgrim first approaches the beach. Described in similes as both dark and light, the guardian's eyes also represent the general economic relations of gains and losses: they are characterized in terms of rot, "decayed as the jungle" (podridos como la selva), and compared to the quality of gold, "precious as the gold" (atesorados como el oro). The black part of his eyes functions as a sign of renovation in decay, and the light part as the sign of abundance held in reserve. *Atesorados* (amassed, precious) suggests two possible meanings. Clearly, its primary use corresponds to the figurative meaning, which gives the eyes a quality of fullness and virtue; in the comparison to gold, the eyes receive the qualities of abundance and beauty. Its literal meaning, however, implies a treasure (of gold), a wealth that is hoarded, "amassed," and thus noncirculating. (In totemic economies wealth is determined not by the accumulation of vast fortunes, but by expenditure and the distribution of goods.) Moreover, the image as a whole establishes a parallel, elliptical relationship: each of the opposite terms integrates an opposition between excess and deficiency.

Furthermore, the jungle and the gold each lose an aspect of their quality in the above oxymoronic figurations (the jungle as the abundance of decay, the exuberance of gold as something held in reserve). This corresponds to Severo Sarduy's thesis regarding baroque language, namely, that it favors the supplement, and thus the excess and partial loss of its object. The mother's breast, excrement (and its metaphorical equivalent, gold), the gaze, and the voice—in short, the *partial object* is "everything that man can comprehend and assimilate from the other and from himself." The baroque favors the supplement due to this relation of loss in the partial object, which in turn has the internal structure of the supplement. In this respect, the supplement has two aspects: it is a surplus that has an accumulating function, and it fills a void.[3] This general economic relation between accumulation and emptiness is fundamental to the baroque.

In the ancient's eyes these relations of loss, the decay and reserved abundance, correspond to the repeated exchanges of gazes, objects, and existences that Pilgrim narrates. The repetition of the supplements throughout "The

3. Sarduy, *Barroco*, 100. See also Derrida, *Of Grammatology*, 144–45.

New World," the useless gold and rotted jungle, and the predominance of their repetition in several rhetorical figures determine the excessive baroque play of the narrative discourse, while also functioning within an insistent economy of signs oriented around a fundamental debt—to the Earth Goddess.

This scene from "The Ancient's Legend" also manifests a neobaroque play of exchanges and alliances between exteriority and interiority, and in particular between light and dark. The chiastic play of chiaroscuro in the ancient's visage forms a neobaroque configuration because the balance between light and dark is complementary, whereas in Renaissance and baroque painting, for example, the distribution of light and dark tends to distort or emphasize (or both) one of the terms of the contrast with the complete withdrawal of the other. Significant figures in a painting are brightly highlighted and surrounded by areas of shadow; such a contrast tends to orient the attention and view of the spectator to the highlighted areas. (Here we can think of Caravaggio.) For Sarduy, this had a didactic effect and was designed to convince with authority by doing away with nuances and suppressing the transition from one term to another. In rhetoric, ellipsis had a similar function with respect to the elision of certain metaphors in Góngora's poetry wherein words of improper values, "the ugly, the uncomfortable and disagreeable," are taken out of Góngora's verse in order to heighten and illuminate other words. With regards to the monstrosity of the cyclops Polifemo, Dámaso Alonso clarifies, however, that the baroque in Góngora is defined not by the presence or absence of any particular element, but by the clash between opposites. The cyclops's hideous appearance contrasts with the soft beauty of his voice, and in this sense the baroque is not defined by either of these elements, but by the clash between them. The Baroque is an enormous "coincidentia oppositorum."[4] In *Terra Nostra*, such opposites complement each other and often correspond to other sets of contrasts. Within an elliptical relationship, geometrically determined as having two centers, the two terms are contiguous and evident, unlike in the obscurantist usage of ellipsis. With the neobaroque nothing is suppressed; meanings are not obscured but multiplied, and they flow into each other, maintaining their autonomy in integrated oxymoronic or complementary relationships or both.

In the contrast of light and dark, "The New World" maintains comple-

---

4. Sarduy, *Barroco*, 17–18, 70; Alonso, *Góngora y el "Polifemo,"* 1:228. Sarduy refers to Alonso's commentary on Góngora's obscurantism in Alonso's edition of Luis de Góngora y Argote, *Las soledades*, 60.

mentary distributions of these opposites throughout its narration. The association of the rotting jungle with the black in the old man's eyes, for example, follows a distribution of light from the beach scene early in "The New World," in the chapter "Whirlpool of the Night." Before his arrival on the beach, when shipwrecked by the nocturnal whirlpool and its disorienting vortical energy, Pilgrim makes the following observations about light and dark, including other oppositions:

> I closed my eyes, nauseated, choking, blinded by the cataracts of black spume in this ocean tunnel . . . and in that vertigo, light and dark were one, silence and clamor, my being and that of the female who gave me birth, wakefulness and sleep, life and death, all one. (*TN*, 365)

> (Cerré los ojos, mareado, ahogado, cegado por las cataratas de negra espuma de este túnel del océano . . . y en ese vértigo se confundían la luz y la oscuridad, el silencio y el clamor, mi ser de hombre y el ser de la mujer que me parió algún día; la vigilia y el sueño, la vida y la muerte, confundidos.) (*TN*, 372)

Opposites are confused in his delirium, as he seems to pass from life to death, and then to life again.

This representation of delirium and semiblindness, moreover, is reminiscent of Sor Juana Inés de la Cruz's "Primero Sueño," above all its opening and the lines 495–540, in which reason struggles to make order of a chaotic universe. Nevertheless, whereas Sor Juana's dream is a reflection on the limits of reason and the soul's effort to overcome the impediments of the body, Fuentes's Pilgrim experiences his journey viscerally, through the full array of the body's senses.[5] Hunger is the sensation that first makes him realize that he has survived the shipwreck, and that he has not died.

When Pilgrim arrives at the beach in "The Beyond," his dreamlike delirium and his exhaustion lead him to believe that he has died, and to wonder whether the beach is indeed paradise. He has not figured out yet that he is reborn, and attributes his distorted perception to death. Once away from the confusion of the whirlpool, he approaches a shore defined by the contrast of "white beaches and black forests" (*TN*, 366) (blancas playas y los negros bosques) (*TN*, 372). The brightness of the beach allows him to separate the contrasts, but in terms consistent with a neobaroque aesthetic; not only are

---

5. Cruz, *Obras completas*, 183–201; Paz, *Sor Juana Inés de la Cruz, o las trampas de la fe*, 497.

the contrasts momentarily and dynamically presented in a relation of mutual dependence, but also the figural language used to convey this relationship is chiastic:

> I say white and black in order to be understood, but I do not speak of whiteness as we know it in life, the white of bone or sheet, or of the blackness of the crow or of the night. Imagine, if you can, Sire, their simultaneous existence; side by side, at once illuminating and obscuring, the white white because the contrast of black permits it, and the black made black because white lights its blackness. In life these colors are divorced, but when at the hour of death I opened my new eyes of sand, I saw them forever united, one the color of the other, unimaginable alone: white beaches, black jungles. (*TN,* 366; translation modified)

> (Digo blanco y digo negro para ser comprendido; mas esa blancura no es la que conocemos en vida, la de hueso o sábana, ni esa negrura la de cuervo o noche. Pensad, más bien, su pareja existencia. Lado a lado, iluminándose y oscureciéndose al mismo tiempo, blanco el blanco porque el contraste del negro se lo permite, y negro el negro porque alumbra su negrura el blanco. La vida divorcia estos colores; al abrir mis nuevos ojos de arena en la hora de la muerte, los vi para siempre unidos, el uno el color del otro, imcomprensibles en la separación: blancas playas, negras selvas.) (*TN,* 372–73)

The relationship between black and white is complementary; although the two terms of the relationship are mutually exclusive, they are meaningless if separated. In his book on Niels Bohr, Abraham Pais makes a general observation on this type of relationship: "Complementarity can be formulated without explicit reference to physics, to wit, as two aspects of a description that are mutually exclusive yet both necessary for a full understanding of what is to be described." Arkady Plotnitsky, referring to this passage from Pais, points out that "a complementarity theory must employ diverse—and at times conflicting or mutually incompatible . . . —configurations, double or multiple, operative within the same framework." These configurations, moreover, should not lend themselves to a "full synthesis, Hegelian or other. Such a matrix entails introducing and accounting for both heterogeneous and interactive operations of pairs or clusters of concepts, metaphors, or of conceptual and metaphoric networks."[6] In Fuentes's fiction, such complementary

---

6. Pais, *Niels Bohr's Times, in Physics, Philosophy, and Polity,* 24; Plotnitsky, *Complementarity: Anti-epistemology after Bohr and Derrida,* 73.

relationships are expressed through the use of extended chiasmi, dynamic oxymoronic images, and various parallel structures such as double phrasing *(difrasismo),* which will be described below.

Through this description of the light on the beach Pilgrim as narrator interprets the contrasts of paradise on its own terms, as opposed to the common tendencies of early chroniclers to relate the things of the New World according to resemblances with things in Europe (bone, sheet, crow). In other words, the complementary relationships he discovers between light and dark, life and death, and between many of the opposites he mentions are indicative of an underlying duality rooted in Aztec cosmology and its precursors that informs his narration. Pilgrim is seeing the land from a pre-Columbian vantage point where opposites, including life and death, simultaneously and perpetually interact. Death complements and clarifies life, and vice versa. According to Miguel León-Portilla, at the center of Aztec cosmology there is a fundamental creative force, Ometéotl ("place of duality" or "dual-god"), which was conceived as a single force of a dual nature:

> The Nahuas, in attempting to explain the origin of all that exists, arrived metaphorically—by the path of "flower and song"—at the discovery of an ambivalent being, an active generating principle which was at the same time a passive receptor capable of conceiving. The powers of generation and of conception—requisites for the appearance of life in our world—were thus combined in a single being. The affirmation is made, first implicitly and later, in other terms, explicitly, that the *nelli téotl* [the "true god"] or Ometéotl is the cosmic principle by which all that exists is conceived and begotten.[7]

Ometéotl is the creative force of the universe, and its supremacy is based precisely on the complementarity of its "perpetual generating faculty and universal sustaining action." Life and death, sky and earth, heat and cold, light and darkness, masculine and feminine are all complementary pairs and varying manifestations of the Ometéotl. It is also curious to note that for the *tlamantinime* the truth of this can be arrived at only through poetry, or "flower and song."[8]

The expression "flower and song" is a double phrasing *(difrasismo),* the pairing of two terms that, though they are sometimes similar, have important differences that add nuance and precision to the concepts. As León-Portilla

7. León-Portilla, *Aztec Thought and Culture,* 83.
8. Ibid., 76, 83.

states, this mode of figuration is intimately bound up in the duality of Ometéotl: "this mode of thought concerning the duality of Ometéotl paralleled a dual quality within the Nahuatl language itself. So strongly inclined to conceive in terms of duality were the minds of the tlamantinime, that when they wanted to endow an idea with maximum clarity and precision, they always isolated two of its qualities, employing what has been called *difrasismo.* Thus they evoked in the mind images that were not abstract and cold, but rich in meaning, fresh, vigorous, and dynamic." This is important in *Terra Nostra* because the modes of figuration in the passage from "The Beyond" are complementary: the chiastic figuration of light and dark; the parallelism of "I do not speak of whiteness as we know it in life, the white *of bone or sheet,* or of the blackness *of the crow or of the night,*" and the double phrasing in "I saw them forever united, one the color of the other, unimaginable alone: *white beaches, black jungles*" (el uno el color del otro, incomprensibles en la separación; *blancas playas, negras selvas*). The chiasmus and the succeeding *difrasismo* are doubly complementary. The first pair of comparisons in the parallelism describing whiteness and blackness is part of a refusal to describe the two opposites separately, in terms of their resemblances to specific things Europeans would recognize, *sheet* in particular. (These are also "improper" objects that would be obscured in a baroque ellipsis.) In this manner a Nahua rhetorical strategy is used with terms that evoke possible European resemblances. While *difrasismo* is used in European languages, according to León-Portilla its use is very rare in comparison to its frequency in Nahuatl, where it is "one of the principal and peculiar characteristics of this language."[9] In the succeeding double phrasing, "white beaches, black jungles," which could be considered two interweaving *difrasismos* (white/black, beaches/jungles), the terms are all general, lacking any specific resemblances, and the complementarity is spelled out: "unimaginable alone" (incomprensibles en la separación). The whole *difrasismo* serves as a metaphor for the land that is governed by the duality of Ometéotl. Thus, the chiasmus in this paragraph, it might be said, is a European rhetorical figure used for the comprehension of a way of viewing the world that would be evident to a native of that coastal terrain when expressed in the deceivingly simple *difrasismo.*

From this analysis I conclude that Fuentes's neobaroque style involves the complementary interplay of classical European and pre-Columbian Mexican textual strategies. This interplay is elliptical in that the two poles or centers

9. Ibid., 102, 75.

interact at the level of figuration. At another narrative level, however, the traditional mode of ellipsis and obscurantism might be functional in terms of Aztec cosmology, seeing that Pilgrim does not remember the majority of the days he spends in that land, once he has heard the legend and been incorporated into it. The destructive side of the mythic duality that Pilgrim assumes as Plumed Serpent/Smoking Mirror is excluded from his narrative memory; as with the dark fields in a painting of the chiaroscuro style, the forgotten time illuminates what is remembered. Moreover, when the Lady of the Butterflies tells Pilgrim that he is the Plumed Serpent in what he remembers and the Smoking Mirror in what he does not remember (*TN*, 445), only the effects of what he does, the destruction he leaves behind as a conquistador, are seen in scattered fragments.

Pilgrim is destined to spend twenty-five days in the land before he can be reunited with the Lady of the Butterflies whom he encounters once the ancient has died. Only five days and five nights will he remember, and these make up the time of the narration. They are the "masked days" and correspond to his destiny as Plumed Serpent (Quetzalcóatl), who is known as the bearer of truth and the "Giver of Life." The other twenty days correspond to Smoking Mirror (Tezcatlipoca), the destructive, mischievous complementary opposite of Plumed Serpent. These twenty days are not narrated, but the effect of their occurrence is felt throughout the novel. It becomes clear in the third part of the novel that Pilgrim's forgotten time corresponds to the character Guzmán, who wreaks havoc throughout the New World as a conquistador, as Cortés. Moreover, what Pilgrim forgets is a series of events that takes place in the future, after his narration; this implies a narration governed by the simultaneity of future, past, and present.[10]

From Reciprocity to Complementarity: Fuentes and Góngora

Now that I have established the complementary play of light on the beach scene as an indicator of both Nahuatl figural strategy and a modification of chiaroscuro, I can focus on a more directly comparative analysis of the initial

10. For a discussion of the significance of the numerical division of the days remembered and forgotten in terms of the Aztec calendrical system, see Springer, "Iconological Study," 96–102.

beach scene in "The New World." This scene is in several respects an in-version of the opening stanzas of Góngora's *Solitudes.* In *Terra Nostra,* when Pilgrim is shipwrecked and separated from his companion Pedro while at sea, he arrives alone on the beach of a strange land that proves to be inhospitable. The scene parallels a similar scene in *The Solitudes,* in which Góngora's *forastero* (stranger, wanderer)[11] finds a more welcoming reception, thus offering us insight into the general economic disparities be-tween the two scenes. Góngora's shipwrecked *forastero,* after having been compared to Arion for the sweet tones of his lament to the sea, is saved from his shipwreck by a wooden plank from his destroyed boat. The wooden spar, or plank *(tabla),* in turn, is compared to the dolphin that saves Arion from drowning:

> Torn from a mountain pine, with Auster's blast
> > Unendingly at war,
> > A charitable spar
> Was dolphin yet enough to keep afloat
> The unthinking pilgrim who had dared to trust
> His pathway to the ocean's Libyan waste,
> > His life to a fragile boat.[12]

> (Del siempre en la montaña opuesto pino
> > al enemigo Noto,
> > piadoso miembro roto
> —breve tabla— delfín no fué pequeño
> al inconsiderado peregrino
> que a una Libia de ondas su camino
> > fió, y su vida a un leño.)

The associations of the wooden spar to the dolphin and to the pine tree that resists the wind elevate the wood, a mundane, natural object, to an almost heroic or mythic status. Throughout *The Solitudes* there is an exaltation of nature, life, and the golden age, more often than not accompanied by a deri-

---

11. Góngora uses the terms *peregrino* (pilgrim) and *forastero* (stranger, outsider) to refer to the protagonist of *The Solitudes.* It is no coincidence that Fuentes uses the same term *pilgrim* as the name of the narrator-protagonist of "The New World," who is also a "pilgrim of love," so to speak, referring to the hurt wanderer of the courtly love tradition. To avoid confusion, I will use the term *forastero* to distinguish Góngora's pilgrim.

12. Góngora, *The Solitudes of Luis de Góngora,* 6–7; page references are hereafter cited par-enthetically in the text.

sion of courtly life.[13] In this respect, Góngora's allusion to the myth of Arion is by no means an arbitrary artifice; the myth offers a moral commentary on the dangers that come with wealth and displays of luxury.

Throughout *The Solitudes* the values and luxuries of courtly life are juxtaposed with the embellished images of use values and the generosity of commoners in the pastoral setting of the first *Solitude*. Arion, being the inventor of the dithyramb and a talented musician, also suggests another moral of the myth: that the most valuable gifts are not the material gifts that can be taken from him, but those that only he can offer, which in turn were bestowed on him by the gods—the natural gifts of his talent. This establishes a fundamental relation between art and generosity that is opposed to the materialist values and ostentatious luxuries of courtly life.

Furthermore, the elevation of natural and common objects corresponds to the baroque sensibility and desire to provoke the viewer. Dámaso Alonso refers to this elevation of nature as a "panic spirit of exaltation" in which the image-object nearly breaks out of its poetic confines. With the shipwreck, this panic sumptuousness accentuates both the threat of the wind and waves as well as the great need of the dolphin and the wooden plank. A little of Arion's desperation is thus transferred to the *forastero*'s situation. In addition, the exaltation is a figural excess that "overloads" the image of nature and, by doing so, conveys the general abundance or fecundity of nature in terms that are *felt*, than understood as such.[14]

José Lezama Lima also considers this exaltation to be both a lifting of the object and the "empowering and seizure of incitement." In this context, the relationship between the excesses of the figural and potlatch becomes clear: the figural excess that leads to a loss of meaning implies an increase of sensuality, of corporeality in the verse. In addition, the object is empowered with respect to the reader: through the production of an excess, the poet moves the

13. Arion laments because the sailors who are taking him home want to kill him for the riches he carries, gifts he had received upon winning a music contest in Taenarus. Seeing that there is no mercy to be found among the sailors, Arion asks to be allowed to sing one last time. He "invoked the gods with impassioned strains, and then leaped overboard," but his song attracts a school of music-loving dolphins. One of them rescues him and carries him to shore. Arion is then able to reveal the treason and duplicity of his would-be assassins, who claim that he is still in Taenarus. The dolphin, interestingly enough, chooses not to leave Arion's side and accompanies him to court, "where it soon succumbed to a life of luxury. Arion gave it a splendid funeral." See Robert Graves, *The Greek Myths*, 1:290; and Alonso, *Góngora y el "Polifemo,"* 1:128, 2:218–21.

14. Alonso, *Góngora y el "Polifemo,"* 1:128.

reader. Furthermore, the exaltation also prepares the object for a sacrifice: the object will lose the fixity of its meaning as it becomes an offering.[15]

Lezama Lima, when contemplating the exaltation of objects in the metaphoric light of Góngora's images, refers to the "fury and height" as being of a "gothic impulse." While his use of the term *Gothic (gótico* and *goticismo)* might lead to some ambiguity, his discussion of the object as being prepared as an offering for sacrifice clearly suggests the importance of the gift in ancient Greece, as conveyed through Góngora's classicism. This is not far removed from Bataille's discussion of potlatch: the appropriation of a power (in Lezama Lima this empowerment takes place in the image-object) depends on the useless consumption or sacrifice of something—in figural terms, the useful thing sacrificed corresponds to the normative function of communication, the literal meaning of the object. Furthermore, Lezama Lima states that the Greek and Roman allusions in Góngora's poetry actually turn off the light, or radiance, of Góngora's metaphors. The fury and passion of Góngora's images pertain to a pre-Renaissance sensibility, a medieval taste for the audible or corporeal image, which is perhaps dulled by the mythical references. While I believe Lezama Lima is right, the quaintness he finds in the classical allusions might also reflect the distance of a twentieth-century reader. With respect to the shipwreck, the wooden spar becomes a "votive offering," as the *forastero* gives it to the rocks as a gesture of gratitude:[16]

> Sucked down to the watery depths, then to the air
>   Spewed up again, beside
> A reef upon whose craggy head he spied
> Cots of warm feathers twined with well-dried reed,
>   Still with salt spray and weed
> Crusted he found hospitality where
>   Jove's bird had found a nest.
>
> Kissing the sand, the plank that once had graced
>   The broken ship, and floated
> Him shorewards, to the rock he now devoted;
> For senseless stones still know
>   The flatteries that grateful gifts bestow.
>   (*The Solitudes,* 6–9; translation modified)

15. Lezama Lima, "Sierpe de Góngora," 192–96.
16. Ibid.; Alonso, *Góngora y el "Polifemo,"* 2:220.

(Del océano pues antes sorbido,
　　y luego vomitado
no lejos de un escollo coronado
de secos juncos, de calientes plumas
　　—alga todo y espumas—
halló hospitalidad donde halló nido
　　de Júpiter el ave.

Besa la arena, y de la rota nave
　　aquella parte poca
que le expuso en la playa dió a la roca;
que aun se dejan las peñas
　　lisonjear de agradecidas señas.)

Through its comparison to the dolphin as well as its activity as the subject of the verb *to float* ("floated him" [le expuso]), the plank is almost personified by the heroic exaltation, by its function as savior. The rocks, to which the plank is offered, are sensitive to the gesture of gratitude: covered with feathers the rocks house the nests of eagles, the birds of Jupiter. This lord of the Greek and Roman pantheon is also known as the god of hospitality that protects strangers and outsiders. Because of the contiguity of "found hospitality" and "where Jove's bird had found a nest," the offering of the plank can also be read as gratitude toward this god, and perhaps a plea to continue the protection.

Thus opens Góngora's first *Solitude* with the shipwrecked *forastero*'s offering of gratitude, a mundane object elevated in its ritual function. The shipwreck scenario with Fuentes's Pilgrim, however, shows a curious play on this gesture of gratitude, and an exaggerated employment of figures to frame the conflicts of his narration. First, pearls and shells accompany Pilgrim when he approaches the shore, and he pays special attention to the changes and contrasts in the light around him, as I noted earlier. The confusion he experiences in his discerning of the landscape parallels a similar confusion that Góngora's *forastero* feels upon touching ground in *The Solitudes:*

Soon as the horizon's boundaries
(Whose line, now scarce distinguishable, turned
Waves into hills and mountains into seas)
　　Sunset no longer burned,
The unhappy outcast, having donned again

> The vesture rescued from the cruel main,
> Trod down the twilight in the thorny shade
> And, less exhausted than discomfited,
>   Rocks that might well have daunted
> The swiftest pinion's daring flight, he mounted.
>   (*The Solitudes,* 9)

> (No bien pues de su luz los horizontes,
> —que hacían desigual, confusamente,
> montes de agua y piélagos de montes—
>   desdorados los siente,
> cuando—entregado el mísero extranjero
> en lo que el mar redimió fiero—
> entre espinas crepúsculos pisando,
> riscos que aun igualara mal, volando,
>   veloz, intrépida ala,
> menos cansado que confuso, escala.)

The immediate coastal landscape is rocky and the surf rough, wave and rock being confused in the blurred horizons of twilight. More confused than tired, and feeling the difficulty caused by the dimming light, the *forastero* climbs the crags whose summit is so high that even birds would have trouble reaching it.[17] Although the landscape that Pilgrim encounters is very different, it has elements that, in their effects, parallel the opening lines of *The Solitudes.*

Pilgrim lands on a beach that is not rocky or rugged at all, but flat and calm, perhaps suggestive of a tropical scene. The light he sees is a morning light, instead of twilight, with contrasts so stark that he is unable to discern the things on the beach. As we have seen, Pilgrim's perception of light and dark shifts from confusion to a clear view of their contrast as a complementary whole. He then experiences another shift in his perception of the beach: birds fly over, and the light is obscured, permitting the clear perception of the things on the beach. The light that allows him to construe the beach as paradise he describes as a pearly light, and he compares it to twilight:

> Perhaps I slipped from swoon to sleep. When I came to myself I seemed to be reclining. My head rested on the sandy beach. . . . I stepped onto the beach and was bathed in light. It was as beautiful as the sunset: a light slanting horizontally across the beach it bathed in a glossy grayish luster. I told myself that was the light we had in life called pearly.

17. Alonso, *Góngora y el "Polifemo,"* 2:221n42.

I stopped looking at the light and turned to see what things it revealed. (*TN*, 367)

(Quizás pasé del desmayo al sueño. Cuando vine en mí, me sentí reposado. Mi cabeza descansaba en la arena de la playa. . . . Pisé la playa y me bañó la luz. Le otorgué los atributos del ocaso: una luz horizontal como la playa la iluminaba con tersos brillos grisáceos. Díjeme que ésa era la luz que en vida llamábamos perlada.
Dejé de ver la luz para ver qué cosas revelaba.) (*TN*, 373–74)

By comparing this pearly light to twilight, he relates it to Venus. This association is by no means arbitrary: the multicolored birds that block the light, the pearls and seashells that accompany him as he floats toward shore (*TN*, 367), the twilight and Venus—are all attributes of the god Quetzalcóatl, Plumed Serpent. These attributes announce the god's arrival in the person of Pilgrim.[18]

The light is also a play on the twilight in the first *Solitude*. In *Terra Nostra*, "a horizontal light" that would parallel the horizontal plane of the beach contrasts the rising and falling movements in the stanza from *The Solitudes*,

> Soon as the horizon's boundaries
> (Whose line, now scarce distinguishable, turned
> Waves into hills and mountains into seas)
> Sunset no longer burned.

As the *forastero* scales the cliffs, the sun descends in the sky. The shift from noun to adjective produces an effect that is both similar and different: where the *horizons* are confused by twilight in *The Solitudes*, in *Terra Nostra* the *horizontal light* softens the blinding contrasts and allows Pilgrim to observe the things on the beach.

As Pilgrim moves his focus from the light to the things it reveals, the sun comes out, and he is struck by the exuberance of a beach covered with pearls. He ponders his own death and the life he might have if he were alive with such wealth: "I moaned. The only person who would profit from theses riches was one who could remember nothing either of his life or of his death. . . . Neither the fortress of the warrior, nor the palace of the King, nor the portals of the Church, nor the honor of a Lady, I told myself at that moment, could possibly resist the seduction of the man who owned such opulence" (*TN*,

18. Springer, "Iconological Study," 92.

368–69). Presented with such an opulent treasure, Pilgrim can feel only an absence of passion and ambition in his existence; he is reminded of his amnesia, his ignorance of any self-possessing identity. Moreover, his ruminations on the seductive power of the wealth are reminiscent of Guzmán's complaints about money's ability to "enslave" the castle walls that represent the landed nobility. It also suggests a general complementarity of abundance and scarcity: the opulence inspires a feeling of emptiness, in this corresponding to Felipe's ostentatious palace dedicated to death.

Although this feeling of emptiness before such wealth conveys an elliptical, baroque sensibility, Pilgrim's representation of the pearls becomes more complex as he refers to himself as the hypothetical "owner" of the opulence, and then encounters the "true masters" of the beach and therefore the pearls. Pilgrim, later to be named "Giver of Life," makes a gestural offer to give away his newly acquired wealth to "the land of death." His gesture, however, is not received with the same appreciation and hospitality as the offering received in *The Solitudes:*

> With outstretched arms, fists filled, I offered the pearls to the land of death. My shining gaze was returned by the veiled and inhospitable stares of the true masters of this beach. Only then did I see them, for their enormous carapaces blended with the color of the jungle behind them. I saw gigantic sea turtles, scattered along the verge where the sand ended and the jungle thicket began. And those sad veiled eyes reminded me of my old friend Pedro, and as I remembered him, I felt that the pearls in my hands grew soft and faded and finally died. (*TN,* 369)

> (Ofrecí las perlas, extendiendo los brazos con mis puños llenos de ellas, a la tierra de la muerte. Me devolvieron la mirada—brillante la mía, veladas, inhóspitas las suyas—las verdaderas dueñas de la playa. Sólo entonces las vi, pues sus inmensos caparazones se confundían con el color de la selva. Las vi: las gigantescas tortugas, echadas en la frontera donde terminaba la arena y comenzaba la espesura. Y esos ojos tristes, envelados, me recordaron a mi viejo amigo Pedro; y al recordarlo, sentí que las perlas, en mis manos, hacíanse blandas, envejecían y, al cabo, morían.) (*TN,* 375)

This is a curious play on the scene in *The Solitudes* in which Góngora's *forastero* makes the offering to the rocks and the eagles' nest. Instead of eagles and hospitality, Pilgrim finds unwelcoming turtles. It becomes clear later on that the markings the turtles have on their shells are associated with the Earth

Goddess. In "The Ancient's Legend," the ancient not only mentions the turtle as one of the animals carrying the mark of the fires of creation, which takes place in the womb of the Earth Goddess, but also explains that the land is a divinity and cannot be owned. Speaking of Pedro's offense, he says: "He defied us. He raised a temple for himself alone. He wished to make himself owner of a piece of the earth. But the earth is divine and cannot be possessed by any man. It is she who possesses us. . . . Your friend wished only to take. He wished to offer nothing" (*TN*, 387–88). The episode with the turtles has a direct intertextual relationship with Inca Garcilaso's *Comentarios reales*, in particular the story of the castaway Pedro Serrano.[19] Fuentes rewrites this story of survival, integrating it into the larger mythological and sacrificial schema of the Earth Goddess he re-creates in "The New World." This is another example of how Fuentes rewrites the chronicles *(crónicas)* in a way that challenges and undermines the very notion of property and the right of conquest, reinforcing the principle of generosity based in a collective relationship with the land. This encounter on the beach with the turtles, moreover, foreshadows many exchanges to come. For example, it is precisely Pilgrim's realization that he does not own that land, nor the pearls for that matter, that saves him. Pedro was unable to learn such a lesson.

Unlike the welcoming that Góngora's *forastero* receives, the turtles are weary and distrustful of Pilgrim. In addition, because he believes himself to have died and arrived at "the land of death," he finds no promise of protection in these unwelcoming creatures. The turtles, then, at first appear to be for Pilgrim the opposite of what the birds and rocks were for Góngora's *forastero*. The inhospitable reception of the turtles is conveyed, moreover, in the exchange of glances, a visual chiasmus described in general economic terms: "I offered" (ofrecí); "They returned my gaze" (me devolvieron la mirada). Pilgrim's reference to turtles as "the true masters [owners] of this beach" (las verdaderas dueñas de esta playa) also enhances the sense that he is an outsider, and that his gesture of offering the pearls is somehow misguided.

With regard to the pearls as a votive offering, these are precious and not mundane like the wooden plank in *The Solitudes*. The pearls suffer a process opposite to that of the wood in *The Solitudes:* instead of a mundane object being exalted through exaggeration, classical allusion, and figural excess, the thought of the death of Pilgrim's fellow castaway, Pedro, causes the pearls to soften and die. Although this irregularity of the pearl is at first suggestive of

19. Garcilaso de la Vega, *Comentarios reales*, 16–20.

the baroque seed pearl that lasts only an instant *(aljófar caduco)*, the pearls are revived by contact with Pilgrim's flesh. This magical effect is repeated, but in the opposite direction, when Pilgrim is forced to take the ancient's place after he has killed him: "What happened, then, Sire, was something like death. They placed me in the ancient's basket, my knees touching my chin; they poured the pearls over my body and I felt their nacreous grayness revive at contact with a skin aflame with ignorance and fear" (*TN*, 398). This play of balance and imbalance is most revealing earlier, once Pilgrim becomes aware of his own hunger and that of the mosquitoes that suck his blood. He slays one of the turtles and feasts on its eggs. At this point, once gorged, he makes the following comparison between the pearls and the eggs:

> And those nests of turtle eggs had not deceived me: they were the opposite face of the pearls, for in the pearls I saw another death image. Without the contact of living flesh, pearls grow old and their luster dims: pearls are a moribund promise; the turtle eggs, pearls of nascent life. (*TN*, 371)

> (Eran [los huevos] como los rostros de las perlas, pues en éstas podía yo ver una imagen más de la muerte: las perlas sin el contacto de piel viva, envejecen y declinan, son moribunda promesa; los huevos de las tortugas eran perlas de naciente vida.) (*TN*, 377)

After a violent encounter Pilgrim constructs this complex image comparing the eggs to the pearls as a metaphor for the coexistence of life and death. This balance also exhibits a general economic distribution of gains and losses: the pearls *decline*, whereas the eggs are nascent, beginning to grow. In this way, the pearls and eggs function in the image as partial objects that are reorganized into both complementary and supplementary relations that affirm the baroque syncretism of the New World.

The dying pearls associated with Plumed Serpent, the Giver of Life, and the eggs associated with the Earth Goddess, the land of death, imply an elevation of nature more complex than in Góngora's *Solitudes*. This is because the dark side, death, forms a complementary relationship with life in a particular way: in *Terra Nostra* the mode of this integration is informed not only by Nahuatl and baroque figural strategies, as I have shown, but also by the Mexican Indian attitude toward death as a continual presence in everyday experience and reality. This is how the images of the pearls and the eggs represent Ometéotl, the universal creative principle of Aztec cosmology.

Perhaps the most important aspect of this figuration is that Pilgrim becomes aware of this complementarity after slaying the turtle and feasting on its eggs. He turns the scissors on the turtles in a way that can be considered sacrificial, given the previously mentioned economies of life and death. The sacrifice and consumption, on the one hand, satisfy his hunger, but at the level of the sacred, they allow him to understand the necessity of death in life. Moreover, the extraction of surplus meaning from this sacrifice and the consumption of the eggs correlate to the challenge of potlatch or gift; the violence of the gift also produces an excess of meaning. In this respect, Deleuze and Guattari's discussion of the "surplus value of code" in relation to both feasting and Marcel Mauss's notion of the "spirit of the thing given" is crucial: what is gained or lost in a signifying chain produces "phenomena of excess and deficiency, phenomena of lack and accumulation, which will be compensated for by nonexchangeable elements of the acquired-prestige or distributed-consumption type."[20] In potlatch, the imbalance and the impossibility of equal reciprocation produce the surplus of code, the appropriation of power, as Bataille would put it. Furthermore, the metaphoric image of the eggs and pearls integrates Pilgrim into the whole debt cycle of "The New World." It also attempts to put back into balance the segments and supplements that have been extracted from the signifying chain—the consumed eggs and the revived pearls. (In other words, not only does Pilgrim's arrival on the beach entail a reorganization of the general balance of life and death in the New World, but it also initiates a subtle and complicated commentary on the auratic nature of the baroque object.) The eggs represent life in their consumption; they take on the *sacred* meaning of life when they are killed. In this sense, the turtle eggs are a gift from the ultimate provider: Mother Earth.

Pilgrim's partially empty gesture to return the pearls can be interpreted as a metaphor for the baroque image of the golden age: even with those Europeans not obsessed with greed, their utopian image of the New World was imposed on the natives and partly led to their demise. The illusion that they had found paradise led the Europeans to miscomprehend and to ignore the reality of the world they had found. In this respect, the commercial values of the pearls that Pilgrim at first describes do not adequately represent the pearls' sacred and tributary functions in the economies of the New World. They do, however, imply the contamination of European market values and the thirst for wealth. (This does not negate their role as tribute.) As Pilgrim

20. Deleuze and Guattari, *Anti-Oedipus,* 150.

engages the turtles and begins to see the life and death associations between the pearls and the eggs, he approaches a more native understanding of his surroundings. Pilgrim's observations of the turtles, the pearls, and the eggs also represent yet another intricate dimension of the integration of baroque and Nahuatl figural modes.

Fuentes deconstructs the utopian vision of the golden age by demonstrating that there is always an underlying cruelty in human existence, a cruelty, nonetheless, that binds tribes and peoples together through ties of obligation. This we will explore further in the next chapter. *Terra Nostra*'s neobaroque economy of exuberance by design forces its readers to reintegrate the Americas' multiple legacies in the face of a utopian modernity that negates them. The integration of European and Nahua representational and textual strategies reaffirms the syncretism of Spain's and Mexico's different cultural heritages. In this vein, the stylistic techniques from writing and painting serve as the mediating hinge between forces that at first seem binary; the violence of writing determines the necessary interrelation of such complementary pairs in Ometéotl, life and death being the most apparent. This integration coincides with a specific affiliation among writing, the sacred, and the economy of debt in "The New World."

4

Markings in the Flesh

The Sacred Bond of Writing

IN THE PREVIOUS CHAPTERS we have seen how the gift serves
as one of the organizing principles that shape the novel, at the same time
that it encourages the reader to reconsider the fundamental relationship between gift giving and art in general. The gift also implies a relationship to
writing as a material and social reality, and in this respect the novel follows a
decidedly poststructuralist line of inquiry. In *Terra Nostra* we find deconstructive operations that are reminiscent of Derrida's deconstruction of the
Saussurian primacy of speech over writing, and we also find in the novel's
style a breakdown of inside-outside and surface-depth dichotomies.

Writing, in this sense, extends throughout the fictional world of *Terra
Nostra* as a play of surfaces that also encompass architectural structures that
in turn serve as representational sites of power: El Escorial, Felipe's ostentatious offering to god and death, but also the Mesoamerican temples of "The
New World." Furthermore, writing and inscription combine with architecture in ways that extend, produce, and represent allegiances between peoples,
and also allegiances that can be considered sacred in the profane sense that
Bataille elaborated, namely, that the sacred implies a debt relationship among
peoples, institutions, and the divine.

In Pilgrim's description of the ancient Lord of Memory who sits within a temple, the old man's eyes contain the *image* of the temple as writing. *Contain* is somewhat of a misnomer because writing, emanating as an image from his eyes, will extend outward from within the temple to encompass, to permeate, the whole fictional world of "The New World." This produces a breakdown of the inside-outside dichotomy that marginalizes writing, at the same time that inscription, pictograph, and writing in general become the representational modes of the fictional world of "The New World." To understand how this happens, and how writing produces general economies in *Terra Nostra,* a reexamination of "The New World" through the lens of Gilles Deleuze and Félix Guattari's theory of territorial representation will be crucial, for in "The New World" every representation of violence and inscription signifies an allegiance of sorts, and the understanding of this obliges the reader in turn to recodify, or rewrite, the representational-sign system of the entire novel.

As I have already begun to demonstrate, through his encounters with people and things Pilgrim discovers certain keys for deciphering the social codes and the sacred patterns of the New World; these moments, however, are marked by tension and sometimes violence. I have shown that Pilgrim receives the most important key from the ancient, the enigmatic old chieftain who recounts the legend of the world's creation. This emblematic image is so important to the novel that we must return to it. In "The Ancient's Legend" Pilgrim describes the Lord of Memory in a series of parallelisms: "For a long time he looked at me with his sad eyes as black and decayed as the jungle, as etched and hard as the temple, as brilliant and precious as the gold" (*TN,* 396) (Me miró largo tiempo con sus ojos de tristeza, negros y podridos como la selva, duros y labrados como el templo, brillantes y atesorados como el oro) (*TN,* 402). The second simile points to another underlying economy in *Terra Nostra.* The temple, a figure reiterated at several points in the narration, is a locus of sacrifice, the site of the commemoration of an originary debt. The sacrifice of a victim appeases the god and delays general destruction. Thus, the temple is at once the monument and memory of the *past* debt, and in its sacrificial function it delays the destruction and postpones the debt's payment. Moreover, in the simile the adjective *etched* (labrados) both suggests the idea of carved stone and evokes the visible pattern found in the iris of the eye. *Labrados* can also be translated as *worked, plowed, wrought* (as in metals), and *embroidered,* in short, the necessary techniques for the elaboration of a complex or baroque work of art.

Above all, the stonework is a form of recording, and the pattern of the iris follows the general pattern of inscriptions and traces that commemorate the sacred debt to the Earth Goddess. When the ancient of memory tells of the creation of the world by Mother Earth, he explains that all the animals that emerged from the goddess's fiery womb bear the mark of their creation:

> From earth's belly of fire were also born the companions of men, the beasts that escaped from her pyre, and all of them bear on their skins the mark of their birth from the ashes: the spots of the snake, the dark blackish feathers of the eagle, the singed ocelot. And so, too, the wings of the butterfly and the shell of the turtle and the skin of the deer all show to this day their refulgent and shadowed origin. (*TN*, 391)

> (Del vientre de fuego de la tierra nacieron también los compañeros de los hombres, las bestias que escaparon del brasero, y que todas tienen marcado en la piel el sello de su parto de cenizas: manchas de la culebra, hoscas y negruzcas plumas del águila, chamuscado tigre. Y así las alas de la mariposa como el techo de la tortuga como la piel del venado muestran hasta este día los fulgores y las tinieblas del origen.) (*TN*, 397)

These animals and the mention of their markings are frequent throughout the novel. The patterns inscribed in the old man's eyes function as part of the signifying chain of images that remembers this creation. Nevertheless, in Pilgrim's encounters with the Lady of the Butterflies, she appears to be associated with Mother Earth, though under the tutelage of Smoking Mirror. The Lady of the Butterflies, moreover, becomes older with each encounter with Pilgrim. In their first encounter in "The Burning Temple" she appears as a young maiden, and transforms herself into a spider whose web or thread she pays out to Pilgrim to guide him on his journey to the inner regions of the New World. This manifestation of the goddess as a spider has its relation to the Greek myth of the Three Fates, the *moira*, who in turn are associated with the three manifestations of the Moon-Earth Goddess. In "The New World" by the second time Pilgrim encounters the Lady of Butterflies, in "Day of the Smoking Mirror" (*TN*, 425–37), she has aged considerably and has taken on the aspect of the Aztec goddess Tlazolteotl, the "Filth-Eater" who hears the confessions of warriors. Pilgrim's last encounter with the Lady of Butterflies finds her a crone, devoured by age and thus reminiscent of the old witch figure in *Aura* (*TN*, 462–64). In "The Old World" and "The Next World" Celestina also appears in different aspects of the Earth Goddess: as maiden, nymph, and crone. The snakes tattooed on her lips as writing correspond and remember not only the heretical traditions of Europe but also the Mesoamerican cosmology re-constructed in "The New World."[1]

In "The New World" the word *etched* (labrado) not only evokes the mem-ory of the debt to the Mother Earth Goddess but also represents the mode of her remembrance: writing. This conception of writing is not, however, lim-ited to phonetic scriptural writing (or writing that is limited to the represen-tation of speech), but rather includes modes of representation such as pictographic writing, hieroglyphs, stone carvings, and any marking of the flesh such as tattooing, scarring, cutting, and burning. The use of the term *labrado* and the images it evokes operate, nevertheless, at two different layers of inscription that in turn correspond to two types of affiliation. The marks on the beasts function as a *debt inscription* on the surface of living tissue, in this way remembering the specific debt all life has to Mother Earth. On the other hand, the use of *labrados* has another function in "The New World." The representation of the animals carved in stone corresponds to the tribu-tary economy of the New World. It becomes an *overcoding* in that an animal image carrying a mark or trace on its body is then represented on yet another surface, thus making the debt inscription an abstract reproduction as op-posed to a direct marking.

In this part of my inquiry, debt inscription and its overcoding are modeled after Deleuze and Guattari's theory of territorial and despotic representation in *Anti-Oedipus.* Deleuze and Guattari use the term *territorial representation* to refer to the inscription process in communitarian societies that commem-orates the debt to the land and affirms allegiance through this memory. Despotic representation corresponds to societies ruled by a despotic lord; in the case of "The New World" this would be Moctezuma, the Lord of the Great Voice, and in the rest of the novel Felipe plays that role as "El Señor." In despotic societies the despot uses the state to appropriate the coding of the debt inscription, thus reproducing the code on infinite surfaces. This over-coding becomes the primary mode of despotic representation. The "code" in Deleuze and Guattari is produced through an event, the marking and in-scription, which implies a relation outside of language.[2] In "The New World"

---

1. Graves, *Greek Myths,* 1:14; Springer, "Iconological Study," 87–88.
2. While J. F. Lyotard has been very critical of terms such as *code* for its association with fixed meanings, Deleuze and Guattari's use of the term suggests more the practice of marking or inscription as actions and events that produce *political relations* (that is, of affiliation and debt, or binding obligations). These are somewhat analogous to the relations of power that are exercised on the body, as defined by Michel Foucault in *Discipline and Punish: The Birth of the Prison,* particularly the first part that deals with the spectacle of public torture.

Pilgrim observes two types of economies oriented around two kinds of affili-
ations: a communal living among the peoples he first encounters that ac-
knowledges allegiance and debt to the earth, and the same people are subjected
under a despot who exacts tribute by redirecting the debt to the earth. All the
forms of tribute Pilgrim witnesses can be described in terms of overcoding
and despotic representation. The territorial modes of representation are,
however, very important for conceiving the relationship between writing and
debt in "The New World," and early on they frame the way Pilgrim begins to
relearn how to interpret the world. His perceptions and representational organization of this New World appear most starkly in "The Beyond" when he
first arrives on the beach and imply yet another dimension to the interpretation of the scene.

Pilgrim's First Encounter with the Earth Goddess

Once Pilgrim has made his observations on the blinding contrasts of the
light and dark regions of the beach, the sun's light is blocked by a flock of
birds, which allows him to notice the details of the scene. He shifts his attention to the things around him in the water, and is surrounded by shells that,
along with the birds, associate him with the destiny of Quetzalcóatl, Plumed
Serpent.[3] Then he sees and hears something in the water that terrifies him:

> I thought I had returned to life; I tried to shout; I tried to shout a single
> word: "Land!"
> But instead of the impossible voice of a dead man I heard a bellow of
> pain; I looked and saw a floating wineskin adrift in the current of a
> sleepy river that emptied here into the sea; I saw an enormous monster
> with the body of a hairless pig, boiled or singed by fire; the monster
> moaned and stained the limpid waters with red. . . . When I saw it, I
> tried desperately to grab hold of the floating shells around me; I said to
> myself, this is God-the-Terrible; I said, I'm looking at the very Devil,
> and I think I fainted from terror. (*TN*, 367)

Before he can cry out he hears a howl of pain, and the sight of charred flesh
and suffering shocks him so much that he faints. Pilgrim falls unconscious
because he is overwhelmed by the horror; he does not understand the natural
relationship between the debt and its representation, the marking of flesh.

3. See Laurette Séjourné, *Burning Water: Thought and Religion in Ancient Mexico*, 144.

Both he and the reader have not yet learned that the sign of burned flesh functions as the living memory of the Earth Goddess's sacrifice, and that this is part of the natural balance of life and death in the New World. Therefore, the memory of the pain will still be pregnant with the horror he felt at what he *saw*. And even if the wounds can be traced to those inflicted on the Earth Goddess, the pain carries the debt's burden more so than any concept of it. This gives the image its force and enigma: it traces back to the terror felt before the debt and sacrifices of the New World's progenitors, yet without any rational explanation.

There are three modes of "territorial representation" operating in this passage that are designed to shock the senses of the spectator, and to produce a metaphysical response that is still undefined in the narration. The modes of representation form a composite of voice, graphism, and eye pain, and function in the text in the following ways: (1) the voice independent of, but coordinated with inscription; the monster's howl of pain; (2) a graphism independent of the voice (debt inscription); the monster's burn marks; and (3) the eye that extracts enjoyment from pain; Pilgrim's reception of the scene, the terror he feels. Of this last mode Deleuze and Guattari remark that "eye pain" involves a collective or divine eye that discerns the "subtle relationship between the sign engraved in the body and the voice issuing from a face—between the mark and the mask." These three modes of representation form, according to Deleuze and Guattari, a "theater of cruelty" that produces allegiance to the earth or, in other terms, that commemorates the sacred debt. Furthermore, as a form of memory territorial representation serves "*to breed* man, to mark him in his flesh, to render him capable of alliance, to form him within the debtor-creditor relation." In this sense, on his journey through the New World Pilgrim is being bred for a particular alliance through the gift of memory that the old man has given him. It might also be said that he himself, both in his capacity as Pilgrim–Plumed Serpent and as narrator-protagonist, is imparting an education in both the Old and the New Worlds.[4]

Clearly, Deleuze and Guattari have borrowed this concept of the theater of cruelty from Antonin Artaud who sought to reinject into the theater a metaphysical and spiritual profundity that can be produced only through a concrete language "half way between gesture and thought." In Artaud's con-

4. Deleuze and Guattari, *Anti-Oedipus*, 189–90. See also Juan-Navarro, "Sobre dioses, héroes y novelistas," for a critical study of Fuentes's interpretation of Quetzalcóatl and the pedagogic role of the *tlamantinime*, the wise men who educate by putting a mirror to one's face. According to Juan-Navarro, Fuentes sees himself in this role.

ception of a theater of cruelty, gestures, objects, screams, cacophonous and rhythmic noises, smells, and lighting form a general hieroglyphic system independent of speech that seeks to introduce a metaphysics, that goes beyond the rational and the discursive. The element of cruelty is key: for Artaud, we have become so desensitized to the sacred that "it is through the skin that metaphysics must be made to re-enter our minds."[5]

In "The New World" Fuentes constructs a world in which cruelty and violence play an integral part in the memory of sacred debt. "The New World" is in a sense a theater of cruelty; aside from Pilgrim's initial experience on the beach with the agonizing monster he encounters in the water, the objects he carries (the scissors, the mirror, the pearls), his almost staged gesture of offering the pearls, the sound of drums, and the smell of charred flesh are all elements of this theater. Pilgrim, the narrator of "The New World," moves through this theater, learns its language, and becomes conscious of his role as its protagonist. Although as a protagonist Pilgrim has yet to inherit the collective memory of the New World, it should be remembered that as a narrator he highlights the contrasts in the environment he describes with the purpose of conveying the order of that land: the complementarity of Ometéotl. At the same time he interprets what he sees in European terms—hence the God-Devil association.

What is at stake in the passage between Land *(Tierra)* and "terror"—our land, our terror, "terra nostra"—is the collective memory and inheritance of the debt as it is transmitted in the writing and reading of the novel as a theater of cruelty. Although the terror of the debt, as the memory and hegemony of the past, is a common theme in Fuentes's works, rarely has the debt inscription operated so explicitly and as originally as in "The New World."

The Economic Life of the Natives: Sharing and the Debt to Mother Earth

During Pilgrim's initial encounter with the indigenes on the beach, the fact that he receives the "golden grains" in exchange for his scissors is no small matter at that point in Pilgrim's narration. The appearance of money in the form of the golden seeds indicates not so much the movements of commerce or any active mercantilism, but rather the extension and machinations

5. Artaud, *The Theater and Its Double*, 89, 99.

of a tributary state. It later becomes clear that the golden grains and the pearls are what the coastal people trade for food and protection from another more powerful society. They also must send members of their families as tribute to the despot who rules in the name of the Earth Goddess.

Nevertheless, the internal communal allegiances are still predominant. When Pilgrim gives his scissors to the coastal natives, he is not selling them. The importance of the reciprocation he receives lies more in the alliance he forms with the natives than in the equity of the exchange. At first feeling himself a captive when taken back to the village after the encounter on the beach, Pilgrim comes to realize the necessity of the exchange that took place: "I again became aware of my situation when the black-plumed chieftain showed everyone the scissors and urged me to show my cloth filled with the golden grains. They all nodded enthusiastically and the nearest women smiled at me and the old men touched my shoulder with their trembling hands" (*TN,* 381). Pilgrim decides to stay among the coastal people and makes various observations on the social and economic life of the village. He notices that, similar to the utopian commune described in Pedro's dream (*TN,* 117–18), the coastal people seem to share everything, including the labor of gathering food: "I rapidly learned that here everything belonged to everyone: the men hunted deer and captured turtles, the women gathered ant eggs, worms, and several kinds of lizards, and the old men were still dexterous in capturing snakes—whose flesh isn't bad to eat; then these things were routinely divided among the whole community" (*TN,* 381). In spite of the quasi-anthropological gaze reminiscent of the earlier chroniclers, there is in this passage and throughout "The People of the Jungle" a subtle play between the economic description of what is consumed and the debt inscription I previously described. The animals that the natives hunt and gather are more or less the same as those the ancient of memory later describes as bearing the marks of the fires of creation. *Even the most utopian forms of economic intercourse and social organization are therefore coded in the theater of cruelty that produces sacred debt.*

As Pilgrim endeavors to integrate himself as an anonymous member of the group, and as he tries to answer the many questions he has about the events that have transpired, it becomes clear that the people, the jungle, and the entire world are marked by the fire: "This curiosity was not easily reconciled with my intent to assume the color of a stone or a tree, like a lizard. That, at least, was not difficult to do; as they filtered through branches and thick treetops, the rays of the austral sun covered bodies and houses and all the objects of the inhabited area with undulating patterns of light and shadow that blended spectrally into random jungle forms" (*TN*, 382). The contrast of his two desires, his curiosity about the economic life of the natives and his will to remain anonymous, parallels and reinforces the chiaroscuro distribution of light and dark: "Fool that I was, I came to believe that that phantasmal movement of light and shadow did in effect disguise me as it did the lizards, and that I could be two things at once, both curious and invisible" (*TN*, 383). The visual description of the contrasts encodes the entire scene with the debt to the full body of the Earth Goddess, here represented as the jungle terrain. The lizard pattern not only is an incidence of debt inscription but also refers to the "Day of the Lizard" during which tribute is paid to the goddess: "when all the things of the world would bleed unless the goddess of the earth—who on this day suffers bitter cold until she is sprinkled with human blood—was fed" (*TN*, 401). Nevertheless, since the ancient Lord of Memory has yet to speak of the world's creation and of human life's debt to the goddess (*TN*, 387–97), this contrast has no meaning to either the narratee—Felipe who listens to Pilgrim within his royal chambers at El Escorial—or the reader, unless the reader is familiar with Mesoamerican cosmologies. Perhaps an attentive reader might decipher the encoding during a second reading, or remember it as a foreshadowing. In any event, after the ancient of memory recounts the legend, the pattern will have a different function altogether.

The Temple in the Jungle: The Ceremonial Site of Tribute

The beginning of "Words in the Temple" marks the limit of a new region and destination for Pilgrim. At this point in the narration Pilgrim sees for the first time the great temple hidden in the jungle's foliage where he encounters the ancient and receives from him the memory of the creation and the debt. He also learns of his own role in that legend. Once the old man has died from the effect of Pilgrim's mirror, Pilgrim must face the despot's emissaries who have come from the interior to collect tribute from the ancient. The chapter titled "The Tributes" marks a crucial transition, for Pilgrim is presented with another figure, the Lady of the Butterflies, who sends him on a journey to his final confrontation with the despot, the Lord of the Great Voice. The Lady of the Butterflies is one manifestation of the Earth Goddess and bears the tattooed serpents on her lips, making her a counterpart to the Celestine lineage. As Alice Gericke Springer has pointed out, however, she is subordinated to Plumed Serpent's double, Smoking Mirror or the Lord of the Great Voice, and she collaborates in "the eternal struggle to seduce" Pilgrim.[6] In this respect, not only is the temple the site of tributary exchange, but it also marks the territorial limit where the allegiances are no longer paid to the Earth Goddess, but rather to the despot. This will have striking consequences for the modes in which economic relations and sacrifices are represented.

In "The New World," once Pilgrim reaches the temple, the way debt is inscribed changes with the predominance of tribute. The familiar pattern that in the preceding chapters was inscribed through the play of light and dark on the jungle landscape, or marked directly on living flesh, is now artificially reproduced on the tributary surfaces: the red ocher painted on the sacrificial victims (*TN*, 401), the serpents sculpted or etched in the temple (*TN*, 386), and the embossed deerskins covering the baskets of pearls and gold that are likewise painted with ocher (*TN*, 381, 399). The tribute that the ancient stores in the temple in expectation of ritual payment, and the treasures and piled bones Pilgrim finds in the palaces and temples of Tenochtitlán, is further evidence of the machinations of a despotic state. In such tributary societies, this form of the production and distribution of goods "is organized in the main through collection, storage, and redistribution, the pattern being focused on the chief, the temple, the despot, or the lord."[7]

With respect to the tributes, therefore, the marking of living flesh as debt inscription gives way to a more abstract representation: the overcoding of despotic representation. Whereas in the "primitive territorial" form of representation the marks on the skin, or on different surfaces, refer to *the debt to the full body of the earth*, in tributary societies the land is subdivided and the debt shifts to the despot. Tribute is then paid to the despot, who receives it in the name of the god, or in this case the goddess. It is in this sense that "the blocks of debt become an infinite relation in the form of the tribute. The entire surplus value of code is an object of appropriation." Furthermore, in primitive representation (territorialization) debt inscription occurs as an event involving pain, or as the trace of that event, and in this sense it has a figural function, but the overcoding (deterritorialization) loses the event to which the mark refers as it redirects the debt; the debt is inscribed on dead or inanimate surfaces.[8]

Lost is the more or less direct relation to the goddess's pain during the creation, a pain reproduced through sacrifice and ritual in the theater of cruelty:

6. Springer, "Iconological Study," 92, 105.
7. Polanyi, *Primitive, Archaic and Modern Economies*, 14–15.
8. Deleuze and Guattari, *Anti-Oedipus*, 194–95.

the mark, the voice of pain, and the eye pain. The overcoding in the form of animal representations now emphasizes the demand for a calculated repayment, the specific amounts necessary to satisfying the tribute. In this context sacrifice becomes less a practice of the community and more a machination of the despotic state. In addition, the tribute requires a cadre of scribes and managers who ensure the proper payment to the despot; this cadre is clearly represented by the emissaries who collect the tribute from the coastal people.

In "The Tributes" Pilgrim realizes that the coastal people trade the pearls and gold for a red grain they need for sustenance during the rainy season, and in exchange for the protection of the Lord of the Great Voice they must offer their village's members for sacrifice and servitude. When the young warrior representing the coastal people presents the tribute to the emissaries, the latter count the tribute and dictate its number to scribes who make a record of it: "Now the warriors descended the steps, carrying the gold-and pearl-filled baskets, and delivered them into the hands of the man with the plumed crest, and he examined the contents of the baskets and then dictated words to the men with the paper scrolls, who traced signs on them with small sharp sticks with different colored points" (*TN*, 400). The scribes and the men with fans, who serve as accountants, are part of the "bureaucratic writing machine" created in the conversion from the "primitive," territorial representation to the despotic form. This involves what Deleuze and Guattari describe as a synthesis of inscription: a bureaucracy of scribes, accountants, and architects, or monument builders.[9] As the despotic state appropriates the representation of the debt, it replaces the concrete signs of the earth, the markings of the flesh, with abstract signs that record and redirect debt to the despot. The scene of the payment of tribute demonstrates this to the letter: in "The Tributes" all the tributes offered bear the painted or embossed lizard pattern. Furthermore, whereas the emissaries and the scribes keep numerical accounts of the debts paid, the temple serves as the monument to the debt, as well as the limit or border of the two territories under the despot.

The Language and Ceremony of Tribute, Exchange, and Gift

The participants in the tribute make it very clear that the tribute is paid in exchange for the protection of a lord: the Lord of the Great Voice. Their discussion establishes a dialogic relation to Guzmán's complaints about the

9. Ibid., 195–97.

breakdown of feudal reciprocity in "Guzmán Speaks." For both Guzmán and the Spanish nobility, the sovereign's protection is critical. For the people of the jungle in "The New World," this protection also defines the tribute: "Then the strange bearers added the baskets of gold and pearls of the people of the jungle to their loads and the young warrior of the black feather belt asked whether all was well, and the man with the crest nodded and said yes, the Lord Who Speaks, or the Lord of the Great Voice—for thus I translated his words—would be content with the tributes of the men of the jungle and would continue to protect them" (*TN*, 400). The tribute of the gold and the pearls, which also function as money, is exchanged for grain and cotton, necessary items for the coastal natives. Pilgrim notes this exchange, and what is more he believes the exchange to be finished, consummated. But the tributary exchange also implies subordination; he observes how the young warrior representing the coastal people prostrates himself before the emissary and kisses his feet (*TN*, 400). Though Pilgrim's observations on the warrior's deference are noteworthy, the economic terms he uses are striking for their difference from those used by the natives directly involved in the tributary exchange. Pilgrim uses the terms *ritual (rito), barter (trueque), exchange (cambio)*, and *gift (don)* to describe the reciprocity, whereas the natives mainly speak in terms of one thing "in exchange for" *(a cambio de)* another, or of gifts, *(regalos)* (*TN*, 400–401). The ancient of memory, on the other hand, never refers in the narration to these exchanges as such, but rather gives gifts and with his questions challenges the receiver to return with a countergift. Thus, while those engaged in tributary exchange recognize the reciprocity and allegiance, they do not name them in the way that Pilgrim does. Pilgrim's observations represent a further removal and abstraction from the actions taking place, and from the debt inscription.

Nevertheless, his role as both narrator and protagonist will, to an extent, break these tributary exchanges and practices, the law of exchange *(trueque)* in general. But whereas the *trueque* of the gold and pearls for the grain and cotton at first appears to Pilgrim to be an equivalent exchange, he notices another type of payment that suggests that the discussion of what is exchanged is grossly euphemistic, and that the tribute has yet to be paid in full: "Then, sadly, [the warrior] stood silent while the man of the crest waited with folded arms for him to continue. . . . [T]he men of the river and the jungle offered gold and pearls in exchange for bread and cloth. What more, then, did the man of the crest expect in payment for grain and cotton? The warrior of the black plumes again spoke: 'In exchange for your protection, we deliver unto you our fathers and women and children gathered here'" (*TN*, 400–401). The tribute, the payment for allegiance and protection, involves human sacrifice; the coastal people give away their parents and their children to be sacrificed or to be servants. And it is this sacrifice that reveals the truly imbalanced nature, the false reciprocity, of the tributary exchange.

The Goddess and the Despot

While the coastal warrior describes the surrendering of his people as an exchange for protection, the emissary with the *panache* (crest) demonstrates the despot's control of the debt to the earth by justifying the tribute in terms of the Earth Goddess's thirst. According to Pilgrim, "I saw that the old men and women and children were painted with the red ocher that had been so laboriously collected. The lord of the crest counted them and dictated words to the scribe and said that this number was good, that it would calm the furies of the day of the Lizard, the day when all the things of the world would bleed unless the goddess of the earth . . . was fed" (*TN*, 401). The goddess's thirst is satisfied through payment to the despot, a payment that is conspicuously counted, calculated, and recorded. The tribute is made to the goddess only indirectly; the despot will supervise the sacrifices and the distribution of the gold and pearls in her name. Above all, the despot protects the coastal people from the goddess's anger and thirst, which implies his power over her. This becomes evident with the Lady of the Butterflies who is described as "the beautiful goddess of the swamps of creation" (*TN*, 401).

The pact that the ancient of memory maintained with the despot, however, is annulled once the emissaries realize that the old man, who had been "the guardian and executor of the pact" (*TN*, 400), is dead and that Pilgrim has taken his place. As the latter tries to return to the temple, only to find it burning, he encounters the Lady of the Butterflies. She is clearly the overseer of the Aztec emissaries who collect the tribute, for when the man in the *panache* rejects Pilgrim, he goes to her for direction (*TN*, 401). The maiden orders the tributes returned, which implies the dissolution of the alliance with the coastal people, and therefore an increase in tensions.

When the Lady of the Butterflies first arrives with the procession of emissaries, she is carried in a palanquin. The elaborate and superimposed animal markings in its decor suggest both her prominence and her subordination to the tributary relations: "And at the end of the procession came other similar men, naked, who bore upon their shoulders a palanquin of woven reeds covered on all four sides by worked and embossed deerskins painted with the yellow heads of plumed serpents and adorned with heavy bands and medallions of purest silver" (*TN*, 399). The Lady of the Butterflies is, in effect, confined within the skins bearing the appropriated signs of the Earth Goddess. The embossment on the deer hide parallels that of the serpents carved in stone and the "worked" skins in the temple used to cover the tribute of the pearls. From this point on, the incidence of overcoding, particularly of the animals carved in stone and embossed in hide, becomes more frequent as Pilgrim penetrates the mountain region, the domain of the Lord of the Great Voice.

In the case of the Lady of the Butterflies, the layering of debt inscription and overcoding is pronounced: while overcoding generally includes the original debt inscription underneath its infinitely reproducible surfaces, the lady herself is adorned with living elements that signify her own territorial divinity:[10] "She wore a crown of butterflies on her head, not a reproduction, not metal or stone or any glass were they, not a garland even of dead butterflies: hers was a crown of living black and blue and yellow and green and white butterflies that wove a fluttering wreath above the head of the being I call woman" (*TN*, 406). Whereas previously she was confined to the palanquin, when she uses magic to attract Pilgrim she appears in the open, in the jungle. The emphasis on the living adornment as opposed to the artificial is crucial: the moment is ruled by desire as the two embrace, a desire expressed in terms of the figural and the magical. In this sense, the chiastic figure of her directed gaze, her *living* gaze, contrasts with all that previously represented the tribute: "And she was that, for if I seem to describe something painted or dreamed or some carved statue, her eyes were living and the life of their gaze was directed toward me. And behind the woman, the burning temple" (*TN*, 406). This emblematic image is characteristic of the neobaroque, and what has often been called "magical realism." The image attempts to recover the auratic through the very undermining of the artificiality of overcoding. And although it affirms the reality of the image, of what is seen, the crown of butterflies remains magical and therefore improbable. If the artificial markings represent the allegiance to the despot (the painted or carved serpents, the

---

10. The objects, the organs, the persons, and the groups associated with the territorial machine (the mode of representation that affirms allegiance to the earth, in short debt inscription) become nothing more than the working parts of the "Despotic State apparatus. . . . The old debt-inscription remains, but is bricked over by and in the inscription of the State" (Deleuze and Guattari, *Anti-Oedipus*, 196).

embossed deerskin), the live butterflies that Pilgrim describes represent the desire for a direct allegiance, for a bond, between Pilgrim and the Lady of the Butterflies. Through an erotic encounter there is an attempt at reterritorialization.

With the disruption of the tribute on the day of the lizards, and the subsequent tension it provokes, a different bond and exchange are established; because the tributary relation between the coastal natives and the interior empire is annulled, another allegiance takes its place. Pilgrim's desire for the Lady of the Butterflies becomes the motivation for his journey to the center of the empire.

The Collective Poetic Voice as Homage to Mother Earth

After Pilgrim has confronted his double and prepares to leave the New World, his use of the term *labrado* redefines the debt inscription I have analyzed: Pilgrim will reconfigure its employment in a way that links the voice and writing, the invisible and the visible, as complementary processes. He will also redirect the sacred debt away from the despot and back to the earth, a reterritorialization of sorts.

When Pilgrim encounters the ancient of memory for the last time in Tlatelolco, he walks through the crowds in the great market and hears "scribes and poets . . . speaking loudly or in calm tones of friendship, of the brevity of life, the delight of love, the pleasures of flowers" (*TN,* 476) (Escribanos, poetas que hablaban en alta voz o con sosegados tonos de la amistad, la breve vida, el gusto del amor, el placer de las flores"). It is not by chance that he refers to these poets as "clerks" (or, following a more archaic and therefore a contemporaneous definition, "scribes"), for the poetry they recite, flower and song, allays itself with the inscription economy that commemorates the debt and allegiance to the earth:

> "My flowers will never cease . . ."
> "My song will never cease . . ."
> "I raise it . . ."
> "We, too, raise new songs here . . ."
> "Also, new flowers are in our hands . . ."
> "With delight the assemblage of our friends . . ."
> "With them dissipate the sadness of our hearts . . ."
> "I gather your songs; I string them like emeralds . . ."

> "Adorn yourself with them . . ."
> "On this earth they are your only riches . . ."
> "Will my heart fade away, solitary as the perishing flowers?
> "Will my name one day be nothing?
> "At least, flowers; at least, songs . . ." (*TN*, 476)

The flower and song are characterized as gems of the earth, and the poet invites the listener to adorn himself with them. By doing so the listener in effect recognizes and reaffirms the bond to the Mother Earth, the true source of wealth. While the poems lament the passage and the wasting effects of time, they also celebrate the principle of renewal. In this sense the persistence of writing, of one's poetic voice after death, is both doubtful and celebratory; the delight of poetry and the transitoriness of life produce the bittersweetness of the collective voice. The bond established, then, is both to the earth and to the collective.

The random voices that Pilgrim hears are a collage of verses and fragments from several poems that originally treated common themes in Nahuatl poetry, in particular the transitoriness of life on earth and the necessity of enjoying the mortal life. All of the verses derive from different poems gathered together in the sixteenth-century manuscript *Cantares mexicanos* (Mexican Songs). This, according to Santiago Juan-Navarro, fits very well the homage that Fuentes pays to the figure of the writer in *Terra Nostra*. The eighth, ninth, and tenth verses are taken from a Spanish version of a Nahuatl poem in Angel María Garibay's *Historia de la literatura náhuatl* (History of Nahuatl Literature) that begins with "I gather your songs" (Tus cantos reúno). According to Garibay it was very common that Nahuatl poets celebrated each other's work in eulogies.[11] In *Terra Nostra* these verses have the function of reinforcing the solidarity of poetic writing, *la palabra*, as a collective product and possession. The term *palabra (word)* in Spanish does not simply translate as "the word," but has a broader range of meaning akin to "discourse," "speech," or the creative word, implying a dimension of artistry beyond that of simple communication. As in English it can also imply a promise or an of-

---

11. Garibay, *Historia,* 180–85. For Juan-Navarro, Fuentes idealizes the role of the poets, scholars, and *tlatmantinime* of Aztec society. He also argues that the image of Nahuatl poetry that Fuentes presents "does not appear to adjust to the historical reality," and actually transforms the poetry into a utopian defense of the permanent value of the work of art ("Sobre dioses, héroes y novelistas," 115–21). My own sense is that Juan-Navarro overstates this argument and forgets that Fuentes's novel does elevate the image of the writer poet, though this image is somewhat depersonalized as it becomes collective. The writer becomes a conjectural figure much like the characters I discuss in Chapter 5 of this book.

fering. Moreover, Fuentes's choice of other verses reinforces the tensions between writing and time, between renewal and death. Pilgrim has come to understand the complementary duality of renewal and death that is a shared experience and destiny among the populace. In the passage that follows the verses Pilgrim hears, the significance of the collective poetic voice as inscription and as *palabra*, "flower and song," is linked to the question of the gift:

> The old man watched me looking and listening. And when at last I again looked at him, I was possessed by conflicting sensations of happiness and sadness.
> He asked: "Do you understand?"
> "Yes."
> Then the ancient of memory seized my hand and leaned close to me, and his words were like carved air, written air: "You gave the word to all men, brother. And your enemy will always feel threatened because of fear of the word all men possess." (*TN*, 476)

> (El viejo me miró, mirando y oyendo. Y cuando al cabo volví a mirarle a él, poseído yo por un conflictivo sentimiento de alegría y tristeza, me preguntó:
> ¿Comprendes?
> —Sí.
> Entonces el anciano de la memoria tomó con fuerza mi puño y acercó mi rostro al suyo y sus palabras eran como aire labrado, aire escrito:
> Hablan; y todo el poder del Señor de la Gran Voz no puede impedirlo. Diste la palabra a todos, hermano. Y por temor a la palabra de todos, tu enemigo se sentirá siempre amenazado.) (*TN*, 484–85)

Pilgrim's gift of the collective word, "la palabra," is associated with the ancient's words, which Pilgrim describes metaphorically in the anaphora "carved air, written air" (aire labrado, aire escrito). This *difrasismo* is clearly oxymoronic, linking spoken poetry to debt inscription, speech to writing. The terms *labrado (carved)* and *escrito (written)* function like a *difrasismo* in that the two terms are similar but different. They complement each other in their syntagmatic combinations with the term *aire*, and thus serve as a metaphor for a kind of debt inscription that breaks with all servitude to the despot. In other words, the written air reterritorializes the debt to the goddess and to the collective in the writing itself: the poetic voice of the scribes *(escribanos)* reappropriates the mode of territorial representation, debt inscription. Yet the debt to the goddess is generalized in the lamentations of the passing of time; the memory of one's name and voice in succeeding generations prevails over the sense of indebtedness and the sacrifices to the goddess, as overseen by the despot. In this sense, the scribes and poets practice writing in a manner different from the scribes who recorded the tribute in front of the temple of the coastal natives.

The Gifts of Plumed Serpent: The Fruits of Labor and the Voice

Thus, clearly allied with writing, *la palabra* as a collective voice subverts the singular despotic voice of the Lord of the Great Voice. The collective poetic voice allies itself with the debt inscription that commemorates yet generalizes the Earth Goddess's self-sacrifice. This signifies a resistance to and a breakdown in the economy of tribute. The break with despotic representation, moreover, implies a specific relationship between economy and language. In an earlier passage the ancient describes the difference between Plumed Serpent and his opposite, Smoking Mirror: "And always you were accompanied by an enemy brother, a double, a shadow, a man who wanted for himself what you wanted for everyone: the fruit of labor, and the voice of men" (*TN,* 474–75). The underlying principle behind the Giver of Life, behind Pilgrim as Plumed Serpent, is the redistribution of wealth and the freedom of speech in the face of the despot's desire to appropriate these for himself exclusively. *La palabra* as a collective voice is to be shared like the fruit of collective labor. In this sense, Pilgrim's utopian desire reappropriates writing as a possible form of resistance.

This utopian principle of language as a collective possession corresponds to Fuentes's preoccupation in *Cervantes; or, The Critique of Reading* with the difference between words and things: "Things do not belong to everyone, while words do; words are the first and natural instance of common property" (*CCL,* 110). In *Writing the Apocalypse,* Lois Parkingson Zamora arrives at a similar conclusion as she examines the final chapter of the novel, when Polo Febo "bids farewell to utopia." He then enters a library where he reads in a number of manuscripts the silenced voices of men from another time who have survived Polo's time. Of this Zamora maintains: "For Fuentes, it is in these texts, if anywhere, that utopia may be located: Words are their communal property, and the literary tradition their antidote to time's annihilation."[12]

12. Zamora, *Writing the Apocalypse,* 172.

The similarity between "the Lord of the Great Voice" and Felipe, as he is described in "The Old World," is established when the ancient of memory declares: "Enclosed in his palace. Imagining there is no voice but his own. Lord of the Great Voice! Hear the voices of all those in this plaza. Know that you are more defeated that all your victims" (*TN*, 476). As Pilgrim narrates this passage, he challenges Felipe's conception of the world, and after having delivered the free poetic voice to the people of the New World, a similar process takes place in the Old. His narration usurps both worlds: as the protagonist, he destabilizes the New World and, in effect, rewrites the legend in which he participates; the story he narrates to Felipe reshapes the Old World.

In "The New World," when the Lord of the Great Voice gives to Pilgrim the wealth and power of Tenochtitlán, Pilgrim's attitude is opposite of those of Felipe and the Lord of the Great Voice. Curiously, it can be said that Pilgrim does not allow himself to be enslaved by the temptations of wealth and power. When offered the riches of the despot's empire, his only desire is to return them to the subjected peoples, more specifically to the natives he lived with on the coast, and to the victims of sacrifices with whom he empathized. His hands full of jewels, he rejects the wealth he was given, a more authentic gesture that echoes a previous scene:

> Return to your true owners! Restore these treasures to those who wrested them from the jungle, the mines, the beaches, to those who worked and set and polished the stones! Restore the lives of all who died for these treasures! Revive in each pearl a girl given as a whore to a warrior, in every grain of gold revive a man sacrificed because the death of the world was feared, revive the entire world, I will water it with gold, sow it with silver, and bathe it in pearls, let everything be returned to the people, deliver everything I here possess to its true owner—my people of the jungle, my forgotten children, my violated women, my sacrificed men. (*TN*, 460)

Though echoing the ostentation of the nobles in "The Old World," Pilgrim's gesture does not entail the same principle of ostentatious consumption to appropriate power; rather, it is an expropriation that implies the principle of generosity. The gesture also produces, nevertheless, a surplus value—Pilgrim appears morally superior to the Lord of the Great Voice and in this way appropriates a power. The play of difference and similarity between Pilgrim and Felipe is further reinforced by the fact that Pilgrim shouts this from on top of the temple of thirty-three steps that warehouses the treasure. The temple steps repeat a similar set of thirty-three steps in El Escorial where Felipe had ascended supposedly to learn of what might lie beyond his death. Whereas Felipe hoards the wealth of the land in celebration and tribute to death, much like the Lord of the Great Voice, Pilgrim throws the jewels, gold, and pearls down the four sides of the pyramid, a gesture that recalls both his initial encounter with the turtles on the beach and the later sacrifices of men and women whose decapitated and mutilated bodies are hurled down the temple steps once their hearts have been wrenched (*TN*, 460).

But as his initial gesture was somewhat futile, nor can this one return to him what death has already claimed. Pilgrim is once again faced with an irremediable loss that plagues him throughout his journey in the inner regions: "It was to the water, to the stone, and to the bones I threw all treasures that my hands could hold, and not, I told myself, to the forever lost inhabitants of the nomadic villages of the river, the jungle, and the mountain" (*TN*, 460). Moreover, before Pilgrim's exclamation that the treasure should be returned to the subjected peoples of the empire, he contemplates the wealth before him and the solitude that it brings. At this moment he also reiterates the two "sovereign desires" that have ultimately led him to make the choices that allow him to survive in the New World: his desire to return with Pedro to the "happy beach of the new world and to return with the Lady of the Butterflies to the happy night of my passion" (*TN*, 459). The impossibility of returning to the Lady of the Butterflies, or of resuscitating the dead, leads Pilgrim to his passionate rejection of the wealth he inherits, and ultimately to the futility of this expropriation. Nevertheless, it is this repudiation of wealth and power that ultimate allows him to persevere and to generate new life, the twenty Spanish-speaking youths he rescues from the Lords of Death (*TN*, 446–49).

Pilgrim's "sovereign desires" are representative of the alliances he maintains with Pedro, the people of the jungle, the Lady of the Butterflies, and the twenty youths he rescues from the Kingdom of Death. In each case, with the possible exception of the twenty youths, the people are violently sacrificed or give some part of themselves to Pilgrim so that he may continue his destiny as Plumed Serpent. His desire in this sense is coded by the debt owed to the people he has loved. I have shown that the debt and thus the alliance, as representations of social relationships, directly result from inscription—not the exchanging of goods or identities, but the marking of bodies. In each scene where an exchange has taken place, the defining relations of these "exchanges" were not the exchanges themselves, but the inscription and writing events that reveal the imbalances or incompleteness of the exchanges. Be it the violence or a cut on the hand in "The Exchange," the striped lizard patterns of the jungle light in "The People of the Jungle," or the tributes paid but carefully recorded and marked in "The Tributes," all these scenes only apparently affirm the law of exchange *(trueque)*. They are each defined by writing events, from the marking of the flesh to the visual opacities of the figures and letters on the page.

The memory produced from these flows of desire pertains to the figural dimension in the writing of the narration. In this light, it should be recalled that the Lord of the Great Voice insisted that the principle of the land was the number two: the two brothers always in opposition, always at war with each other, a binary system of constant exchanges between life and death. The ancient of memory, on the other hand, claimed otherwise: three are the brothers, the ancient himself being the third term; as the third term he represents memory, which binds life and death to each other. In "The New World," memory thus affirms the complementarities of Ometéotl and prevents the absolute negation of either of the opposing terms. Through the complementary relationships between apparent opposites, then, there is always a hinge between them: memory as inscription. In the ancient Lord of Memory's eyes, "as black and decayed as the jungle, as etched and hard as the temple, as brilliant and precious as the gold," the middle term recalls the original debt but also the possibility of reunion with the earth. (In this sense the temple is also a representation of the mountain.)

In summary, "The New World" deconstructs the utopian vision of the New World as a peaceful paradise, precisely through the elaboration of the violent coexistence between life and death. Not only is the land ruled by a tyrant who exacts tribute and demands sacrifices, but the original relationship to the land itself is governed by a "theater of cruelty" that marks the destiny of its inhabitants with a fundamental debt to the Earth Goddess. Yet, as Pilgrim discovers, there still exists the hope of reunion, of a primordial reconciliation. This is to be found in the collective space of poetic endeavor, in which the voice as writing resists the bonds of despotism. It is also found through passion and erotic experience, as Pilgrim's sovereign desires attest.

5

Conjectural Legacies

History, Memory, and the
Reinventions of Identity

IN TERRA NOSTRA the burden of the past is a constant dilemma throughout the work, and is also complemented by a principle of reinvention, the promise of a future difference. Indeed, the entire project of *Terra Nostra* is predicated on the renovation of an inherited heterogeneous legacy, and responds to this legacy in several ways. Of particular importance is how the concept of *herencia* (inheritance, heritage, legacy) operates throughout the novel. (I prefer not to translate this word into English because to do so might limit its meaning.) More than a concept, the word *herencia* functions in the novel much like a "metaphysical name" in the sense that Derrida reads the Heideggerian "unique word": the term *herencia* is understood as a pliable, interchangeable reference to the past, with a spectral impact on the present as trace; it functions as "the Being" of the past, present, and future "speaking through language" (see "Différance" by Derrida). It also carries the sense of debt and obligation, of gift-countergift or potlatch, the play between memory and forgetting, and above all the possibility of renovation and reinvention through the conjectural genealogy of fiction after Borges. As Fuentes puts it in *Geografía de la novela* (Geography of the Novel):

In the story "Pierre Menard, author of the Quixote," Borges suggests that the new reading of any text is also the new writing of that same text, which now exists on the shelf next to all that happened between its first and last readers. Far from the petrified stories, and with fists full of archival dust, Borges's story offers it readers the opportunity to re-invent, to re-live the past, in order to continue inventing the present. Thus literature is directed no only to a mysterious future, but also toward an equally enigmatic past. The future depends on that.[1]

La herencia as the subject of inquiry in *Terra Nostra* takes on a certain nonfix-ity and resists nostalgia as it offers up the possibility of rethinking the past. This is what is meant by "conjectural legacy": the past itself is open to rein-terpretation and reinvention, which in turn destabilizes any essentialist or singular notions of identity for both the present and the past of Spain and Latin America. *Terra Nostra* posits, but also questions, the many possibilities that were available in the past, and in doing so it reconfigures the identities of the novel's characters through their recombination and interexchange. This is often played out through the familial structures present in the novel, and in the interaction between traditional literary characters (Don Juan, Don Quixote, and Guzmán de Alfarache, for example) and the historically based characters (Felipe, Isabel, Inés, and the Mad Lady [Juana La Loca]).

Related to these exchanges of identity, and crucial to any understanding of the functions of *herencia* as renovation in *Terra Nostra,* is the idea of an inherited guilt. Such guilt is represented through the persistence of a funda-mental error or transgression that corrupts a family lineage. The belief in a hereditary guilt and corruption originates, in part, in the ancient pre-Hellenic world. I refer here to E. R. Dodds's conception of guilt culture, in which the crimes of one's ancestors were believed by the ancient Greeks to follow their descendants: "The family was a moral unit, the son's life was a prolongation of his father's, and he inherited his father's moral debts exactly as he inherited his commercial ones. Sooner or later, the debt *exacted its own payment.*" This accursed inheritance and the law of *moira* depended in large

---

1. Fuentes ends this chapter of *Geografía* with a tribute that expresses his gratitude to Borges (54–56). Clearly, in Fuentes's treatment of Borges there is a definite relationship be-tween, on the one hand, the consciousness of reading as rewriting, as infinite renovation in the present and future, and, on the other, the sense of obligation and debt to the past, the solidar-ity of gratitude and acknowledgment.

part on the belief that souls were partially reincarnated, a belief heretical to later Christian tenets as presented in *Terra Nostra*'s cultural backdrop. Moreover, the inheritance of a debt and the exacting of its payment in comparison with the crime of a descendant and its punishment further tie the concept of *moira,* of destiny, to that of economy. In this sense the destiny of an individual marks the reappropriation of a lot, of a destiny, of knowledge of the self and of lands and properties. This suggests the "Odyssean structure" of narrative: *The Odyssey* is also concerned with ensuring the remembrance of one's property and destiny: the bestowing of an inheritance to an heir. Telemakos's search for his father is in large part predicated on the fact that Penelope's suitors are squandering Ulysses' wealth and abusing the hospitality of his house. Alongside the laws of distribution and partition, economy also includes exchange and circulation. These are closely related to the figure of the circle, a figure with profound implications for any economic narrative. As Derrida points out, the "motif of circulation can lead one to think that the law of economy is the—circular—return to the point of departure, to the origin, also to the home."[2] This becomes a problem when what is inherited is debt or the curse of an ancestral crime.

Absolutism and Its Corruption

This idea of corruption, furthermore, takes on a peculiar nuance when we consider it in relation to the concept of inherited guilt. For the ancient Greeks, following Dodds's study, the ignorance and the forgetting of the inherited guilt intensify the terror that such an inheritance produced, for the crimes handed down were unpredictable and often forgotten:

> There is no trace in Homer of the belief that pollution was either infectious or hereditary. In the archaic view it was both, and therein lay its terror: for how could any man be sure that he had not contracted the evil thing from a chance contact, or else inherited it from the forgotten offence of some remote ancestor? Such anxieties were the more distressing for their very vagueness—the impossibility of attaching them to a cause which could be recognised and dealt with.

With respect to *Terra Nostra,* nonetheless, it should be remembered that Felipe sees himself as belonging to a Christian universe, however threatened

2. Dodds, *The Greeks and the Irrational,* 34 (emphasis in original); Derrida, *Given Time,* 6–7.

by heresies. The Christian sense of guilt distinguishes itself from the more archaic form of inheritance that operates in the novel. Whereas the Christian's guilt expresses itself in "the haunting fear of falling into mortal sin," and is thus "a condition of the will, a disease of man's inner consciousness," the more archaic pollution is the automatic consequence of an action, and belongs to the world of external events.[3] For Felipe as a Christian, then, the terror is intensified: while he expects the crime and sin to originate from within, a torment that Felipe consistently tries to remedy through his ostentatious displays and false largesse, he nevertheless finds himself confronted with unexplained external causes, disruptions of his order that increasingly mock his inner sovereignty. He cannot control what he cannot see within himself, yet these uncontrollable external signs of pollution all point inward.

In this respect, Felipe's sense of terror is symptomatic of his desire to contain all knowledge of the world within what he can see, can read, and can warehouse in El Escorial. A fortress against the outside world that he can no longer control, the palace is repeatedly penetrated by the signs of his ancestors' crimes, as well as the hauntings of his own offenses. But the palace, like his own body, is the site of a profound irony: regardless of his efforts to be pure and chaste, including the excessive number of sermons and prayers he demands of the palace clergy (*TN*, 209, 651), his body and his palace diminish and decay: "He lay swooning within his solitude, illness, and shadow of two twin bodies: his palace and his own" (*TN*, 742). The decay of Felipe's body can be further understood in relation to Fuentes's interpretation of José Lezama Lima's Catholic conception of the body:

> Behind every reality there are other, many realities and here, in this one, there are death and the dead. The manner, but also the reality of this metaphoric reunion is what Lezama Lima calls *supernaturalness.* . . . Supernaturalness leads to a *superabundance* whose name is God. But its paradox is that the road from the first to the second passes through sin and death. The body is the site of the fall and of the land of death. And yet it is the object of ceremony and homage. Why? Because it will be resuscitated. If it is not as such, God does not exist.[4]

Felipe's body manifests the primordial crime in its decay, but is still the site of regeneration and thus of the general economy of gains and losses. The rot and the sin pay homage to the exuberance of God, of nature, of exuberance

3. Dodds, *The Greeks and the Irrational*, 36.
4. Fuentes, *Valiente mundo nuevo*, 240–41.

itself. In Felipe's case, with the decay and his ostentatious celebrations of death, there is the hidden promise of a redemptive future—resuscitation of his body that takes place, but always in a different form, hence his reincarnation as a young man and then a wolf.

The sense of Felipe's corruption, moreover, is not limited to these final scenes. According to an early conjecture by the palace nuns, Felipe's refusal to leave an heir suggests a fundamentally corrupt family legacy: "Is that why our Señor doesn't have children, Madre Milagros, because he inherited the malady and can't or because he can but fears he will transmit the infection?" (*TN,* 181). (The French malady that Felipe supposedly inherits is symptomatic of a larger illness.) More important are the scenes in which Celestina discusses the three heirs, whose presence, she suggests, points to an originary crime:

> "The founders, Ludovico?, Felipe?," said Celestina. . . . "This I bequeath to you: a blind, pertinacious, and painful return to the imagination of the future in the past as the only future possible to my race and my land . . ." Beneath all the suns, said Ludovico, in all times, two brothers have been the founders, two brothers have fought each other, one brother has killed the other, and then everything has been founded once again upon the memory of a crime and the nostalgia for death. (*TN,* 593–94)

Like a Borgesian metaphor, the crime is repeated throughout time in its diverse intonation. This describes the story of an abomination and its memory as characteristic of a universal culture. In this context, the struggle between Ludovico and Felipe is placed within a more universal history of the struggle between brothers, Cain and Abel, Osiris and Set, Plumed Serpent and Smoking Mirror, and their argument over the love of the forbidden women: Eve, Isis, and the Lady of the Butterflies (*TN,* 594). Hence, the crime is related to this fundamental separation and implies a desire expressed as nostalgia for death, for a future or a past future of unity, a utopian space that cannot exist in the present. This common space "before birth" deals with a lost bond in which all were united, and produces the legacy of a desire for reunion. Often in *Terra Nostra* this utopian desire manifests itself in the present as the desire to merge sexually with others, to join bodies in the same space and time. Nonetheless, the originary crime that directly haunts Felipe's lineage is that of Tiberius, who placed a curse on his descendants, as is revealed in his dialogues with Theodorus, his chronicler (*TN,* 678, 693–95).

The Crimes of Tiberius

In *Terra Nostra* the anguish and terror that Felipe faces with respect to his desire to leave no descendants are provoked by the threats to his singularity, the signs of Tiberius's curse. Felipe, however, does not recognize the signs of the Caesar's curse for what they are: he does to some extent see himself reflected in the three heirs—as a group they are consistently referred to as "the three heirs"—but he does not learn of Tiberius's crime and curse until very late in the novel. The crosses marked on their flesh, the six toes, are not associated with Tiberius until Felipe reads the chronicler Theodorus's reports on the public accusations circulating against Tiberius, and Caesar's response to the news of Pontius Pilate and of the Nazarene's crucifixion.

Felipe's desire to be the last and the greatest of his line, at the same time that his power and the insular world he constructs around himself (El Escorial) disintegrate, derives from Tiberius's ancestral curse.[5] Tiberius's absolutist desire to be the last of his line is intimately linked to his wish that Rome be the culmination of history, and that all future nations dream of Rome's unity in the face of a progressive dispersion in which they will fight among each other: "And from this growing fragmentation let new wars be born resulting in multiplied and absurd frontiers dividing minuscule kingdoms ruled by less and less important Caesars, like your Pilate, struggling to be a third Rome, and so on, and so on, without end" (*TN*, 694). With respect to this desire for absolute individuality, Zunilda Gertel highlights the all-important role that the narrators and literary characters have in Fuentes's reconfiguration of history and in the dispersion of the subject: "The identity of the narrators is masked in a protean I-you-he (we) that hides and reveals the absence of all individuality. Narrators and characters appear, change and reappear transformed in the three parts of the novel. . . . Paradoxically, the more a character tries to prove his uniqueness, the singularity of his self, the more the novel's discourse shows the dispersion of the subject, of that self."[6]

The sign of the cross, for Tiberius the sign of the body's torture and death, is part of the inheritance he bestows on his descendants. The birth mark in the form of a cross functions as a sign of dispersion, and is found on three identical strangers who appear in Felipe's kingdom several centuries later but

---

5. For further analysis of these characters, including other secondary characters who bear the mark of the cross, such as Johannes Agrippa, see Luz Rodriguez Carranza, *Un teatro de la memoria: Análisis de "Terra Nostra" de Carlos Fuentes*, 41–49.

6. Gertel, "Semiótica," 65.

who appear earlier in the novel in "The Old World." As part of the curse and as a cruel joke, Tiberius will divide his empire among his three sons, who will in turn divide their lands, and so on. And in order that his descendants remember their ancestral origin, he will have them "promise to copulate with she-wolves so that the heirs would be born from these beasts, and that as a secret jest, each bears the incarnate cross of the Nazarite upon his back; they would be my heirs, but in a different time, in a time of defeat and dispersion" (*TN,* 695). Felipe is thus haunted by pale and farcical repetitions of himself, not exact repetitions to be sure, but his own image exaggerated and multiplied. The dispersion occurs at the level of Felipe's kingdom as well. The empire is inverted and doubled in the New World, and is partitioned in the Old World through the sale of the land and the indebtedness of Felipe's estate to El Comendador.

The curse that Tiberius describes matches the occurrences in "The Old World": Felipe's father, Felipe the Fair, fornicates with a wolf, and later in the chronological sequence three shipwrecked youths, the Idiot, Don Juan, and Pilgrim, appear in Spain all bearing the mark of the cross. The three youths, moreover, have extraordinary and phantasmal characteristics: one is a half-wit and is transformed by the Mad Lady into a farcical heir to the thrown, the other is a seducer with diabolic powers, and the last is Pilgrim, who retains no memory of his life before his recent adventure to the New World. As the offspring of Felipe the Fair's copulation with the wolf, these youths are Felipe II's half brothers, and therefore potential heirs. Furthermore, they all through different means pose a threat to the stability of Felipe's power: the Idiot is the instrument of the Mad Lady's thirst to reclaim power; Don Juan runs off with Inés, the one illicit love in Felipe's old age; and Pilgrim bears the news of another world, the conquest of which Felipe cannot carry out without further ceding his reign to the Guzmáns and *comendadors* (knight commanders).

Tiberius's crime was not simply that he chose to be the last emperor of Rome, but that he had killed the true heir to the empire. Moreover, Tiberius was obsessed with the public accusations circulating about the crime. Much in the way that Felipe satiated his need to know and understand the heretical beliefs of his time, Tiberius used Theodorus to discover what his enemies were saying about him. But more than a strategic need to know, Tiberius's curiosity reveals a guilty conscious that desires to legitimate his "aberrant" succession (*TN,* 678–79). The nature of the crime and its consequences represent for Theodorus an aberrance in the continuity of the Roman order of things, of the very foundations of the Roman nation.

This discontinuity, moreover, strikes at the heart of the Roman understanding of history as Theodorus describes it: while Tiberius's crime disrupts the very manner in which history is chronicled, the deviation as event should be written so as to support the founding act, the formation and supremacy of the Roman Empire: "For the ancient Greek chroniclers, who lived in an unstable world, subject to invasions, civil wars, and natural catastrophes, the reaction was clear: history can concern itself only with what is permanent; only that which does not change can be known; what changes is not intelligible" (*TN*, 688). For Roman chroniclers who have inherited the idea that only that which is permanent can be the subject of history, the accident, or deviation, must be written and remembered such that it also legitimates and maintains the continuity of the imperial order (*TN*, 688-89). In this sense, Tiberius's crime obliges the chronicler to suffer the conflict of his own historical conscience and awareness of the imperative in the face of the discontinuity.

Paradoxically, Theodorus must legitimate, on the one hand, the illegitimate succession of the Caesar and, on the other, reveal the public judgment against this illegitimacy to the very usurper, Tiberius. This is key because the founding of the Roman nation, and therefore the basis of all legitimation, is the collective itself. Roman law is an act that defines a whole series of events: "paternity, possession, marriage, inheritance, and contracts. None of these events would be legitimate without reference to the principle, the act, the general norm—superior to the individual's—that legitimize them. And what is the base of this legitimacy? The nation itself, the Roman nation, its origins, its foundation" (*TN*, 688–89). The Caesar, as a singular phenomenon, is pitted against the collective, the only true source of his legitimacy. Tiberius does not seek the legitimacy of his constituency regardless of the fact that in the Roman Empire his actions need popular approval. Thus, the sovereign subject, while depending on his subjects to vindicate his lordship, both affirms and denies the foundation—he curses his descendants as an act of loyalty designed to continue Rome's centrality as the universal empire. By doing so he destroys any possibility of a future empire that would surpass Rome. Yet his legitimacy is not affirmed by the Roman collective; Tiberius remains a usurper. In a sense Theodorus's discussion of Tiberius's legitimation crisis is reminiscent of Guzmán's complaints against Felipe's neglect of his duty to protect the Spanish nobility: both lords are determined to undermine any future greater than their own present.

This corruption that Theodorus witnesses leads him to consider taking action to modify his historical reality, but to do so would invite his own death. His only recourse is to create within himself a utopian space that can remain pure and untouched by the corruption and aberrance of his master. Nevertheless, while this internal space contradicts and undermines the external threat, it also entraps him in a dichotomy similar to the one Felipe faces—he seeks a place where he can remain singular and control the realm of his existence, if only an internal one:

> I know that my questions imply a temptation: that of acting, of intervening in the world of chance and placing my grain of sand upon the hazardous beach of events. If I succumb to it, I may lose my life without gaining glory; my kingdom is not that of necessity but that of whatever fragile liberty I can gain for myself in spite of necessity. To the temptation of action I oppose a conviction: since I neither want nor can influence the events of the world, my mission is to conserve the internal integrity and equilibrium of my mind; that will be the manner in which I recover the purity of the original act; I shall be my own citadel, and to it I shall retire to protect myself against a hostile and corrupt world. I shall be my own citadel and, within it, my own and only citizen. (*TN*, 689)

The metaphor of the citadel corresponds to a utopic internal space that serves as a bastion of freedom for Theodorus. Yet the singularity that this would suggest for him is illusory, as he immediately recognizes upon contemplating himself as narrator: "I confess here that the only temptation to which I shall truly succumb is that of presenting myself to myself—when I write about myself in the third person—in a more worthy, more sympathetic light. The truth is not so beautiful" (*TN*, 689). For both Theodorus and Felipe, the "corruption" of the world forces them to seek insular shelters that in the end serve as mirrors; they multiply the images of these two characters and reveal their internal impurity. Yet whereas Theodorus is conscious of the corruption's source, Felipe is not aware of it until very late.

The Servitude of Lordship and the Unattainable Object of Desire: The Land

For Felipe, who yearns for a way to cleanse himself of contagion and a second chance to re-create his history in light of his own crimes, confession to one who appears untouched and pure offers him the momentary illusion of renouncing his past and the legacy of his ancestors. When Felipe speaks to

Inés in "Crepusculum" he regrets the missed opportunities they might have had if they had met when both were young: "We would have fled from this place, renouncing everything, with you I would have abdicated time before crime and inheritance collected their toll, we would have fled together on the aged Pedro's ship, we would have found a new land, together" (*TN*, 257). That the crimes and the inheritance exact a payment in terms of tribute clearly suggests an economy not unlike the tributary economy in "The New World," where the allegiances and debt are directed to the despot instead of to the land. Felipe, moreover, imagines that he and Inés could have left for the New World, which represents a space in the past that might have erased his stain. Following the suggestion of his vassal, Guzmán, Felipe projects this space onto the body of Inés and wonders if he will not contaminate her instead: "Inés, Inés, will you be what Guzmán said, new earth for my exhausted seed, will my corrupt seed be cleansed in your womb, or will my corruption impose itself upon your purity?, will I infect your very entrails, ravage your skin?" (*TN*, 259). As an analogy of a New World that would receive the contagion and purify the polluted monarch, or conquistador, this image of Inés's body presupposes an appropriation: Europe's utopian possession of the Americas. The image of the exhausted seed, moreover, reminds one of the usury and white mythology of Western writing, of the exhausted signs of the Old World.

Furthermore, Felipe's desire for salvation and consummation is predicated on the idea that the differences he must confront in life will be subsumed in an absolute identity produced through death:

> Now there is no salvation: there is only time that, however long it lasts, Inés, is never the same for two living beings. . . . [O]nly in death are we identical; and if this were not true, if death were only another form of difference, then what?, would our guilt and our sorrows never end?" (*TN*, 257; translation modified)

> (Ahora no hay salvación: sólo hay un tiempo que, mientras se vive, Inés, nunca es igual para dos seres vivos, . . . y sólo la muerte es idéntica, sólo en la muerte somos idénticos . . . si la muerte resultase ser otra forma de la diferencia, ¿entonces qué, nunca terminarán nuestras culpas y nuestros dolores?)

Felipe clearly desires the consummating identity that death would give him, an idea that parodies the Hegelian absolute. In Hegel's celebrated chapter on lordship and sovereignty in *The Phenomenology of Spirit*, the master who seeks the absolute truth of his existence must risk death to do so, but must also stay alive in the process. The scenes in *Terra Nostra* when Felipe climbs the thirty-three steps in El Escorial with the mirror in his hand, horrified at the image of his face progressively aging with each step, seem a parody of the Hegelian *Aufhebung* (sublation: a process of both elevating and conserving) and the dialectic of lordship in which the lord risks his life to learn its meaning yet must not die. Felipe cannot bring himself to the top of the stairs until he is already certain of his death, and thus has nothing to lose, nothing to put at stake. Because Felipe is also unwilling to risk his life for others, or to become other, he is thus doubly farcical.

In this sense, as a literary parody *Terra Nostra* burlesques the process of the Hegelian *Aufhebung* through dramatic imitation in language and imagery. Fuentes seeks to distance his novel and himself from Hegel's philosophical discourse, as did many twentieth-century writers who sought lines of escape from the Hegelian dialectic. Yet this is not an easy task, which is why an author such as Fuentes would resort to parody to treat a subject he might indeed take seriously. Literary parody, as Mikhail Bakhtin has observed, serves to "distance the author still further from language, to complicate still further his relationship to the literary language of his time, especially in the novel's own territory. The novelistic discourse dominating a given epoch is itself turned into an object and itself becomes a means for refracting the new authorial intentions." Moreover, the parodic attitude in novels also destroys the "preceding novelistic worlds," which implies a critique more radical than simply the parody of verbal forms. Indeed, with Rabelais, the "parodic attitude toward almost all forms of ideological discourse—philosophical, moral, scholarly, rhetorical, poetic and in particular the pathos-charged forms of discourse (in Rabelais pathos almost always is equivalent to lie)—was intensified to the point where it became a parody of the very act of conceptualizing anything in language." In the Hispanic tradition, often seen as lacking the critical influence of the Reformation and Enlightenment, writers and poets have shown such "critical passion" through their literary production, and in particular through parody and burlesque. Miguel de Unamuno emphasized the figure of Don Quixote as the critical but irrational tenor of the Spanish character.[7]

---

7. Bakhtin, *The Dialogic Imagination,* 309; Octavio Paz, *Los hijos del limo: Del romanticismo a la vanguardia,* 121–30, 232–35n2; Unamuno, *Del sentimiento trágico de la vida en los hombres y en los pueblos,* 248–71. See also Unamuno's prologue to *Amor y pedagogía: Tratado de Cocotología* for his playful jabs at his own use of parody and burlesque to speculate on serious matters (9–14).

Felipe's attitude represents, in part, the principle of self-preservation in G. W. F. Hegel, a rationality for life that annuls the meaning to be gained from the risk of death. Self-consciousness, according to Hegel, is saved from itself as it learns "that *life* is as essential to it as pure self-consciousness." In his discussion of the laughter in Georges Bataille's reading of Hegel, Jacques Derrida explains the comedy of this dialectic: "Through this recourse to the *Aufhebung,* which conserves the stakes, remains in control of the play, limiting it and elaborating it by giving it form and meaning . . . this economy of life restricts itself to conservation, to circulation and self-reproduction as the reproduction of meaning; henceforth, everything covered by the name lordship collapses into comedy." The falling back into rationality is what reduces the lord's subjectivity to servitude, for it is the bondsman, as the other of the lord, who works and thus gives meaning to the lord's power. In this way the lord never escapes the servitude of rationality, of dialectics, and is forever dependent on the bondsman's subordination as the other of himself.[8]

In a world where Felipe is merely one life in a series that makes up an individual, his death will be a form of difference that condemns him to bear the weight of the past. He is master of neither time nor space; he knows that time escapes his control, but it is Inés who undermines his faith in his lordship over the land when she speaks to him: "She walked to the threshedhold that led to the chapel and there, sweet, distant, barefoot, she found words; words crowned her, transported her, possessed her; perhaps they were not hers, perhaps she was but the vehicle and they spoke through her tongue: 'Señor, your race has made Heaven and Hell one. I want only the earth. And the earth does not belong to you'" (*TN,* 259). After she pronounces the dictum that the land does not belong to him, Felipe would remember those words and carry them with him until his final ascent to the absolute truth he hopes to find at the moment of death: "El Señor would never, even before he knew they had been her last, forget Inés's words. He would repeat them to the end, until the moment when older and more ill than ever, astounded at his own survival but certain of his mortality, he again ascended the stairs of his chapel in search of the final light and truth" (*TN,* 259). That the words possess Inés, and that they do not belong to her, suggest that she is possessed by a collective poetic voice allied to the earth, as we discussed in the previous chapter with regard to the *difrasismo* "carved air, written air" at the end of

8. Hegel, *The Phenomenology of Spirit,* 114-15; Derrida, *Writing and Difference,* 255–56. For an in-depth discussion of Hegel's spectral presence in *Terra Nostra's* writing, see Djelal Kadir, *Questioning Fictions: Latin America's Family Romance,* 105–40. Kadir describes Fuentes's attitude toward Hegel as both ambivalent and ironic.

"The New World." The words and the land belong to no one and to everyone at the same time, but most important, as the ancient Lord of Memory said of our relation to the land, we belong to words.

In this light, Inés's possession by the words is indicative of a sovereign operation in part because it destroys the idea that the land can be possessed; the words that possess her deconstruct the idea of property as the basis of Felipe's legitimation. The words act on and through her: "words crowned her, transported her, possessed her." For this reason, her function as a conduit is what makes their expression a sovereign operation; the words she voices are moved by an energy "outside of reason," by her desire: "I want only the earth."

Inés's utterance is also combined with the visual figure of her body framed by the chapel. The phrase "la coronaron," taken metaphorically, parodies Felipe's lordship; she is crowned and therefore the designated sovereign, the bearer of power and truth. As a visual element, however, the words *crowned her* might suggest an iconic image of a saintly figure with a halo of words, or even a crown of spikes if we consider the visual form of the letters. Her bare feet may suggest pilgrimage and the arrival at a higher spiritual place, or they could imply a direct connectedness to the earth. In this way her saintly image is an epiphany and at the same time a baroque emblem that resists absolutism and affirms its ties to the earth. It is no wonder that Inés later becomes more directly associated with Sor Juana Inés de la Cruz.

The Art of Memory in *Terra Nostra*

The image of Inés crowned by her words is representative of a technique designed to associate the image with a memory. In the acknowledgments to *Terra Nostra,* Fuentes expresses his debt to Francis A. Yates as the source for his incorporation of the art of memory in his novel. Yates's treatise outlines the development of the art of memory from the classical era to the Renaissance. In this art, grotesque, shocking, disturbing, or unusually beautiful images were used to recall specific ideas or information that one needed to remember for oratorical discourses, or for intellectual and didactic purposes. Yates quotes the *Ad Herennium* as one of the earliest sources of this practice:

> We ought, then, to set up images of a kind that can adhere longest in memory. And we shall do so if we establish likenesses as striking as possible; . . . if we assign to them exceptional beauty or singular ugliness; . . . or

if we somehow disfigure them, as by introducing one stained with blood or soiled with mud or smeared with red paint, so that its form is more striking, or by assigning certain comic effects to our images, for that, too, will ensure our remembering them more readily.

Yates further comments that the author of the *Ad Herennium* "has clearly got hold of the idea of helping memory by arousing emotional affects through these striking and unusual images, beautiful or hideous, comic or obscene."[9]

Although the image of Inés framed by the chapel certainly has distinctive elements that make it memorable (the crown, her bare feet, as well as the visuality of the words that "crowned her"), her image is not as striking as others in the novel. Isabel and the Mad Lady's mutilations are much more effective as images in this respect.[10] Isabel's grotesquely violated body is juxtaposed with Felipe's body marked with the corrupt legacy of his family; both are visual reminders of the repression of desire within the frame of Felipe's absolutism and the curse of his legacy (*TN*, 161–68). The Mad Lady's mutilation must also be understood in the context of her frustrated desire for union with her late husband. The amputation of her limbs, moreover, becomes symbolic of her desire for compensation and power; the loss of her limbs corresponds to her own sense of martyrdom and her affirmation of the principle of sacrifice and loss as the only honor and glory (*TN*, 181–86). The visual impression of these disfigured bodies is naturally more memorable than Inés's epiphany. This is partly due to the intensity of the images and also to their reiteration; Isabel's mouse, the Mad Lady's amputated limbs, and Felipe's rotting body become essential traits of their representation as characters. These traits function as the traces of a repressive past, but also as signs for the present's dispersion and the frustrated possibilities of the future.

Furthermore, the memory and forgetting of these images do not depend solely on the number of repetitions, or on the intensity of the image; the novel's massive accumulation of cultural knowledge and narration produces what José Miguel Oviedo has called a "risk of saturation," and within such a narration much of the detail of the earlier sections is forgotten by the time the reader has progressed to "The Next World."[11] Yet through their reiterations

9. Cicero, *Ad Herennium: De ratione dicendi (Rhetorica Ad Herennium)*, 3.22, p. 221; Yates, *The Art of Memory*, 10.

10. For a detailed treatment of these mutilations and their overall significance in the novel, see Kristine Ibsen, "'El teatro de la memoria': Transtextuality and the Activation of the Reader in Fuentes' *Terra Nostra*," 111.

11. Oviedo, "Fuentes," 195–96.

and their recombinations, the images and events involving the principal characters are retrieved as forgotten memories, and reinvented. Zunilda Gertel develops this relationship of memory and forgetting with respect to history's function in the narrative:

> In the narrative process of *Terra Nostra*, history assumes a semiotic function as spatial-temporal separation. But one should not think of history in the abstract, but rather in the manner in which Fuentes as author and compiler reads history. The true function of the historical fact, according to Fuentes, resides in its ability to repeat itself, lose itself and return again. This alternation of memory and forgetting allows each cyclically reiterated historical sign, each diachronic sign, to be reinscribed in the synchronic space of a different context.[12]

The return to existence, as Gertel suggests, implies both the return to a forgotten memory as well as the possibility of renewal and change. The historical fact's ability to repeat itself, to lose itself—to be forgotten—and to return implies that an event, image, character, or person may return to being the same, while at the same time being other, but is never simply a return to the same. What counts is the difference that is produced in the new context, but also recovered in memory.[13]

This difference is a constant in the transformational semiosis of the novel's characters, according to Gertel: "Somebody is always an Other that had existed before and that will exist again."[14] Felipe, in this vein, dreams of himself as if he were three different men: "the three a single man although possessing three different faces in three distinct times; the three, always, captive in the stony valley with no exit but the sky" (*TN*, 138). At the end of the novel, in the chapter "The Thirty-three Steps," as Felipe lies dead in his coffin he is approached by a ghost who tells him to choose between three representations of the three different times he has lived. These he views reflected in the triptych hung in his palace:

> He looked toward the triptych on the altar: it had become an enormous mirror of three panels, and in them Felipe saw himself in triplicate: one,

---

12. Gertel, "Semiótica," 68.

13. This is very reminiscent of Borges's fiction and essays, in particular Borges's "Pascal's Sphere" in which he he states, "Perhaps universal history is the history of the diverse intonation of a few metaphors" (*Other Inquisitions, 1937–1952*, 9).

14. Gertel, "Semiótica," 67.

the youth of the day of the wedding and the crime in the castle; another, the man of middle years who had conquered the heretics of Flanders and ordered the construction of this necropolis; the third, the pale, ill old man who in life had rotted with this rotting-house. "Choose," said the voice of the phantom. (*TN*, 754)

Realizing that death has given him a second chance, Felipe chooses to be young again and is transformed into the image of his youth, dressed as he had been on his wedding day. He then follows the ghost to the stairway, but beforehand, upon passing his coffin, he removes his cap and exchanges it for the crown on the elder Felipe's rotted cadaver: "He did not know what he did then, or why he did it; he did not know whether he felt love, hatred, or indifference for those remains; he merely experienced a passion, a necessary passion, neither homage nor profanation: a transport that determined his action. He removed his cap. He removed the crown from the body. He placed the cap on the body. He placed the crown upon his head" (*TN*, 755). The exchange of the cap and the crown is significant in that it condemns Felipe to receive the legacy he so desires to avoid, namely, that of his resurrection as a wolf. After he ascends the stairs and passes into the future, modern-day Spain, he encounters an old tourist guide at the base of the giant cross at the Valley of the Fallen (Valle de los Caídos). Felipe appears to the guide as a young man, but the old man recognizes him for who he is. At this instant, significantly, the recognition is accompanied by the guide's throwing down his cap, an act that, compared to Felipe's choice to exchange his cap, seems to alter Felipe's destiny: in the following paragraph, night has fallen, and it becomes evident that Felipe has returned as a wolf to a time that may or may not be the same as that of the guide (*TN*, 758–60).

The Stairway to the Future

This final ascent of the stairs leads to another possible interpretation aside from the epiphany as a parody of the Hegelian *Aufhebung*. As Felipe ascends the stairs for the last time, the ghost of Mijail ben Sama speaks to him with a doubled voice that simultaneously pronounces opposing axioms and declarations with each step Felipe takes. Visually, these are organized in two columns on the page, beginning on the first step with opposite ideas of who the creator is:

> Androgenous creator of being   Father creator of an incomplete
> invented in his image and likeness   man: where is woman? (*TN,* 756)

The axioms are divided according to the general tension in the novel between the principle of heterogeneity and that of singularity and absolutism. As Felipe ascends the stairs he is told to look at the world this time, as opposed to previous times when he looked into the mirror at himself, and the world "on each step the world offered the temptation to choose anew" (*TN,* 756). He appears not to choose as he ascends, but in truth he has lived according to the axioms of the second column and by not choosing the first, he by default has already chosen the second when he took back his crown in place of the cap. At the top of the stairs he is transported to his new existence in the future.

The stairs and the axioms at each step are modeled after Ramon Lull's "ladder of being" as described by Yates in *The Art of Memory.* According to Yates, Lull's art of memory was based on moving internal images, depicted by signs within movable concentric circles that would allow for multiple combinations, and the ladder of being on which the intellect could ascend and descend. These two elements are represented in a sixteenth-century cut in which Intellectus holds such a figure of concentric circles, the inner circle being the moveable one, as he moves to ascend the ladder of being (fig. 2). He ascends the scale of creation, "the various steps of which are illustrated with, for example, a tree on the plant step, a lion on the brute step, a man on the step *Homo,* stars on the step *coelum,* an angel on the angel step, and on reaching the summit with *Deus,* the intellect enters the House of Wisdom." In this case the "bonitas" (goodness, one of the attributes of God) of each step is represented by its visual or material association: the plant, the lion, the angel, and so on. On the ladder the elemental structure of the world combines with the divine structure "to form the universal art which can be used on all subjects because the mind works through it with a logic which is patterned on the universe."[15]

In Fuentes's "ladder of being" each step represents a different choice to be made between two opposing worldviews. The apparent opposition, though, is not reflective of the universal pattern implied in the two columns. The third term, the subject who must choose, is the mediating factor, which implies not a world divided between two poles that cancel each other, but one in which there are always other possibilities. The remembering subject can al-

15. Yates, *The Art of Memory,* 173–85.

Figure 2. The Ladder of Ascent and Descent. From *Liber de ascensu et descensu intellectus*, edition of Valencia, 1512.

ways decide between complementary poles. At the top of the stairs, more-over, the wisdom one achieves at the moment of death is the knowledge that comes from the passage to a *different* life and time, but within the same space more or less.

Felipe's desire for singularity and lordship, the passion that leads him to exchange the cap for the crown, is indicative of his inability to accept the multifaceted nature of his soul, and the possibility of being different. Felipe's cap, part of his wedding dress, is symbolic of the desire to join with another and, when considered in relation to the guide's cap, to be a common man, which is what he might have been had he joined Pedro, Simón, Ludovico, and Celestina in his youth. This can be surmised from the two representations of himself that he sees and imagines:

> He saw in the mirror of the painting his own features at sixteen, genteel, almost feminine but marked by the stigmata of his house: prognathic jaw, thick, always parted lips, heavy eyelids. But above everything else he was aware of his young body, the body of the imaginary voyage on Pedro's boat in search of the new world, accompanied by Simón, Ludovico, and Celestina: his skin tanned, his hair bleached by ocean gold, his muscles strong, his flesh firm. (*TN*, 754–55)

The general aspect of an imaginary body that has worked and been at sea contrasts with Felipe's face, marked by the traits of his family line, and thus suggests an alternative. Nevertheless, when Felipe puts on the crown he unwittingly chooses the destiny burdened with Tiberius's curse: to be reborn a wolf, hunted in his own lands by his descendants (*TN*, 150–51, 154–55, 755, 759). Nevertheless, Felipe's awareness of his three selves, and the opportunity to choose among them at the moment of his death, is not exclusively a trait of his character. The characters that share this tripartite existence are the literary figures Fuentes has re-created in his novel.

The Conjectural Identities of Traditional Characters

The combinations that the literary characters experience, however, are of a different order than that of Felipe, who chooses between and is aware of three principal stages of his life—a temporally ordered existence. In the case of Don Juan, whose existence intersects at different times with Don Quixote, the combinations are not straightforward and do not necessarily involve a "synthesis" with other characters. In other words, the novel's characters are not *identified* with each other; each combination represents a conjectural difference in the spirit of Borges. The characters from the Spanish literary tradition, mainly Celestina, Don Juan, and Don Quixote, enter into combinations with other literary and mythological figures in a somewhat conjectural fashion; their existences represent numerous possibilities of combination. In "The Next World" this becomes evident in the interactions between Don Juan and Don Quixote, primarily in their relation to Celestina.

An important indication that the characters follow multiple, conjectural destinies is given by Celestina in the chapter "The Duel," when she witnesses Don Juan's death as the result of a duel. While speaking to the nun, supposedly Inés, who has been abducted by Don Juan, Celestina reveals that Don Juan's death might have had other possible outcomes: "Do you know something, child? The worst of it all is that my fancy is still unsatisfied. Don Juan should not have died this way . . . Perhaps in another life" (*TN*, 528). Celestina is vaguely aware that this is not how Don Juan is supposed to die. Don Juan's last words, furthermore, indicate a clear awareness that he had died once before: "Celestina . . . Celestina . . . Is it you, you are young again? Oh, Mother that I meet you again only as I am again dying . . . I who saw you die before" (*TN*, 527). From Don Juan's last words not only is this at least the second time that he has found her upon his death, but he had also witnessed her die as well.

That Don Juan falls and injures himself while trying to carry off Inés is also reminiscent of Calisto's death in *The Celestina*, though by no means an exact repetition: Calisto dies from his fall, an absurd death, whereas Don Juan in "The Duel" dies from the swords of Inés's brothers. Don Quixote also assumes traits from Calisto in *The Celestina*. In a passage in which Don Quixote scolds Sancho for trying to pass Celestina off as a grand lady, Don Quixote describes himself as having been fooled by Celestina when young: "Though you not believe it, I was once young, and it was at the hands of this same false, stubble-chinned, evil old woman I lost my virtue, for promising to gain me access to the bedchamber of my beloved, she instead in her own chamber drugged me with love philters and took me for herself, I having paid in advance" (*TN*, 531). Don Quixote's depiction of himself as a young man seeking the services of Celestina as the go-between clearly establishes a parallel between him and Calisto, as well as one between Dulcinea and Melibea.

The association, of course, is not exact. In *The Celestina*, the matchmaker *(alcahueta)* does not drug and seduce Calisto in the same manner, nor does she pass Melibea to another suitor. Perhaps what is most intriguing and artful in Fuentes's integration of Don Quixote and Calisto is the desublimation, and perhaps even the commodification, of Dulcinea. The Don Quixote of

The Adventures of Don Quixote de la Mancha would never have bought the services of Celestina, nor sought the carnal satisfaction of such an illicit encounter with Dulcinea. Don Quixote's ideal of courtly love is profaned by his contact with Celestina and Don Juan, a double impact of renaissance and baroque disillusionment. This results in his conscious affirmation of the possible correspondences between fiction and reality: "Do you think I am blind? Do you think I do not recognize the real reality of things? Windmills are giants. But Celestina is not Dulcinea" (*TN*, 531).

Don Quixote, in the remembrance of his youth, is both combined and integrated with Don Juan. In *The Joker of Seville* Don Juan murders Doña Ana de Ulloa's father, Don Gonzalo, to whom the king dedicates a statue to honor his memory. The statue comes to life to avenge himself against Don Juan, who had brazenly invited the statue to dinner. The animated statue appears at Don Juan's home and drags the latter down to hell. By comparison, in *Terra Nostra*, Don Quixote refers to the statue of Dulcinea's father as the source of the spells and enchantments that confound those around him: "See what my fate has been, sirs, that I see the truth of things which others hold to be a lie; the enchantment lay upon the others; and greater the enchantment of my enchantment, as I saw that only I, cursed by the statue of Dulcinea's father, saw giants where others, as if enchanted, saw only windmills" (*TN*, 578). The statue, as Dulcinea's father, automatically associates a series of feminine literary characters and reaffirms their interchangeability in the novel: associated with Doña Ana are Inés, Dulcinea, and Melibea. Likewise, Inés's father, El Comendador, becomes part of a series of possible associations with Don Gonzalo (knight commander de Calatrava) and Pleberio from *The Celestina*. The most direct association that Don Quixote has to Don Juan, however, is his own reference to the exchanges that take place between him and Don Juan: "I lived the youth of Don Juan. Perhaps Don Juan will dare to live my old age. You, my boy . . . I cannot remember . . . I believe I looked like you in my youth. You, lad, would you agree to continue living my life for me?" (*TN*, 578–79). The exchange of existences suggested here and in the passages cited above implies not the synthesis of these characters, but their interchangeability in a myriad of possible combinations. Don Quixote recognizes that he is both different from and the same as Don Juan, following the general scheme described by Gertel. This passage, moreover, echoes a similar passage from the chapter "A Piece of Land" in which Pedro questions Pilgrim's resolve and willingness to exchange destinies (*TN*, 376).

Celestina's Kiss and the Theater of Memory

In *Terra Nostra* the character Celestina is a curious reinvention of a Spanish literary archetype. Fernando de Rojas's matchmaker/madame/witch *(alcahueta)* is perhaps the most representative figure of the confluence of Spain's multiple cultural heritages: Christian, Jewish, and Muslim. Rojas's *Celestina*, moreover, illustrates the abhorrence that Jews and the new converts *(nuevos conversos)* felt toward the corruption among the Catholic clergy, particularly with respect to their employment of *alcahuetas* and prostitutes.[16] Fuentes could not have chosen a better figure from the Spanish literary tradition than Celestina in *Terra Nostra* to counter Felipe's desire for purity and absolute singularity. Both in Rojas's work and in *Terra Nostra*, Celestina poses a threat to the ideological order of the Inquisition due to her heretical views and practices.

Moreover, through her guidance of Pilgrim in Fuentes's novel, Celestina, as we have seen, is the instigator and disseminator of the news of the New World, and thus injects a sense of difference in Felipe's one-dimensional understanding of the world. She is the go-between for Felipe and Pilgrim, and by extension between the Old and New Worlds. While Fuentes emphasizes the Jewish element in Celestina, her association with the Muslim, Moorish heritage is not quite as explicit. This one would have to surmise from the general influence of Hispanic-Arabic erotic and lyrical traditions in Celestina's poetic function as a narrator and usurper. She uses language to motivate the passions and desires of other characters, to pass on a secret knowledge that can be revealed only through love:

> I want you to break the order of this place as you would shatter a perfect goblet of finest crystal; . . . my name is Celestina; my tattooed lips can repeat it all, my lips forever engraved with the burning kiss of my lover, my lips marked with the words of secret wisdom, that knowledge that separates us from princes, philosophers, and peasants alike, for it is not revealed by power of books or labor, but by love; not just any love, my companion, but a love in which one loses forever, without hope of redemption, one's soul, and gains, without hope of resurrection, eternal pleasure. (*TN*, 251)

---

16. Marcel Bataillon, *Le Celestine selon Fernando de Rojas*, 168; Francisco Márquez Villanueva, *Orígenes y sociología del tema celestinesco*, 148–49.

In *Terra Nostra,* Celestina is a seemingly immortal character whose soul transmigrates through several different lives: Celestina, friend of Felipe in his youth; the page who brings Pilgrim to Felipe; La Madre Celestina who forgets her past; the young woman Polo Febo encounters in 1999, Madame Zaharia, among others associated with Celestina. Through a kiss from her tattooed lips she transmits the memory of her past lives and in this way also takes over the lives of those through whom she wishes to carry on her legacy and the wisdom she has inherited.

This is clearly described in "Memory upon the Lips" when Celestina revisits the moment she passed on her memory to a young girl, who is later to become the androgynous page that finds Pilgrim on the beach once he has returned from the New World. The girl responds with an excessively anaphoric and mechanical "yes madam" *(señora sí):* "*señora sí,* I give you my life, continue it, *señora sí,* I give to you my voice, I give to you my lips, I give to you my wounds, my memory is upon your lips, men infected me with illness, the Devil with wisdom, daughter of no man, lover of all, I am poisoned" (*TN,* 539). The wisdom Celestina imparts is the heretical knowledge that no one exists as a singular being, and that the separation between men and women is a plague: "There will be no well being for man upon earth as long as a single black hole of sulphur and flesh and hair and blood exists, there will be no well-being for woman upon earth while the hairy black scorpion commands, the whip of flesh, the erectile serpent, remember me, child, *señora sí*" (*TN,* 540). Celestina represents, moreover, the conscious memory of the "contagion" of evil that results from the separation of the sexes, and the wisdom she inherited from the devil, namely, that in the ancient texts men had suppressed the name of Yahweh's wife, and that the first being created was both masculine and feminine, "made in the same image and likeness of the Divinity in whom both sexes were joined; in His place they invented a God of vengeance and anger, a bearded goat; they expelled woman from Paradise, to her they assigned guilt for the Fall" (*TN,* 524–25). Celestina's mission, and the mission that she passes on to those who receive her memory, is that of undermining the power of men, which is opposed to love: "power without mystery, cruel, divorced from love, separated from real time, which is woman's time, simultaneous time: the power of man is captured within a simple succession of events which in their linear progression lead every thing and every being to death" (*TN,* 525). The desire for reconciliation through love corresponds to this concept of simultaneity in which multiple lives and destinies can converge in a single space and is manifested in the final scene of the novel when Celestina and her young lover, Polo Febo, merge into a single hermaphroditic entity.

Celestina's kiss functions through memory to bring together in a single space the times that the migratory souls of Felipe and Pilgrim have lived, much in the same way that Valerio Camillo's Theater of Memory combines the possibilities of the past. Before Celestina and her lover merge, her kiss transports him to Camillo's theater: "You feel you have been transported to the Theater of Memory. . . . [Y]ou draw away from the kiss of the girl with tattooed lips; you are filled with memories, Celestina has transmitted to you the memory that was passed to her by the Devil disguised as God, by God disguised as the Devil" (*TN*, 774). At this moment the last youth, Celestina's lover in 1999, realizes that history has had its second chance and that Spain's past was revived in order to choose again but that little had changed; the same crimes and errors have been repeated. If the curse of Tiberius is the desire for singularity against a legacy of dispersion, Celestina's kiss bestows the memories of multiple legacies—Arab, Jewish, Christian, Aztec, Mayan— along with the wisdom that we are incomplete without our counterparts, the others who help compose the multiple identities that make us. Her kiss remembers the debt owed to those other forgotten legacies—man's debt to woman, Christianity's debt to Judaism, Judaism to Arab culture, and vice versa. Thus, *the kiss from the tattooed lips also functions as a form of debt inscription:* the memory of the past that Polo Febo receives through her kiss is designed to motivate him to join with her and to put the world back in its rightful order through love; in other words, to fulfill the promise made at the beginning and to resolve the debt owed to Celestina, to the goddess. Polo Febo subsequently renders himself to Celestina and to pleasure, and by this he merges his body and soul with hers.

The conscious remembrance of our legacies allows us to make decisions and to modify the future, but also to imagine what the past might have been like. Celestina's kiss and the Theater of Memory produce spaces where different times can converge; in this sense Celestina's lips are analogous to the space of writing—the inscription of or on a body—and Camillo's theater, the space of a reading in which many possible readings are combined. Both Celestina's kiss and Camillo's Theater of Memory are gifts of memory in the sense that they are presented to others as a challenge. The inventor of the Theater of Memory in "The Next World" wonders what he could receive in exchange for such an invention, as he explains its function to the character Ludovico:

"What will they give me, the kings of this world, in exchange for this invention that would permit them to recall what could have been and was not?"

"Nothing, Maestro Valerio. For the only thing that interests them is what really is, and what will be."

Valerio Camillo's eyes glistened as never before, the only light in the suddenly darkened theater: "And it is not important to them, either, to know what never will be?"

"Perhaps, since that is a different manner of knowing what will be.'"

"You do not understand me, monsignore. The images of my theater bring together all the possibilities of the past, but they also represent all the opportunities of the future, for knowing what was not, we shall know what demands to be: what has not been, you have seen, is a latent event awaiting its moment to be, its second chance, the opportunity to live another life. History repeats itself only because we are unaware of the alternate possibility for each historic event: what that event could have been but was not." (*TN,* 561; translation modified)

The question "What will they give me, . . . in exchange for this" (¿Qué me darán, a cambio . . . ?) places the Theater of Memory within the conflicting economies of gifts and exchanges in the novel, with the same tension between the giving of gifts and the expectation of a return in exchange. Moreover, Valerio Camillo's question can be read as a rhetorical question implying that no value can be placed on such a splendid and powerful gift. Yet Ludovico takes the question literally, and, not divining the meaning of such a gift, deems it to be useless to the kings. The visual description of Valerio's eyes upon hearing Ludovico's response juxtaposes the light of his eyes and the dark of the theater to highlight his confrontational attitude as he explains the value of the theater. This recalls the play of light and shadow in the confrontation between Pilgrim and the Lord of Memory; the chiaroscuro that accompanies potlatch intensifies the sense of difference and imbalance in the potlatch.

The Theater of Memory's function, according to its inventor, offers the possibility of a second chance: aside from affirming the essential burden of the past's legacies on the present, and this includes all that never happened and all that has been silenced, the theater also represents the possibility of renovation and renewal precisely through this understanding of what might have been and what was. In other words, the memory of what had been forgotten allows for past possibilities to be revived in the future. Nonetheless, it is Celestina's kiss that identifies the error committed and the debt to be paid.

The kiss, as memory inscribed in the body, and the theater are both triggers and representations of the play between memory and forgetting in the novel. They initiate series of events that converge and diverge, leaving open the possibility of infinite reconfigurations. This corresponds with what Gilles Deleuze wrote about baroque narratives, the bifurcation of stories that enclose one in the other: "A bifurcation, like the exit from the temple, is called a point in the neighborhood of series' divergence. Borges, one of Leibniz's disciples, invoked the Chinese philosopher Ts'ui Pên, the inventor of the 'garden with bifurcating paths,' a baroque labyrinth whose infinite series converge or diverge, forming a webbing of time embracing all possibilities."[17] Celestina's kiss and Valerio Camille's Theater of Memory produce such series and bifurcations, much as Borges and Cervantes created spaces and characters that produce repetitions and series opening into infinity. Borges's shaman, who in "The Circular Ruins" realizes that he is a simulacrum, an invention of another shaman or god, is not so far removed from Alonso Quijano, inventor of Don Quixote, who becomes aware that he too has been written about. And in each case reader and writer become confused with each other as the reader reinvents these stories, perhaps inserting himself into the series. Throughout *Terra Nostra* this play, moreover, operates according to a baroque economy of gains and losses, always implying that what did not exist "clamors" to exist, clamors for its place in the series, that in the void there persists a latent exuberance.

17. Deleuze, *Fold*, 61–62.

Conclusion

S ACRIFICE, POTLATCH, unsurpassable gifts, "El trueque"—ex-changes of looks, objects, existences—usury, the legacy of the debt—these economic metaphors predominate in *Terra Nostra* and expand the novel's inquiry into the tricky logics of the gift. An *accursed share* that binds us together, the gift of writing as "la palabra" fuels a frustrated utopian desire in Carlos Fuentes's work. The author himself reveals this desire in *Cervantes; or, The Critique of Reading* when he declares that "things do not belong to everyone, while words do; words are the first and natural instance of common property" (*CCL*, 110). This sharing, however, is not straightforward, particularly for the writer. The work of art, as Lewis Hyde asserts, belongs primarily, but not exclusively, to the sphere of the gift. And this points to the fundamental tension at the heart of *Terra Nostra:* the necessary violence of the gift and of writing within the context of utopian desire. When I speak of the violence of the gift, I take into account Jacques Derrida's radical conception, namely, that the condition of its possibility is its impossibility, that the moment it is recognized as a gift it ceases to be a gift. Or, as Hyde suggests when he discusses the mystery of the gift, one cannot really speak of the gift for the mystery can be shown, can be witnessed or revealed, but "it cannot be explained."[1] *Terra Nostra* also shows that to even speak of the gift implies a transgression, the forceful imposition of a meaning, a debt, a power relationship.

Terra Nostra self-consciously theorizes the gift, but this has attracted sparse

1. Hyde, *Gift,* 273, 280.

attention among its critics. I demonstrated that the novel presents characters who not only engage in gift giving, and the economic relationships that annul the gift, but also attempt to define their social and political environs through such gifts and exchanges. According to Gloria Durán, what *Terra Nostra* has in common with Fuentes's first novel, *Where the Air Is Clear,* is the novel's diverse social setting. Characters from different classes are represented, they have a broad scope of action, but in *Terra Nostra* the main characters, nevertheless, are more archetypal than realistic.[2] I point out in this study that the gift, at times through its supplements—potlatches, sacrifices, transgressions, and excesses—is one of the preeminent economic metaphors that define the characters in their social and cultural milieu; it not only colors their most private beliefs and desires but also marks them as archetypes: Pilgrim as Plumed Serpent, "the Giver of Life."

I have also shown that these economic metaphors determine how the characters are represented: the usury of Felipe's faded image on coin; the excessive image of his body wasting away; the very concept of *herencia* that ties Felipe to the curse of Tiberius's hideous crime and that fuels the former's obsession with absolutism during a time of dispersion. The "exchanges" of identity between literary and mythical characters, Don Quixote and Don Juan, Pilgrim as Plumed Serpent and Smoking Mirror, also follow the general pattern of economic metaphors. Furthermore, Felipe and the Mad Lady's ostentatious tributes to death, the processions of mummified remains and the necropolis El Escorial, evince an economy of wasteful expenditure. Such ostentation betrays an ignoble form of feudal largess in which the self-interest of both characters is exaggerated to the extent that the "power" they gain from such displays pales, and appears illusory, before the not-so-invisible machinations of the usurer and of Guzmán, Felipe's violent liegeman. To this economy of loss El Comendador Don Gonzalo de Ulloa, first introduced as "the usurer," opposes a principle of accumulation.

The metaphor of usury functions as the sign of the dispersion of Felipe's power: the division and sale of the land, its abstraction through capital, and the commodity fiction. Felipe's body suffers a similar desublimation as a symbol of authority. In this way power relations shift; as Felipe's image fades with his power, the usurer becomes more influential and, ironically, seeks prestige through bonds of obligation with the king. This attests to the interdependence between the rising merchants and a weakened nobility with restored,

2. Durán, *The Archetypes of Carlos Fuentes: From Witch to Androgyne,* 151–2.

but limited, seigneurial privilege. The encounter with the New World furthers the merchants, and rogues such as Guzmán, in their efforts to empower themselves. The encounter represents an initial decentralization of seigneurial power rooted in Spain as real commercial power is transferred to the margins of the empire—the lands of the Americas, on the one hand, and the commercial centers of Europe, on the other: Genoa, Porto, Antwerp, Danzig.

The ancient Lord of Memory, on the other hand, attests to another form of debt related to the land as a signifier of power. Also referred to as "the guardian of the pact," he serves as the overlord of the tributary pact between his people and the Aztec empire. The old man's visage contains the sign of tribute: the simile of the very temple in which he resides as the guardian. The temple and the legend he recounts commemorate the sacred debt to the earth that, according to the old man, defines all human destiny (*TN,* 392). I determined that the mode of this commemoration is a form of writing, a debt inscription that marks the animals and landscape. This form of representation is appropriated by the despot, the Lord of the Great Voice or Smoking Mirror, who exacts tribute in the name of the Earth Goddess. Pilgrim, however, is the usurper of this despotic order; through his difference and his gifts, he reestablishes a new bond to the land at the moment he must abandon the New World. This new territorial bond involves a reappropriation of writing as the collective space of poetry, and as the homage to the earth.

Fuentes deconstructs the utopian vision of the golden age by demonstrating that there is always an underlying cruelty in human existence; a cruelty, nonetheless, that binds tribes and peoples together through ties of obligation. The European invention of the Americas as a utopia imposed an ideal order: On the one hand, Europeans sought to bind the Americas to Europe by making the New World the ideal image of the Old. On the other hand, the Inquisition sought to purge the New World of sin and error. *Terra Nostra* cautions us against making the same misjudgments about the Spaniards as they made about the Aztecs: in Mexico's heritage both forms of despotism, the Spanish and the Aztec, coincide in their attempts to repress the multifarious legacies of each empire. Just as Felipe's obsessive absolutism in Spain was a source of the kingdom's decay, in "The New World" the despotism of the Lord of the Great Voice perpetuates a stagnant, cyclical legacy of tyranny and sacrifice. Pilgrim usurps the order of both worlds, for what each despot fears is the difference that he represents. Pilgrim offers himself to the New World without realizing at first that he is offering what is already there (the pearls and the legend of Plumed Serpent)—the key is in what he brings as an outsider. He is not aware of his particular gifts, and when they are revealed to him, his time in the New World concludes and he leaves behind a legacy of difference. His narration has a similar destabilizing effect on the Old World, transforming it into "The Next World" (El otro mundo).

Terra Nostra's neobaroque economy of exuberance by design forces its readers to reintegrate the Americas' multiple legacies. I have demonstrated how Fuentes does this at the figural level, where the integration of European and Aztec representational and textual strategies reinvents the syncretism of Spain's and Mexico's different cultural legacies. The stylistic techniques from writing and painting serve as the mediating hinge between forces that at first seem binary; writing determines the necessary interrelation of such complementary pairs that make up the Ometéotl, life and death being the most apparent, and the encounter itself of Spain and Mexico. Fuentes does not employ his complex imagery for purely intellectual designs; his overloaded and at times grotesque, transgressive images serve to *motivate* in the reader a passionate response toward their heritage, and to cultivate a neobaroque sensibility that is informed by the combined legacies of the Americas, Europe, and Africa.

The neobaroque integration of Spanish and Aztec figural modes elucidates a larger economy of universal cultures, namely, that in the encounter between Europe and the Americas neither culture can resist the instability that results from the knowledge of the other. The encounter obliges a certain relinquishment to differences, regardless of how much the despots of each world attempt to stifle the differences from within and without. These cultures must of necessity intermarry—for this is the obligation of the encounter. In order for Pilgrim to survive in the New World he must give of himself to his hosts, and by the time of his departure he has transformed that World.

The tension between gift and exchange, and the strange allegiances produced by it, can result from the mixing of cultural identities, but most important it is what produces these legacies. When the ancient Lord of Memory reiterates his challenge, "What will you give us now?" he affirms the underlying principle of the debt cycles: potlatch and sacrifice. The challenge can initiate a legacy of debt, its memory and its fulfillment. In this sense, when relating the sacrifices the gods made as they created humankind, the old man explains that in order to guide the humans in the payment of their debt, their destinies, "the mother earth and the father sun invented and ordained time, which is the course of destiny" (*TN*, 392).

Albeit in a somewhat profane manner, *Terra Nostra* reproduces the tragic tension between destiny and individual action, between the circularity of time and the freedom of the moment to modify it. This shows how the gift intercedes in narrative time, for the gifts given also form the narrative structure of the novel on a grand scale. I have shown that, in part, "The New World" follows the trajectories of the scissors and the mirrors that Pilgrim offers as gifts (both objects, moreover, appear in Paris at the beginning and the end of the novel). The scissors and the mirror have gift effects correlative of their conventional functions: the mirror operates as a sign of inverted repetition (a chiastic attribute) in the context of Pilgrim's encounter with his double, and the scissors punctuate and split the narrative flow much as Clotho's shears cut the thread of human destiny. In this sense, both objects are signs of dispersion and multiplicity, partition and distribution.[3]

The narration "The New World" itself serves as a gift. Much as the old man's legend challenges and transforms its listener Pilgrim, "The New World" has a similar effect with regard to its narratee, Felipe: the narrative time of "The Old World" is disrupted by the incursion of another narration that challenges and modifies the order of Felipe's world. These narrations interact in a concentric series as a gift ("The Ancient's Legend"), within a larger gift ("The New World"), within the novel itself that gives a resounding challenge to universal literature: "rewrite the (hi)story of the Americas, of the world." The challenge appeals to the readers of the novel to reconsider the multiple legacies of Latin America, and to remember the obligation to recover those legacies that have been silenced by centuries of alliance between absolutism and capitalist modernization. Furthermore, Fuentes's *Terra Nostra* does not simply "demystify" the history and traditions of Latin America, it also recodifies them through the critical rereading and rewriting as resistance to the homogenization and commodification of capitalist modernity. *Terra Nostra* reterritorializes Latin America's cultural legacies as heterogeneous legacies that do not subordinate themselves to any other tradition or cultural center, but that insist on being read and interpreted on their own terms.

And while *Terra Nostra* successfully reclaims the baroque as a critical consciousness, it does so on potentially tenuous ground—the problem of the novel as gift. Within the narration, *Terra Nostra* does not advertise itself as a commodity; if anything, the manuscript in the green bottle is something that is cast away, found, given and multiplied. In *Cervantes; or, The Critique or Reading*, when Fuentes discusses Joyce's potlatch, and by association his own project, he cannot and does not directly declare *Terra Nostra* as a gift or a challenge, for to do so would be to fall into the same traps as Felipe and the

---

3. The splitting and multiplying effect of the scissors and the mirror corresponds to the economy of the "fold" in Deleuze's conception of the baroque (*Fold*, 34–38).

Mad Lady. When these two characters contemplate the nature of their gifts, I found that their conclusions were limited by the desire for compensation—their gifts were interested, they expected to gain power and to master time. They also suffered the same problem as Pilgrim, namely, that they could not give of themselves, sacrifice themselves. In *Cervantes; or, The Critique of Reading* when Fuentes declares that words are the only common property, implied in this assertion is a necessary sacrifice:

> Miguel de Cervantes or James Joyce can only be the owners of words to the extent that they are not Cervantes and Joyce, but rather everyone: they are the poet. The poet is born of his act: the poem. The poem creates its autors, as it creates its readers. Cervantes, everyone's reading. Joyce, everyone's writing. (*CCL* 110)

> (Miguel de Cervantes o James Joyce sólo pueden ser dueños de las palabras en la medida en que no son Cervantes y Joyce, sino todos: son el poeta. El poeta nace después de su acto: el poema. El poema crea a sus autores, como crea a sus lectores. Cervantes, lectura de todos. Joyce, escritura de todos.)

Such an expropriation is natural to the gift, and to writing. The apparent disinterestedness speaks not only to Fuentes's utopian desire but also to the underlying political implication in Fuentes's notions of literature as "common property," and of gift economy. What Pierre Bourdieu states about generosity and disinterestedness can also be said of Fuentes's baroque gifts: "The purely speculative and typically scholastic question of whether generosity and disinterestedness are possible should give way to the political question of the means that have to be implemented in order to create universes in which, as in gift economies, people have an interest in disinterestedness and generosity."[4] For Fuentes, the baroque is an art of resistance that opposes the interested and often miserly ethics of capitalist modernization; the baroque opposes and undermines it with the exuberance of expenditure, the sacrifice of individuality in favor of solidarity, and the sharing and privileging of the cultural "universe" over the economic one.

Yet when an author such as Fuentes speaks of such self-sacrifice, the sacrifice of the writer he describes in relation to Cervantes and Joyce, one begins to wonder what the author expects in return. Certainly, the name Carlos Fuentes has garnished the author much prestige from his previous works, and

---

4. Bourdieu, "Marginalia—Some Additional Notes on the Gift," 240.

guarantees the sale of his books. It is somewhat ironic that one of the few Latin American novelists to successfully make a living from his novels should be the one to make such assertions. Nevertheless, as a writer Fuentes already participates in the realm of the gift, and therefore risks the pitfalls of the debt cycle; by merely writing a novel he plays on the border of the gift and debt. All narrative is gift, but because Fuentes's writing self-consciously discusses the gift he risks the charge of being too interested in proving his mastery.

Terra Nostra's critics are divided amongst two main camps "pitting those who view Fuentes's novel as a fundamentally open and subversive text against those who see *Terra Nostra* as the work of a literary despot intent on lording it over his readers." One of the most useful and eloquent texts from the early criticism on *Terra Nostra* is Juan Goytisolo's essay titled *"Terra Nostra."* Not only does Goytisolo give crucial insights regarding this controversy, but he also gives the reader an invaluable guide for understanding *Terra Nostra*. His own judgment of the novel is similar to my own: "As is still the case for *Don Quixote*, [in *Terra Nostra*] the singular, traditional reading surrenders to a dilemma or a variety of interpretations that preserves our freedom of choice and judgment, thus bestowing on an apparently aesthetic venture a profoundly moral justification that surpasses the limits of literature."[5]

The ostentation of Fuentes's potlatch should not lead one to a reductive conclusion about his intentions, or about the desire for mastery. Fuentes is merely participating in an aggressive competition that is paradoxically infused with solidarity. As much as *Terra Nostra* can be seen as a challenge to the reader to "come up with something better," it also pays homage to those who have come before—hence, the reference to characters and figures from the Spanish and pre-Columbian Mexican traditions, as well as those characters representative of other twentieth-century novelists: Julio Cortázar, Jorge Luis Borges, Juan Rulfo, Gabriel García Márquez, and Mario Vargas Llosa. Not only is *Terra Nostra* a countergift, a gesture of gratitude that recognizes its own debt to Mexico's diverse heritage, but it is also an ostentatious gift that challenges its readers in a particular way: the novel functions as a gift that does not seek to close an exchange, but to oblige the readers to rethink Latin America and Spain's mutual history, to confront its silences, and to reinvent themselves in the process. In this way *Terra Nostra* marks us with the debt to the syncretic heritage of Latin America.

5. For a brief overview of this debate, see van Delden, *Fuentes, Mexico, and Modernity*, 146–47; and Goytisolo, *"Terra Nostra,"* 251.

Bibliography

Abeyta, Michael. "The Metaphor of Usury in *Terra Nostra:* On the Traces of Bataille and Derrida in Fuentes's Writing." *Hispanic Review* 72:2 (2004): 287–305.

———. "Ostentatious Offerings: The Neobaroque Economies of Carlos Fuentes's *Terra Nostra.*" *Confluencia* 18:1 (2002): 103–17.

———. "El trueque y la economía del don en *Terra Nostra* de Carlos Fuentes." *Revista Iberoamericana* 70:207 (2004): 431–41.

Adorno, Theodor. *Aesthetic Theory.* Translated by C. Lenhart. New York: Routledge, 1984.

———. *Negative Dialectics.* Translated by E. B. Ashton. New York: Continuum, 1973.

Alazraki, Jaime. "*Terra Nostra:* Coming to Grips with History." *World Literature Today* 57:4 (1983): 551–58.

Alonso, Dámaso. *Góngora y el "Polifemo."* 6th ed. 2 vols. 1974. Reprint, Madrid: Gredos, 1980.

Artaud, Antonin. *The Theater and Its Double.* Translated by Mary Caroline Richards. New York: Grove Press, 1958.

Avelar, Idelber. *The Untimely Present: Postdictatorial Latin American Fiction and the Task of Mourning.* Durham, NC: Duke University Press, 1999.

Bakhtin, Mikhail M. *The Dialogic Imagination.* Edited by Michael Holquist. Translated by Caryl Emerson and Michael Holquist. 1981. Reprint, Austin: University of Texas Press, 1992.

Bataille, Georges. *The Accursed Share: An Essay on General Economy.* Translated by Robert Hurley. 3 vols. New York: Zone Books, 1988.

————. *Visions of Excess: Selected Writings, 1927–1939.* Edited by Allan Stoekl. Translated by Allan Stoekl, Carl R. Lovitt, and Donald M. Leslie Jr. Theory and History of Literature. 14. Minneapolis: University of Minnesota Press, 1985.

Bataillon, Marcel. *Le Célestine selon Fernando de Rojas.* Paris: Didier, 1961.

Benjamin, Walter. *Illuminations.* Edited by Hannah Arendt. Translated by Harry Zohn. 3rd ed. New York: Schocken Books, 1976.

Beverley, John. "Nuevas vacilaciones sobre el barroco." *Revista de Crítica Literaria Latinoamericana* 14:28 (1988): 215–77.

Beverley, John, José Oviedo, and Michael Aronna, eds. *The Postmodernism Debate in Latin America.* Durham, NC: Duke University Press, 1995.

Blanco, José Joaquín. "Fuentes: de la pasión por los mitos al polyforum de las mitologías." In *Crónica literaria: Un siglo de escritores mexicanos,* 339–71. 1976. Reprint, Mexico City: Cal y Arena, 1996.

Boling, Becky. "A Literary Vision of History: Marxism and Positivism in *Terra Nostra* by Fuentes." *Latin American Research Review* 19:1 (1984): 125–41.

Boone, Elizabeth Hill. *The Codex Magliabechiano and the Lost Prototype of the Magliabechiano Group.* Berkeley and Los Angeles: University of California Press, 1983.

Borges, Jorge Luis. *Obras completas.* 3 vols. Buenos Aires: Emecé, 1989.

————. *Other Inquisitions, 1937–1952.* Translated by Ruth L. C. Simms. Austin: University of Texas Press, 1964.

Bourdieu, Pierre. *The Logic of Practice.* Translated by Richard Nice. Stanford, CA: Stanford University Press, 1990.

————. "Marginalia—Some Additional Notes on the Gift." In *The Logic of the Gift: Toward an Ethics of Generosity,* edited by Alan Schrift, 231–41. Translated by Richard Nice. New York: Routledge, 1997.

Brody, Robert, and Charles Rossman, eds. *Carlos Fuentes: A Critical View.* Austin: University of Texas Press, 1982.

Brotherston, Gordon. *Book of the Fourth World: Reading the Native Americas through Their Literature.* Cambridge: Cambridge University Press, 1992.

Caputo, John D., and Michael J. Scanlon, eds. *God, the Gift, and Postmodernism.* Bloomington: Indiana University Press, 1999.

Carpentier, Alejo. "La novela latinoamericana en vísperas de un nuevo siglo." In *Historia y ficción en la narrativa hispanoamericana,* edited by Alejo Carpentier et al., 19–48. Caracas: Monte Avila Editores, 1984.

Cicero, Marcus Tullius. *Ad Herennium: De ratione dicendi (Rhetorica Ad Herennium)*. Translated by Harry Caplan. London: William Heinemann; Cambridge, MA: Harvard University Press, 1964.

Cortínez, Verónica. "Crónica, épica y novela: *La historia verdadera de la conquista de la Nueva España* y 'El Mundo Nuevo' de *Terra Nostra*." *Revista Chilena de Literatura* 38 (1991): 59–72.

Cruz, Martin de la. *Libellus de medicinalibus indorum herbis: Manuscrito azteca de 1552*. Translated to Latin by Juan Badiano. Mexico City: Fondo de Cultura Económica; Instituto Mexicano del Seguro Social, 1964.

Cruz, Sor Juana Inés de la. *Obras completas*. Mexico City: Porrúa, 1972.

Curtius, Ernst Robert. *European Literature and the Latin Middle Ages*. Translated by Willard R. Task. Bollingen Series 36. Princeton, NJ: Princeton University Press, 1973.

Deleuze, Gilles. *The Fold: Leibniz and the Baroque*. Translated by Tom Conley. Minneapolis: Univeristy of Minnesota Press, 1993.

Deleuze, Gilles, and Félix Guattari. *Anti-Oedipus: Capitalism and Schizophrenia*. Translated by Robert Hurley, Mark Seem, and Helen R. Lane. Minneapolis: University of Minnesota Press, 1983.

———. *A Thousand Plateaus: Capitalism and Schizophrenia*. Translated by Brian Massumi. Minneapolis: University of Minnesota Press, 1987.

Derrida, Jacques. *Dissemination*. Translated by Barbara Johnson. Chicago: University of Chicago Press, 1981.

———. *The Gift of Death*. Translated by David Willis. Chicago: University of Chicago Press, 1996.

———. *Given Time: I. Counterfeit Money*. Translated by Peggy Kamuf. Chicago: University of Chicago Press, 1992.

———. *Margins of Philosophy*. Translated by Alan Bass. Chicago: University of Chicago Press, 1982.

———. *Of Grammatology*. Translated by Gayatri Chakravorty Spivak. 1974. Reprint, Baltimore: John Hopkins University Press, 1976.

———. *Speech and Phenomena, and Other Essays on Husserl's Theory of Signs*. Translated by David B. Allison. Evanston, IL: Northwestern University Press, 1989.

———. *Writing and Difference*. Translated by Alan Bass. Chicago: University of Chicago Press, 1978.

Díaz, Gisele, and Alan Roberts, eds. *The Codex Borgia: A Full-Color Restoration of the Ancient Mexican Manuscript*. New York: Dover, 1993.

Dodds, E. R. *The Greeks and the Irrational.* 1951. Reprint, Berkeley and Los Angeles: University of California Press, 1966.

Donoso, José. *Historia personal del "boom."* Barcelona: Anagrama, 1972.

Dupont, Denise. "Baroque Ambiguities: The Figure of the Author in *Terra Nostra.*" *Latin American Literary Review* 30:59 (January–June 2002): 5–19.

Durán, Gloria. *The Archetypes of Carlos Fuentes: From Witch to Androgyne.* Hamden, CT: Archon Books, 1980.

Echeverría, Bolívar. *La modernidad de lo barroco.* Mexico City: Era, 1998.

———. *Modernidad, mestizaje cultural, Ethos Barroco.* Mexico City: UNAM/El Equilibrista, 1994.

Eco, Umberto. *The Role of the Reader: Explorations in the Semiotics of Texts.* Bloomingtion: Indiana University Press, 1984.

Faris, Wendy. *Carlos Fuentes.* New York: Ungar, 1983.

———. "The Return of the Past: Chiasmus in the Texts of Carlos Fuentes." *World Literature Today* 57:4 (1983): 578–84.

———. "Southern Economies of Excess: Narrative Expenditure in William Faulkner and Carlos Fuentes." In *Look Away! The U.S. South in New World Studies,* edited by Jon Smith and Deborah Cohn, 333–54. Durham, NC: Duke University Press, 2004.

———. "'Without Sin, and with Pleasure': The Erotic Dimensions of Fuentes' Fiction." *Novel: A Forum on Fiction* 20:1 (Fall 1986): 62–77.

Feijoo, Gladys. *Lo fantástico en los relatos de Carlos Fuentes: Aproximación teórica.* Senda de estudios y ensayos. New York: Senda Nueva de Ediciones, 1985.

Foucault, Michel. *The Archaeology of Knowledge and The Discourse on Language.* Translated by A. M. Sheridan Smith. New York: Pantheon, 1972.

———. *Disipline and Punish: The Birth of the Prison.* Translated by Alan Sheridan. New York: Vintage, 1977.

———. *The Order of Things: An Archeology of the Human Sciences.* New York: Vintage, 1973.

Franco, Jean. *Critical Passions: Selected Essays.* Durham, NC: Duke University Press, 1999.

Fuentes, Carlos. *Aura.* Translated by Lynsander Kemp. Mexico City: Era, 1962; reprint, New York: Farrar, 1975.

———. *The Buried Mirror: Reflections on Spain and the New World.* Boston: Houghton Mifflin, 1992.

————. *Burnt Water: Stories*. Translated by Margaret Sayers Peden. New York: Farrar, Straus, and Giroux, 1980.

———— [Talón de Aquiles, pseud.]. "La burra del trigo." *Revista Mexicana de Literatura* 1 (September–October 1955): 93–94.

————. *The Campaign*. Translated by Alfred Mac Adam. New York: Farrar, Straus, Giroux, 1991.

————. *Cantar de ciegos*. Mexico City: Joaquín Mortiz, 1964.

————. *Casa con dos puertas*. Mexico City: Joaquín Mortiz, 1970.

————. *Cervantes, o la crítica de la lectura*. Mexico City: Joaquín Mortiz, 1976.

————. *A Change of Skin*. Translated by Sam Hileman. New York: Farrar, Straus, and Giroux, 1968.

————. *Christopher Unborn*. Translated by Alfred Mac Adam and the author. New York: Vintage Books, 1990.

————. *Constancia, and Other Stories for Virgins*. Translated by Thomas Christensen. New York: Harper Perennial, 1991.

————. *The Crystal Frontier: A Novel in Nine Stories*. Translated by Alfred Mac Adam. New York: Farrar, Straus, and Giroux, 1997.

————. *Cumpleaños*. Mexico City: Joaquín Mortiz, 1969.

————. *The Death of Artemio Cruz*. Translated by Alfred Mac Adam. New York: Farrar, Straus, and Giroux, 1991.

————. *Diana: The Goddess Who Hunts Alone*. Translated by Alfred Mac Adam. New York: HarperPerennial, 1996.

————. *Los días enmascarados*. Mexico City: Los Presentes, 1954.

————. *Distant Relations*. Translated by Margaret Sayers Peden. New York: Farrar Straus Giroux, 1982.

————. *Geografía de la novela*. Mexico City: Fondo de Cultura Económica, 1993.

————. *The Good Conscience*. Translated by Sam Hileman. 1961. Reprint, New York: Farrar, Straus, and Giroux, 1995.

————. *Holy Place*. In *Triple Cross: Holy Place [by] Carlos Fuentes. Hell Has No Limits [by] José Donoso. From Cuba with a Song [by] Severo Sarduy,* translated by Suzanne Jill Levine. 5–144. New York: E. P. Dutton, 1972.

————. *The Hydra Head*. Translated by Margaret Sayers Peden. New York: Farrar, Straus, Giroux, 1978.

————. *Inez*. Translated by Margaret Sayers Peden. New York: Farrar, Straus, and Giroux, 2002.

————. *Inquieta compañía.* Mexico City: Santillana, 2004.

————. *Myself with Others: Selected Essays.* New York: Farrar, Straus, and Giroux, 1988.

————. *A New Time for Mexico.* Translated by Marina Gutman Castañeda and Carlos Fuentes. New York: Farrar, Straus, and Giroux, 1996.

————. *La nueva novela hispanoamericana.* 3rd ed. 1969. Reprint, Mexico City: Joaquín Mortiz, 1972.

————. *The Old Gringo.* Translated by Margaret Sayers Peden. 1985. Reprint, New York: Farrar, Straus and Giroux, 1997.

————. *The Orange Tree.* Translated by Alfred Mac Adam. New York: Farrar, Straus, and Giroux, 1994.

————. *La silla del Águila.* Mexico City: Alfaguara, 2003.

————. *Terra Nostra.* 1975. Reprint, Mexico City: Joaquín Mortiz, 1992.

————. *Terra Nostra.* Translated by Margaret Sayers Peden. New York: Farrar, Straus, Giroux, 1976.

————. *This I Believe: An A to Z of a Life.* Translated by Kristina Cordero. New York: Random House, 2005.

————. *Tiempo mexicano.* Mexico City: Joaquín Mortiz, 1971.

————. *Valiente mundo nuevo: Épica, utopía y mito en la novela hispanoamericana.* Madrid: Mondadori España, 1990.

————. *Where the Air Is Clear.* Translated by Sam Hileman. 1960. Reprint, New York: Noonday Press, 1993.

————. *The Years with Laura Díaz.* Translated by Alfred Mac Adam. New York: Farrar, Straus, and Giroux, 2000.

Gallo, Marta. "*Terra Nostra* divisa est in partes tres." *Filología* 20:1 (1985): 213–22.

García-Gutiérrez, Georgina, ed. *Carlos Fuentes desde la crítica.* Mexico City: Taurus, 1999.

Garcilaso de la Vega, El Inca. *Comentarios reales.* Mexico City: Pórrua, 1998.

Garibay, Angel María. *Historia de la literatura náhuatl.* 2 vols. Mexico City: Pórrua, 1954.

Gass, Joanne Margaret Wells. "Penelope's Tapestry: The Weave of History and Fiction in John Barth's *Letters,* Carlos Fuentes' *Terra Nostra.*" PhD diss., University of California–Irvine, 1990.

Genette, Gérard. *Narrative Discourse: An Essay in Method.* Translated by Jane E Lewin. Ithaca, NY: Cornell University Press, 1980.

Gertel, Zunilda. "El discurso transformacional en *Aura.*" In *Homenaje a Alfredo A. Roggiano: En este aire de América,* edited by Keith McDuffie and Rose Minc, 331–41. Pittsburgh: Instituto Internacional de Literatura Iberoamericana, 1990.

———. "La imagen metafísica en la poesía de Borges." *Revista Iberoamericana* 43 (1977): 433–48.

———. "Semiótica, historia y ficción en *Terra Nostra.*" *Revista Iberoamericana* 47:116–17 (1981): 63–72.

Giacoman, Helmy F., ed. *Homenaje a Carlos Fuentes: Variaciones interpretativas en torno a su obra.* Long Island City, NY: Las Américas, 1971.

Gimferrer, Pere. "El mapa y la máscara." *Plural* 58 (1976): 58–60.

Góngora y Argote, Luis de. *Soledades.* Edited by John Beverley. 4th ed. Madrid: Cátedra, 1984.

———. *Las soledades.* Edited by Dámaso Alonso. Madrid: Sociedad de Estudios y Publicaciones, 1956.

———. *The Solitudes of Luis de Góngora.* Translated by Gilbert F. Cunningham. 1964. Reprint, Baltimore: John Hopkins University Press, 1968.

González-Echevarría, Roberto. *Myth and Archive: A Theory of Latin American Narrative.* Cambridge: Cambridge University Press, 1990.

———. "*Terra Nostra:* Theory and Practice." In *Carlos Fuentes: A Critical View,* edited by Robert Brody and Charles Rossman, 132–45. Austin: University of Texas Press, 1982.

Goux, Jean-Joseph. *Symbolic Economies: After Marx and Freud.* Translated by Jennifer Curtiss Gage. Ithaca, NY: Cornell University Press, 1990.

Goytisolo, Juan. "*Terra Nostra.*" In *Disidencias,* 221–56. 1977. Reprint, Barcelona: Seix Barral, 1978.

Graves, Robert. *The Greek Myths.* 2 vols. 1955. Reprint, London: Penguin, 1960.

Gutiérrez, Carl. "Provisional History: Reading through *Terra Nostra.*" *Review of Contemporary Fiction* 8:2 (1988): 257–65.

Habermas, Jürgen. *The Philosophical Discourse of Modernity; Twelve Lectures.* Translated by Frederick Lawrence. 1987. Reprint, Cambridge, MA: MIT Press, 1992.

———. *Philosophical-Political Profiles.* Translated by Frederick Lawrence. Cambridge, MA: MIT Press, 1985.

Hegel, G. W. F. *The Phenomenology of Spirit.* Translated by A. V. Miller. Oxford: Oxford University Press, 1979.

Helmuth, Chalene. *The Postmodern Fuentes.* Lewisburg, PA: Bucknell University Press, 1997.

Hernández de López, Ana María, ed. *Interpretaciones a la obra de Carlos Fuentes, un gigante de las letras hispanoamericanas.* Madrid: Ediciones Beramar, 1990.

———, ed. *La obra de Carlos Fuentes: Una visión múltiple.* Madrid: Pliegos, 1988.

Hyde, Lewis. *The Gift: Imagination and the Erotic Life of Property.* 1974. Reprint, New York: Random House, 1983.

Ibsen, Kristine. *Author, Text and Reader in the Novels of Carlos Fuentes.* Currents in Comparative Romance Languages and Literatures 16. New York: Lang, 1993.

———. "'El teatro de la memoria': Transtextuality and the Activation of the Reader in Fuentes' *Terra Nostra.*" *Revista Hispánica Moderna* 47.1 (June 1994): 109.

Jameson, Frederic. *The Political Unconsciousness: Narrative as a Socially Symbolic Act.* Ithaca, NY: Cornell University Press, 1981.

Josephs, Allen. "The End of *Terra Nostra.*" *World Literature Today* 57 (1983): 563–67.

Juan-Navarro, Santiago. "Re-contextualizing Historiographic Metafiction in the Americas: The Examples of Carlos Fuentes, Ishmael Reed, Julio Cortazar [*sic*], and E. L. Doctorow." PhD diss., Columbia University, 1995.

———. "Sobre dioses, héroes y novelistas: La reinvención de Quetzalcóatl y la reescritura de la Conquista en 'El mundo nuevo' de Carlos Fuentes." *Revista Iberoamericana* 62:174 (1996): 103–28.

Kadir, Djelal. "Fuentes and the Profane Sublime." In *The Other Writing: Postcolonial Essays in Latin American Writing Culture,* 73–110. West Lafayette, IN: Purdue University Press, 1993.

———. *Questioning Fictions: Latin America's Family Romance.* Theory and History of Literature 32. Minneapolis: University of Minnesota Press, 1986.

Kant, Immanuel. *Critique of Judgement.* Translated by J. H. Bernard. New York: Hafner, 1951.

Keenan, Thomas. "The Point Is to (Ex)change It: Reading *Capital,* Rhetorically." In *Fetishism as Cultural Discourse,* edited by Emily Apter and William Pietz, 152–85. Ithaca, NY: Cornell University Press, 1993.

Kerr, Lucille. "On Shifting Ground: Authoring Mystery and Mastery in Carlos Fuentes's *Terra Nostra.*" In *Reclaiming the Author: Figures and Fictions from Spanish America,* 65–88. Durham, NC: Duke University Press, 1992.

———. "The Paradox of Power and Mystery: Carlos Fuentes's *Terra Nostra*." *PMLA* 95:1 (1980): 91–102.

Las Casas, Bartolomé de. *Brevísima relación de la destrucción de las Indias.* Edited by André Saint-Lu. Madrid: Cátedra, 1991.

León-Portilla, Miguel. *Aztec Thought and Culture: A Study of the Ancient Nahuatl Mind.* Translated by Jack Emory Davis. The Civilization of the American Indian. 1963. Reprint, Norman: University of Oklahoma Press, 1990.

Lévi-Strauss, Claude. *The Elementary Structures of Kinship.* Translated by James Harle Bell, John Richard von Sturmer, and Rodney Needham. London: Eyre and Spottiswoode, 1969.

———. "Introduction à l'oeuvre de Marcel Mauss." In *Sociologie et anthropologie,* by Marcel Mauss, ix–lii. Paris: Presses Universitaires de France, 1966.

Lezama Lima, José. "Sierpe de Don Luis de Góngora." In *Lezama Lima,* edited by Armando Álvarez Bravo, 191–220. Buenos Aires: Jorge Alvarez, 1968.

Loesberg, Jonathan. "Narrations of Authority: Cortés, Gómara, Diaz." *Prose Studies* 6:3 (1983): 239–63.

López Mena, Sergio. "Lectura y recuperación de *Terra Nostra,* un acto de justicia." In *Carlos Fuentes: Perspectivas críticas,* edited by Pol Popovic Karic, 139–55. Mexico City: Siglo XXI Editores, 2002.

Lyotard, Jean François. *The Differend: Phrases in Dispute.* Translated by Georges Van Den Abbeele. Theory and History of Literature 46. Minneapolis: University of Minnesota Press, 1988.

———. *Discours, figure.* Collection d' esthétique. Paris: Klincksieck, 1971.

Mandel, Ernest. *The Formation of the Economic Thought of Karl Marx: 1843 to "Capital."* Translated by Brian Pearce. New York: Monthly Review Press, 1971.

Maravall, José Antonio. *Las comunidades de Castilla: Una primera revolución moderna.* Madrid: Revista de Occidente, 1963.

———. *Culture of the Baroque: Analysis of a Historical Structure.* Translated by Terry Cochran. Theory and History of Literature 25. Minneapolis: University of Minnesota Press, 1986.

Márquez Rodríguez, Alexis. "Aproximación preliminar a *Terra Nostra:* La ficción como reinterpretación de la historia." In *La obra de Carlos Fuentes: Una visión múltiple,* edited by Ana María Hernández de López, 183–92. Madrid: Pliegos, 1988.

Márquez Villanueva, Francisco. *Orígenes y sociología del tema celestinesco.* Barcelona: Anthropos, 1993.

Marx, Karl. *Capital.* Vol. 1. Edited by Ernest Mandel. Translated by Ben Fowkes. New York: Vintage Books, 1977.

———. *Economic and Philosophic Manuscripts of 1844.* In *The Marx-Engels Reader,* edited by Robert C. Tucker, 66–125. 2nd ed. New York: Norton, 1978.

Mauss, Marcel. *The Form and Reason for Exchange in Archaic Societies.* Translated by H. D. Halls. New York: Norton, 1990.

McHale, Brian. *Postmodernist Fiction.* New York: Methuen, 1987.

Ordiz, Francisco Javier. *El mito en la obra narrativa de Carlos Fuentes.* León, Spain: Universidad de León, Servicio de Publicaciones, 1987.

Ortega, Julio. *El discurso de la abundancia.* Caracas: Monte Avila Editores, 1992.

Oviedo, José Miguel. "Fuentes: Sinfonía del Nuevo Mundo." *Hispamérica: Revista de Literatura* 16 (1977): 19–32.

———. Introduction to *Obras completas,* by Carlos Fuentes, 163–202. Vol. 3. Mexico City: Aguilar, 1989.

Pais, Abraham. *Niels Bohr's Times, in Physics, Philosophy, and Polity.* New York: Oxford University Press, 1991.

Paley Francescato, Marta. "Re/creación y des/construcción de la historia en *Terra Nostra* de Felipe Montero." *Revista Iberoamericana* 56:151 (1990): 563–67.

Patrimonio Nacional. *El Escorial: Octava maravilla del mundo.* Madrid: Patrimonio Nacional, 1967.

Paz, Octavio. *Los hijos del limo: Del romanticismo a la vanguardia.* 1974. Reprint, Barcelona: Seix Barral, 1990.

———. *El laberinto de la soledad, Posdata, Vuelta a El laberinto de la soledad.* Mexico City: Fondo de Cultura Económica, 1997.

———. *Sor Juana Inés de la Cruz, o las trampas de la fe.* Mexico City: Fondo de Cultura Económica, 1982.

Plotnitsky, Arkady. *Complementarity: Anti-epistemology after Bohr and Derrida.* Durham, NC: Duke University Press, 1994.

———. *Reconfigurations: Critical Theory and General Economy.* Gainesville: University Press of Florida, 1993.

Polanyi, Karl. *Primitive, Archaic and Modern Economies: Essays of Karl Polanyi.* Edited by George Dalton. Garden City, NY: Doubleday, 1968.

Popovic Karic, Pol, ed. *Carlos Fuentes: Perspectivas críticas.* Mexico City: Siglo XXI Editores, 2002.

Pratt, Mary Louise. "La modernidad desde las Américas." *Revista Iberoamericana* 66:193 (October–December 2000): 831–40.

Pulido Herráez, Begoña. *Carlos Fuentes: Imaginación y memoria.* Sinaloa, Mexico: Universidad Autónoma de Sinaloa, 2000.

Readings, Bill. *Introducing Lyotard: Art and Politics.* Critics of the Twentieth Century. London: Routledge, 1991.

Richard, Nelly. "Un debate latinoamericano sobre práctica intelectual y discurso crítico." *Revista Iberoamericana* 66:193 (October–December 2000): 841–50.

Ricoeur, Paul. *From Text to Action.* Translated by Kathleen Blamey and John B Thompson. Evanston, IL: Northwestern University Press, 1991.

Rodriguez Carranza, Luz. *Un teatro de la memoria: Análisis de "Terra Nostra" de Carlos Fuentes.* Leuven, Belgium: Leuven University Press; Buenos Aires: Danilo Albero-Vergara, 1990.

Sahlins, Marshall. *Stone Age Economics.* New York: Aldine de Gruyter, 1972.

Saldívar, Ramón. *Figural Language in the Novel: The Flowers of Speech from Cervantes to Joyce.* Princeton, NJ: Princeton University Press, 1984.

Sánchez MacGregor, Joaquín. "Composición de *Terra Nostra.*" *Anuario de Letras: Revista de la Facultad de Filosofía y Letras* 14 (1976): 255–70.

Sarduy, Severo. *Barroco.* Buenos Aires: Editorial Sudamericana, 1974.

———. "Un fetiche de cachemira." In *Homenage a Carlos Fuentes,* edited by Helmy F. Giacoman, 261–74. New York: Las Américas, 1971.

Schrift, Alan, ed. *The Logic of the Gift: Toward an Ethic of Generosity.* New York: Routledge, 1997.

Séjourné, Laurette. *Burning Water: Thought and Religion in Ancient Mexico.* Translated by Irene Nicholson. Guildford, Surrey: Thames and Hudson, 1978.

Shell, Marc. *The Economy of Literature.* Baltimore: John Hopkins University Press, 1978.

———. *Money, Language and Thought: Literary and Philosophic Economies from the Medieval to the Modern Era.* Berkeley and Los Angeles: University of California Press, 1982.

Simson, Ingrid. *Realidad y ficción en "Terra Nostra" de Carlos Fuentes.* Editionen der Iberoamericana: Reihe III, Monographien un Aufsätze: Bd. 22. Frankfurt am Main: Vervuert Verlag, 1989.

Sommers, Joseph. *After the Storm: Landmarks of the Modern Mexican Novel.* Albuquerque: University of New Mexico Press, 1968.

———. *Yañez, Rulfo, Fuentes: La novela mexicana moderna.* Caracas: Monte Avila, 1970.

Song, Sang-Kee. "La sombra precolombina en el *ethos* barroco en las obras de Carlos Fuentes, Octavio Paz y Rufino Tamayo." *Revista Iberoamericana* 67:194–95 (January–June 2001): 251–65.

Soto-Duggan, Lilvia. *"Terra Nostra": Memoria e imaginación.* Actas: Simposio Carlos Fuentes, edited by Isacc Levy and Juan Loveluck. Columbia: University of South Carolina Press, 1980.

Spivak, Gayatri Chakravorty. "Scattered Speculations on the Question of Value." In *The Spivak Reader: Selected Works of Gayatri Chakravorty Spivak,* edited by Donna Landry and Gerald MacLean, 107–40. New York: Routledge, 1996.

———. "Speculations on Reading Marx: After Reading Derrida." In *Poststructuralism and the Question of History,* edited by Derek Attridge, Geoff Bennington, and Robert Young, 30–62. Cambridge: Cambridge University Press, 1987.

Springer, Alice Gericke. "An Iconological Study of the New World in Carlos Fuentes' *Terra Nostra.*" PhD diss., Vanderbilt University, 1985.

Taylor, Mark C. "Capitalizing (on) Gifting." In *The Enigma of Gift and Sacrifice,* edited by Edith Wyschogrod, Jean-Joseph Goux, and Eric Boynton, 50–73. New York: Fordham University Press, 2002.

Toscano, Nicolás. '*Terra Nostra* y la pintura." *Cuadernos Americanos* 22 (1990): 191–99.

Unamuno, Miguel de. *Amor y pedagogía: Tratado de Cocotología.* Madrid: Espasa-Calpe, 1987.

———. *Del sentimiento trágico de la vida en los hombres y en los pueblos.* Madrid: Espasa-Calpe, 1980.

Van Delden, Maarten. *Carlos Fuentes, Mexico, and Modernity.* Nashville: Vanderbilt University Press, 1998.

———. "Extremo occidente: Carlos Fuentes y la tradición europea." In *Carlos Fuentes: Perspectivas críticas,* 79–94. Edited by Pol Popovic Karic. Mexico City: Siglo XXI Editores, 2002.

Villalobos, José Pablo. "Carlos Fuentes: Caught in the Modern/Postmodern Crossfire." *Mexican Studies/Estudios Mexicanos* 16:2 (Summer 2000): 401–9.

Villoro, Juan. "Goya y Fuentes: Los trabajos del sueño." In *Efectos personales,* edited by Juan Villoro, 91–103. Barcelona: Anagrama, 2001.

Williams, Raymond L. "Fuentes the Modern, Fuentes the Postmodern." *Hispania* 85:2 (2002): 209–18.

———. *The Writings of Carlos Fuentes.* Austin: University of Texas Press, 1996.

Williams, Shirley. "Mito e historia en *Terra Nostra* de Carlos Fuentes." In *De la crónica a la nueva narrativa mexicana: Coloquio sobre literatura mexicana,* edited by Merlín H. Foster and Julio Ortega, 331–41. Colección Alfonso Reyes 7. Oaxaca, Mexico: Editorial Oasis, 1986.

Wyschogrod, Edith, Jean-Joseph Goux, and Eric Boynton, eds. *The Enigma of Gift and Sacrifice.* New York: Fordham University Press, 2002.

Yates, Francis A. *The Art of Memory.* 1966. Reprint, Chicago: University of Chicago Press, 1984.

Zamora, Lois Parkingson. "Magic Realism and Fantastic History: Carlos Fuentes's *Terra Nostra* and Giambattista Vico's *The New Science.*" *Review of Contemporary Fiction* 8:2 (1988): 249–56.

———. *Writing the Apocalypse: Historical Vision in Contemporary U.S. and Latin American Fiction.* Cambridge: Cambridge University Press, 1989.

Zavala, Iris M. "The Three Faces of the Baroque in Mexico and the Caribbean." In *Literary Cultures of Latin America: A Comparative History,* edited by Mario J. Valdés, 3:174–79. Oxford: Oxford University Press, 2004.

Index